Advanced Turbo C® Programmer's Guide

Related Titles of Interest

Turbo Pascal® DOS Utilities, *Alonso*

Programming with Macintosh Turbo Pascal®, *Swan*

Turbo C® Survival Guide, *Miller and Quilici*

Turbo Pascal Library Units, *Shammas*

Turbo C® DOS Utilities, *Alonso*

Turbo C® and Quick C® Functions: Building Blocks for Efficient Code, *Barden*

The Turbo Programmer's Reference: Language Essentials, *Weiskamp*

Quick C® DOS Utilities, *Alonso*

C Programming Reference: An Applied Perspective, *Miller and Quilici*

C Wizard's Programming Reference, *Schwaderer*

Introducing C to Pascal Programmers, *Shammas*

DOS Productivity Tips and Tricks, *Held*

Advanced Turbo C®
Programmer's Guide

DONNA MOSICH

NAMIR SHAMMAS

BRYAN FLAMIG

John Wiley & Sons, Inc.
New York • Chichester • Brisbane • Toronto • Singapore

Publisher: Stephen Kippur
Editor: Therese A. Zak
Managing Editor: Corinne McCormick
Editing, Design, and Production: Publishers Network, Morrisville, PA

Library of Congress Cataloging-in-Publication Data:

Mosich, Donna
Advanced Turbo C® Programmer's Guide/Donna Mosich, Namir Shammas, Bryan Flamig.
p. cm.

ISBN 0-471-63742-4

Printed in the United States of America

88 89 10 9 8 7 6 5 4 3 2 1

We dedicate this book to
Dennis Ritchie, the designer of C

CONTENTS

Advanced Turbo C®
Programmer's Guide

INTRODUCTION

The advent of Turbo C offers programmers in general and C programmers in particular an exciting implementation noted for its environment and compiler speed. Turbo C gained instant success and acceptance among veteran and novice programmers. This book is aimed at all levels of C programmers. It discusses topics related to aspects of programming that are frequently encountered, such as console I/O, mouse management, pop-up windows, strings, dynamic variables, generic programming, graphics, file I/O, and debugging.

The first two chapters offer a brief introduction (or refresher, if you like) to C and Turbo C. Chapter 1 discusses the basic components of a C program, and Chapter 2 begins with a discussion of functions.

Chapter 3 discusses the practical basics for keyboard, mouse, and screen I/O. The techniques and code discussed in this chapter will be used as a building block in other chapters. Chapter 4 discusses pop-up window management and error-reporting windows. The data structure of windows are presented, along with techniques for stacking, hiding, showing windows, and performing window I/O.

Chapter 5 gives a brief but thorough roundup of the file I/O system supported by Turbo C. Among the topics covered are those that deal with text and binary file I/O; using file pointers versus file handles, DOS file information, standard I/O, and file buffer control.

Chapter 6 presents two basic string libraries that offer an alternate route to Turbo C's string library routines. These routines use indices to assist in the various string functions. Chapter 7 discusses advanced techniques for manipulating pointers and handling memory allocation. In particular, this chapter discusses an implementation of a dynamic string structure.

Chapter 8 tackles the topic of generic sorting and searching. First the generic sorting and searching routines of Turbo C are examined. this is followed by a discussion on how to build your own generic routines. Examples show functions for generic shell and insertion sort; merging sorted array; reversing sorted arrays; binary search, bidirectional linear search, and indexed table search.

Chapter 9 covers C functions that perform DOS directory operations. This includes functions that performs an extended DIR with multiple file specification, file-copying utility with multiple file specification, multi-file lister, and a smart directory jump.

Chapter 10 introduces a Variable Length Record (VLR) package. Along with showing many of the file I/O functions in practical use, the Pop-up Window and Dynamic String packages are put to use as well. The chapter ends with a very simple "slide-show" program, in which graphic objects can be stored and retrieved using variable length records.

Chapter 11 points out the tricks and traps in using the graphics routines. This includes using the mouse and then showing a sample graphics pop-up window package. The methods for overcoming some of the limitations of Turbo C graphics are also presented.

Chapter 12 is an application chapter for a hypertext system that uses the various tools and techniques developed in earlier chapters. It employs pop-up windows, mouse and keyboard I/O, variable length dynamic strings, and file I/O with variable length records.

Chapter 13 discusses the Turbo C debugger and a selection of various popular bugs.

CHAPTER

1

C Program Components

This chapter looks at the basic components of a C program unit and serves as a brief refresher on topics such as:

- Data types
- Declaring variables and constants
- Compiler directives
- Basic console I/O
- Pointers
- Operators
- Expressions
- Decision-making constructs
- Loop constructs

PREDEFINED DATA TYPES

Turbo C supports a large combination of predefined simple data types. This is made possible by combining basic type identifiers and type modifier identifiers. The data type identifiers are:

Data Type Identifier	Byte Size	Class
`char`	1	`character`
`int`	2	`integer`
`float`	4	`floating`
`double`	8	`floating`
`void`	0	`typeless`

The type modifiers are:

Type Modifier Identifier	Effect
`short`	Reduces valid range of values.
`long`	Extends valid range of values.
`signed`	High bit is used as a sign bit.
`unsigned`	High bit is not used as a sign bit.

Table 1.1 shows the combination of simple data types that can be used by combining the basic type and type modifiers.

The **typedef** enables you to replace multi-word data type identifiers with single word identifiers. This is shown in the following example.

```
typedef unsigned int word;  /* define word     */
typedef unsigned char byte; /* define byte     */
typedef double extended;    /* define extended */
```

Table 1.1 Predefined Data Types in Turbo C

Simple Data Type	Byte Size	Value Range	Sample Constant(s)
char	1	-128 to 127	-5, 'a'
signed char	1	-128 to 127	5, 'b'
unsigned char	1	0 to 255	5, 'x'
int	2	-32768 to 32767	-234
signed int	2	-32768 to 32767	-344
unsigned int	2	0 to 65535	65000
short int	2	-32768 to 32767	1230
signed short int	2	-32768 to 32767	345
unsigned short int	2	0 to 65535	40000
long int	4	-2147483648 to 2147483647	1000000
signed long int	4	-2147483648 to 2147483647	-2000000
unsigned long int	4	0 to 4294967295	300000000
float	4	3.4E-38 to 3.4E+38 and -3.4E-38 to -3.4E+38	-1.23e-02
long float	8	1.7E-308 to 1.7E+308 and -1.7E-308 to -1.7E+308	2.3e+100
double	8	1.7E-308 to 1.7E+308 and -1.7E-308 to -1.7E+308	-4.32e-100
long double	8	1.7E-308 to 1.7E+308 and -1.7E-308 to -1.7E+308	12.34e+100

USER-DEFINED TYPES

Turbo C supports three classes of user-defined types: enumerated, structures, and unions.

1. Enumerated types enable you to define a list of identifiers that have implicit values of special significance. The members of an enumerated list cannot appear in any other enumerated list. The general syntax for declaring an enumerated type is:

   ```
   enum <enumerated type name> {<list of members delimited by commas>};
   ```

   Examples for declaring enumerated types include:

   ```
   enum booleans { FALSE, TRUE };
   enum colors { red, blue, green, yellow, white, cyan };
   enum error { no_file, no_mem, no_disk, no_printer };
   enum days { Sun, Mon, Tue, Wed, Thu, Fri, Sat };
   ```

   By default (as is the case with all of the examples given) the first member of an enumerated list is assigned 0, the second is assigned one, and so on. You can explicitly alter the ascending sequence of numbers by assigning values to all or some of the enumerated list members. Consider the case of the enumerated type days. You may assign 1 to member **Sun** (short for Sunday) instead of 0, since it is the first day of the week and not the "zeroth"! The above enumerated type declaration can be rewritten as:

   ```
   enum days { Sun = 1, Mon, Tue, Wed, Thu, Fri, Sat };
   ```

   This also assigns 2 to **Mon**, 3 to **Tue**, and so on. In this example, only one enumerated member is explicitly assigned a value. An extreme case involves assigning a specific value to each member of an enumerated list, as shown in the following example:

   ```
   enum error { no_file = 5,
                no_mem  = 7,
                no_disk = 11,
                no_printer = 21};
   ```

2. Structures enable your application to define data types that contain logically related fields. These fields can have predefined or user-defined types. Thus you can include arrays, enumerated types, other structures, and unions. Structures are declared in C using the following general syntax:

   ```
   struct <structure name> {
                   <type 1> <field 1>;
                   <type 2> <field 2>;
                   <type 3> <field 3>;
                   .................
                   <type n> <field n>;
                 };
   ```

Examples for declaring structures are:

```
struct complex_math {
                         double real;
                         double imag;
                       };
struct pixel_point {
                         int x_coord;
                         int y_coord;
                         enum colors color;
                       };
struct mail_rec {
                      char name[31];
                      struct address_rec address;
                      double loan_amount;
                    };
```

Turbo C also supports **bitfields**, which are special structures that permit you to access specific bits. The general syntax for their declaration is:

```
struct <bitfield name> {
                               <type 1> <field 1> : <bits 1>;
                               <type 2> <field 2> : <bits 2>;
                               <type 3> <field 3> : <bits 3>;
                               .................
                               <type n> <field n> : <bits n>;
                           };
```

The bitfields map on memory locations from the least significant bit to the most significant one. Examples of bitfields are:

```
struct two_chars {
                    unsigned int char1 : 8;
                    unsigned int char2 : 8;
                  };
struct keyboard_status {
                     unsigned int capslock  : 1;
                     unsigned int scrollock : 1;
                     unsigned int numlock   : 1;
                    };


struct two_chars myword;
struct keyboard_status kbd_st;
myword.char1 = 'a';
myword.char2 = 64; /* ASCII code of character 'A' */
```

```
if myword.char1 == myword.char2
    kbd_st.capslock = 0;
else
    kbd_st.capslock = 1;
kbd_st.capslock = 1 - kbd_st.capslock; /* toggle key status */
```

3. **Unions** are structures whose fields are overlaid in memory. Each field offers an alternate form of accessing data and does not complement other fields. The general syntax for declaring a union is:

```
union <union name> {
                    <type 1> <field 1>;
                    <type 2> <field 2>;
                    <type 3> <field 3>;
                    ................
                    <type n> <field n>;
                   };
```

   In the following example a union is declared such that each field occupies eight bytes:

```
union eight_bytes {
                    char   c[8];
                    int    i[4];
                    float  x[2];
                    double y;
                  };
```

DECLARING VARIABLES AND CONSTANTS

Variables are declared in C using the following general syntax:

```
<data type>  <list of variable names>;
```

The variables in a list are delimited with commas and may be initialized. Examples of declaring scalar variables that utilize either a predefined or user-defined type are:

```
int i, j, k = 12;
char ch1 = 'a', ch2 = 65 /* ASCII code of 65 */;
double pi = 31.4;
struct complex a, b, c = { 2.34, 74.5 };
union eight_byte c;
```

Arrays are declared in C by specifying the size of each dimension. The lower bound of each array dimension is fixed at zero. Each array dimension is represented by a separate set of brackets. Examples for declaring and simultaneously initializing arrays are:

```
int numbers[10] = { 1, 2, 3, 4, 5, 6, 7, 8, 9, 0 };
char digits[10] = { '1', '2', '3', '4', '5',
                    '6', '7', '8', '9', '0' };
struct complex x[2] = {  { 1.0, 11.0 },      /* value for x[0] */
                         { 2.3. 9.43 } }; /* value for x[1] */
double matrix[2][2] = { { 1.0, 2.0} ,    /* values for x[0][0..1]  */
                        { 3.0, 4.0} }; /* values for x[1][0..1]  */
```

These examples also reveal that multidimensional arrays store values such that the rightmost index (or indices) changes faster than the one to its left. Initialized arrays can have their sizes removed if the number of data objects in the initialization is also the sought array size. Thus the above examples can be rewritten as follows to take advantage of this feature:

```
int numbers[] = { 1, 2, 3, 4, 5, 6, 7, 8, 9, 0 };
char digits[] = { '1', '2', '3', '4', '5',
                  '6', '7', '8', '9', '0' };
struct complex x[] = { { 1.0, 11.0 },      /* value for x[0] */
                       { 2.3. 9.43 } }; /* value for x[1] */
double matrix[][] = { { 1.0, 2.0} ,    /* values for x[0][0..1]  */
                      { 3.0, 4.0} }; /* values for x[1][0..1]  */
```

Strings are considered by C as arrays of characters with the null character used as the string delimiter. When dimensioning a string, one element must account for the null character. Turbo C provides a library for extensive string management functions. The file **string.h** contains the prototypes for the string functions.

Turbo C supports two access modifiers: **const** and **volatile**. Constants are declared either as macros using the **#define** directive (see the next section), or using the new ANSI const declaration. The latter declares that an identifier has a fixed value and cannot be altered. The general syntax for declaring a constant is:

```
const <type> <constant identifier> = <value>;
```

If the constant type is omitted, the **int** type is assumed by default. Examples for declaring constants are:

```
const DAY_IN_WEEK = 7;
const double PI = 3.14;
const char DELIMITER = '|';
```

Turbo C implements another variable-access modifier, namely, the **volatile** modifier. It informs the compiler that the contents of a variable are also modifiable by the underlying system.

Turbo C supports the following four storage classes:

1. The **auto** storage specifier explicitly declares local variables to be automatic. Local variables found in a function vanish once the function terminates its execution and returns to its caller.
2. The **static** storage specifier indicates that a local variable should be stored in a permanent memory location and retain its value between function calls.

3. The **extern** specifier resolves references to the same objects at link time. It commonly is used in multiple-file projects. In addition, the **extern** specifier is used to access global, compiler, and defined variables, and to prototype runtime library functions.
4. The **register** specifier instructs the compiler to use the hardware's CPU registers to store critical data in order to obtain significant speed performance.

COMPILER DIRECTIVES

Turbo C has the following directives:

1. The **#define** directives defines macros with optional arguments. The general syntax is:

```
#define <macro> <macro text or value>
#define <macro(<list of argument>) <macro expression>
```

Examples for using the **#define** directive are:

```
/* define data type macros */
#define BOOLEAN char
#define BYTE unsigned char
#define REAL double
#define INTEGER int
/* define macro keywords */
#define PRINT printf
#define WRITE printf
#define INPUT scanf
#define READ scanf
#define ReadKey getch()
#define ReadChar getche()
#define WRITELN printf("\n")
#define WRITELN2 printf("\n\n")
#define WRITELN3 printf("\n\n\n")
/* macros for popular shorthand command sequences */
#define readvar(msg,frmt,var) printf(msg); scanf(frmt, &var)
#define read2var(msg,frmt,x,y) printf(msg); scanf(frmt, &x, &y)
#define readchar(msg,var) printf(msg); var = getche()
/* define screen macros (somewhat similar to those in conio.h).
   Requires that the ANSI.SYS driver be in CONFIG.SYS  */
#define clrscr printf("\x1b[2J")
#define gotoxy(col,row) printf("\x1b[%d;%dH",col,row)
#define clreol printf("\x1b[K")
/* define boolean constants */
#define FALSE 0
#define TRUE 1
```

```
/* boolean pseudo-functions */
#define boolean(x) ((x) ? "TRUE" : "FALSE")
#define yesno(x) ((x) ? "Yes" : "No")
/* macros that define pseudo one-line functions */
#define abs(x) (((x) >= 0) ? (x) : -(x))
#define max(x,y) (((x) > (y)) ? (x) : (y))
#define min(x,y) (((x) > (y)) ? (y) : (x))
#define sqr(x) ((x) * (x))
#define cube(x) ((x) * (x) * (x))
#define reciprocal(x) (1 / (x))
/* macros used for character testing */
#define islower(c) ((c >= 'a') && (c <= 'z'))
#define isupper(c) ((c >= 'A') && (c <= 'Z'))
#define isdigit(c) ((c >= '0') && (c <= '9'))
#define isletter(c) ((c >= 'A') && (c <= 'z'))
/* macros used in character case conversions */
#define tolowercase(c) (c - 'A' + 'a')
#define touppercase(c) (c - 'a' + 'A')
```

A simple example of how a macro, with an argument, is expanded by the preprocessor is:

```
int a = 4, b = 7;
printf("Is %d greater than %d : %s",
        a, b, boolean(a > b))
```

This is converted into the following line by the preprocessor:

```
int a = 4, b = 7;
printf("Is %d greater than %d : %s",
        a, b, ((a > b) ? "TRUE" : "FALSE"))
```

When declaring a macro with arguments, enclose each argument in parentheses in the macro expression and enclose the entire macro expression in parentheses. This ensures that the macro-based pseudofunction works properly with expression-type arguments and also within other expressions.

2. Macros created by **#define** are undefined using the **#undef** directive. The general syntax is:

```
#undef <macro name>
```

3. The **#include** directive is used to include the source code from another file.

```
#include <filename>
```

or

```
#include "filename"
```

The two forms differ in the way that the included file is sought. Using the angle brackets, only the special directory for included files is searched. The current directory is not examined.

4. The **#error** error message directive halts program compilation when encountered and displays an accompanying error message. The general syntax is:

```
#error <error message text>
```

5. The **#if, #else, #elif,** and **#endif** conditional compilation directives act in a fashion similar to **if** statements. The only difference is that the outcome involves the decision of whether or not to compile certain code portions. The following is an example for using this set of directives.

```
#include <stdio.h>
#define FORMATTED_INPUT 1
main()
{
   char string[81];
   printf("Enter string : ");
   #if FORMATTED_INPUT == 1
      scanf("%s", string);
   #else
      gets(string);
   #endif
   printf("\n\nYou entered ");
   puts(string);
}
```

6. The **#line** directive enables you to assign a value to the predefined macro **__LINE__** and a filename to the macro **__FILE__**. The general syntax for using this directive is:

```
#line <line number> ["filename"]
```

7. The **#pragma** directive is loosely defined by the ANSI standard as a set of general-purpose directives in the following form:

```
#pragma <directive name>
```

The **#pragma** directives may vary in the C implementations that support them. The rule that is used is *if the directive is not recognized, ignore the* ***#pragma*** *directive altogether*.

There are two **#pragma** directives supported by Turbo C:

7.1 The **#pragma inline** directive informs the compiler that your source code contains in-line assembly language code.

7.2 The **#pragma warn** causes the Turbo C to override warning messages. You can include settings to turn on, turn off, or restore values of warning as they were when file compilation started. These settings are shown:

Directive	Meaning
`#pragma warn +<wrn1>`	Warning <wrn1> is turned on.
`#pragma warn -<wrn2>`	Warning <wrn2> is turned off.
`#pragma warn .<wrn3>`	Warning <wrn3> is restored.

Consult the Appendix C in the *Turbo C Reference Manual* for the complete list of warnings.

BASIC CONSOLE I/O

Console I/O may be classified into formatted and unformatted.

Formatted I/O

This class of I/O enables you to handle the I/O of multiple data items in one function call while simultaneously controlling the format of the data. The champions of this category are the **printf** and **scanf** functions that output and input data via the console, respectively. To use these I/O functions, a C program must include the header file **stdio.h**.

The **printf** function takes a variable number of arguments, the first of which must always be a string constant or a variable. The **printf** may contain a single string-typed argument, in which case it is used to simply output the content of the string itself. However, the **printf** function is primarily designed to use its first string argument as an output format control. Table 1.2 shows some C escape sequences that can be used with strings, and Table 1.3 provides the different options of **printf**. The **printf** function works with single data items as well as with strings (that is, arrays of characters that are properly end with a null character).

Table 1.2 The C Escape Sequences

Sequence	As Hex Value	Decimal Value	Task of Sequence
\a	0x07	7	Bell
\b	0x08	8	Backspace
\f	0x0C	12	Formfeed
\n	0x0A	10	New line
\r	0x0D	13	Carriage return
\t	0x09	9	Horizontal tab
\v	0x0B	11	Vertical tab
\\	0x5C	92	Backslash
\'	0x2C	44	Single quote
\"	0x22	34	Double quote
\?	0x3F	63	Question mark
\OOO			1 to 3 digits for an octal value
\XHHH and \xHHH			1 to 3 digits for a hexadecimal value

Table 1.3 Formatted I/O String Control

```
% [flags] [width] [.precision] [F|N|h|l] <type character>
```

Flag Character	Effect
-	Justify to the left within the designated field. The right side is padded with blanks.
+	Display the plus or minus sign of value.
blank	Display a leading blank if the value is positive. If the output is negative, a minus sign is used.
#	Display a leading 0 for octals. Display a leading 0X or 0x for hexadecimals. Display the decimal point for reals. No effect on integers.

Category	Type Character	Output Format
character	c	single character
integer	d	signed decimal int
	i	signed decimal int
	o	unsigned octal int
	u	unsigned decimal int
	x	unsigned hexadecimal int. The numeric character set used is [01234567890abcdef].
	X	unsigned hexadecimal int. The numeric character set used is [01234567890ABCDEF].
pointer	p	prints only offset of near pointers as AAAA and far pointers as SSSS:OOOO
pointer to int	n	stores a count of the characters printed so far in the specified pointer location
real	f	signed value in the form [-]dddd.dddd
	e	signed scientific format using [-]d.dddd e[+|-]ddd
	E	signed scientific format using [-]d.dddd E[+|-]ddd
	g	signed value using either 'e' or 'f' formats, depending on value and specified precision
	G	signed value using either 'E' or 'f' formats, depending on value and specified precision
string pointer	s	emits characters until a null-terminator or precision is attained

The **scanf** function is the counterpart of **printf**. Its first argument is the string format control. The other arguments must be the addresses of the data objects receiving the information. With scalar variables the **&** operator is used to provide the address of the data object. The following example shows how the **printf** and **scanf** functions are used:

```
#include <stdio.h>
#include "math.h"
main()
{
    int i, j;
    double x, y;
    char c, d;
    char name[81];
    struct complex {
            double real, imag;
            } a;
    printf("Enter you name : ");
    scanf("%s", name);
    printf("\nHello %s, how are you?\n\n", name);
    printf("Enter an integer : ");
    scanf("%d", &i);
    j = i + 1;
    printf("\n%d + 1 = %d\n\n", i, j);
    printf("Enter a real number : ");
    scanf("%lf", &x);
    y = x * x ;
    printf("\n%lf^2 = %lf\n\n", x, y);
    printf("Enter a character : ");
    scanf("%s", name); /* input to a string */
    c = name[0]; /* pick the first character of the string */
        d = c + 1;
        printf("\n%c follows %c\n\n", d, c);
        printf("Enter a complex number (2 reals delimited by space) : ");
        scanf("%lf %lf", &a.real, &a.imag);
        x = sqrt(a.real * a.real  + a.imag * a.imag);
        printf("\nabsolute value of complex number = %lf\n\n", x);
    }
```

Unformatted I/O

Unformatted I/O involves strings and characters. String I/O is performed by the **gets** and **puts** functions that read and write strings to the standard output, respectively.

```
#include <stdio.h>
main()
{
   char name[81];
   int i;
   printf("Enter a string : ");
   gets(name); /* no & operator is needed */

   for (i = 0; name[i] != '\0'; i++)
      /* if lowercase convert to uppercase */
      if (name[i] >= 'a' && name[i] <= 'z')
         name[i] += 'A' - 'a';
   puts(name); /* display uppercase version */
}
```

Character I/O is carried out using **getch** (read a character with no echo), **getche** (read a character with a screen echo), **putchar**, and **putc**. The following is an example of simple character I/O:

```
#include <stdio.h>
#include "conio.h"
main()
{
   char c, d;
   printf("Enter a character : ");
   c = getche(); /* input with echo */
   printf("\nYou typed ");
   putchar(c);
   printf("\nEnter a character : ");
   d = getch(); /* input with no echo */
   printf("\nYou typed ");
   putchar(d);
}
```

POINTERS

Pointers are powerful data objects in C. They hold the addresses of other data objects. C pointers are also associated with data types. This enables the pointer to keep track of the size of the data object to which it is pointing. This feature gives pointer arithmetic powerful capabilities: when a pointer is altered by **n**, for example, its associated address changes by **n * (the size of the object to which it points)**. This enables a pointer to access arrays by scrolling through every array member. The asterisk character is used in pointer declarations. Examples include:

```
int *ptr, i; /* only ptr is a pointer */
```

Once declared, pointers must be initialized with a valid address before they are able to work properly. There are two main routines to initialize a pointer:

1. Assign to the pointer the address of an existing object. In this case, the pointer stores the memory address of another variable (scalar, array, structure, etc.). The ampersand operator is used to return the address of a variable. Examples of this type of pointer initialization include:

```
char c = 'a', *ptr_char;
int i = 11, *ptr_int = &i; /* ptr_int now points to i */
struct complex a = {12.2, 334.9 }, *ptr_cmplx;
ptr_char = &c; /* ptr_char now point to c */
ptr_cmplx = &a; /* ptr_cmplx now points to a */
```

Concerning arrays and strings, C permits the bare array identifier to act as a pointer to the first array element. Thus, for example, if an array is declared as follows:

```
char myname[31];
```

then the identifier **myname** is equivalent to the expression pointing to the first element, **&myname[0].** Therefore, when pointers are used with arrays, the pointer is simply assigned the array name, as in:

```
char myname[31];
char *ptr = myname;
```

2. The pointer is involved in dynamic allocation. The run-time system allocates a new memory area and assigns its address to the pointer. The **malloc** and **calloc** functions are used for new dynamic allocation. The **realloc** function is used to adjust the size of an existing dynamic space. These functions return a **NULL** pointer if the (re)allocation fails. Since they return void-typed pointers, typecasting is required for the addresses of the pointers to be properly accessed. Dynamically allocated memory may be removed later using the **free** function. To use these functions, a C program must include the **alloc.h** header file. An example for dynamically allocating memory using malloc is:

```
struct complex {
                double real, imag;
              };
struct complex *ptr;
/* use pointer type casting since malloc returns a void pointer */
ptr = (struct complex *) malloc(sizeof(struct complex));
```

Pointers are used to access the data objects they point to using the asterisk and operator.

```
#include <stdio.h>
#include "math.h"
#include "alloc.h"
main()
{
```

```
    struct complex {
                    double real, imag;
                    };

    char d, c = 'a', *ptr_char;
    int j, i = 11, *ptr_int = &i; /* ptr_int points to i */
    double x;
    struct complex a = {12.2, 334.9 }, *ptr_cmplx;
    struct complex *ptr;
    ptr = (struct complex *) malloc(sizeof(struct complex));
    ptr_char = &c; /* ptr_char now point to c */
    ptr_cmplx = &a; /* ptr_cmplx now points to a */
    d = *ptr_char + 1; /* ASCII of d = ASCII of c + 1 */
    j = *ptr_int  *  *ptr_int; /* j = i * i */
    /* copy contents of 'a' into dynamic memory using the
       ptr_cmplx and ptr pointers.
    */
    ptr->real = ptr_cmplx->real;
    ptr->imag = ptr_cmplx->imag;
    x = sqrt(a.real * ptr->real + a.imag * ptr->imag);
}
```

In accessing an array, a pointer may employ one of the following schemes, depending on the application:

1. When the members of an array are accessed in a nonsequential order, an offset integer can be used to select the sought element. If **x[i]** represents an element of the array, it is accessed using the pointer **ptr**, by using ***(ptr + i)**. Similarly, the address of that element is available in the form **&x[i]** or **(ptr + i)**. In such access schemes, the pointer is assigned the base address of the array and retains that address.
2. When the members of an array are to be accessed in a perfect sequence, pointer arithmetic can be used. The method normally starts by assigning the base address of the array to the pointer. To access the next array member, the pointer is incremented by one. Thus, the pointer address is constantly changing. Accessing the array members in a perfectly sequential manner avoids using the array identifier and an offset index. The following example initializes an array with values in descending order and sorts it ascending order. Both array access methods are used.

```
#include <stdio.h>
#define SIZE 100
main()
{
   int numbers[SIZE];
   int i, j, tempo, *ptr;
```

```
    /* assign descending values to array members */
    ptr = numbers; /* assign base-address of array to pointer */
    /* scroll through the array */
    for (i = 0; i < SIZE; i++, ptr++)
       *ptr = SIZE - i;
    ptr = numbers; /* reassign base-address of array to pointer */
    /* employ bubble sort to arrange the array in ascending order */
    for (i = 0; i < (SIZE - 1); i++) {
       for (j = i+1; j < SIZE; j++) {
          /* access elements in an imperfect sequential manner */
          if (*(ptr+i) > *(ptr+j)) {
                tempo = *(ptr+i);
                *(ptr+i) = *(ptr+j);
                *(ptr+j) = tempo;
          }
       }
    }
    /* display array in descending order */
    for (i = 0; i < SIZE; i++)
       printf("%d  ",*(numbers+i));
    printf("\n\n\n");
}
```

Concerning the access of multidimensional arrays using pointers, the following scheme is used:

Access Using Indices	Access Using Pointers
`x[i][j]`	`*( *(ptr + i) + j)`
`x[i][j][k]`	`*( *( *(ptr + i) + j) + k)`

The following example illustrates the use of pointers to access two-dimensional numeric arrays. The program prompts the user for the number of rows, the number of columns, the matrix of data, and then calculates the average value for each column in the matrix.

```
/*
  C program that demonstrates the use of pointers to access
  two-dimension arrays. The average value of each matrix column
  is calculated.
*/
#include <stdio.h>
#include "conio.h"
#define MAX_COL 10
#define MAX_ROW 30
main()
```

```
{
    double x[MAX_ROW][MAX_COL];
    double sum, sumx, mean;
    int i, j, rows, columns;
    clrscr();
    do {
        printf("Enter number of rows [2 to %d] : ",MAX_ROW);
        scanf("%d", &rows); printf("\n");
    } while (rows < 2 || rows > MAX_ROW);

    do {
        printf("Enter number of columns [1 to %d] : ",MAX_COL);
        scanf("%d", &columns); printf("\n");
    } while (columns < 1 || columns > MAX_COL);
    for (i = 0; i < rows; i++)   {
        for (j = 0; j < columns; j++)   {
            printf("X[%d][%d] : ",i,j);
            scanf("%lf", *(x+i)+j); printf("\n");
        }
        printf("\n");
    }
    for (j = 0; j < columns; j++)   {
        sum = rows;
        sumx = 0.0;
        for (i = 0; i < rows; i++)
            sumx += *(*(x+i)+j);
        mean = sumx / sum;
        printf("\n\n");
        printf("Mean for column %d = %lf\n\n",j+1,mean);
    } /* for j */
    printf("\n\n");
}
```

OPERATORS

The operators in C can be classified into the following categories (see Table 1.4):

1. **Arithmetic operators** These include the four arithmetic functions and the modulus operator.
2. **Assignment operators** These allow assignments that update a variable to be written in a shorter form. Each assignment operator is made up of an equal sign and an arithmetic or bitwise operator placed to its left. The general syntax for assignment operators is:

   ```
   <variable> <operator>= <expression>;
   ```

which is equivalent to the long form:

```
<variable> = <variable> <operator> <expression>;
```

Examples of assignment operators are:

```
sum += x; /* same as sum = sum + x */
power *= term; /* same as power = power * term */
map |= 0x1F; /* same as map = map | 0x1F */
```

3. **Increment (++) and decrement (—) operators** These operators increment or decrement the value of variables by one. They are placed either immediately before or after the variable name, with no spaces in between. If these operators are placed before the variable name, then the value of the variable is first altered before it may enter into any expression. If these operators are placed after the variable name, then the value of the variable may enter in any expression before the variable is altered. An example is:

```
main ()
{
    int i, j, k;
    i = 10;
    j = 34;
    k = j * i++; /* i contributes a 10 to the expression
                    and then is incremented.  k is assigned 340 */
    k = j * —i; /* i is first decremented from 11 to 10.
                   The value of 10 enters in evaluating k */
}
```

4. **Relational operators** These operators are used in composing logical expressions. Such expressions are false if their value is zero; otherwise, they are true. The conditional operator may be regarded as a miniature form of the **if** statement. The general syntax for a conditional operator is:

```
(<expression>) ? <if-true-value> : <if-false-value>;
```

If the expression is true (i.e., nonzero), the **<if-true-value>** is returned; otherwise, the **<if-false-value>** is returned.

Notably absent is the relation **XOR** operator, which can be simulated. Examples of using relation operators are:

```
#include <stdio.h>
main ()
{
    int i, j, k;
    i = 10;
    j = 34;
    k = (i > 5); /* assign a non-zero value to k */
    k = (!(i > 5)); /* assigns a 0 to k */
```

```
    k = (i >= 11) && ( j == 30); /* assign 0 to k */
    k = (i != 8) || (j <= 0); /* assigns a 0 to k */
    k = (i > 100) ? 100 : -100; /* assigns -100 to k */
}
```

5. **Bitwise operators** These operators alter the bit pattern of a variable. C includes the bitwise version of **AND**, **OR**, **XOR**, and **NOT**.

   Examples of using bitwise operators are:

```
main
{
   int i, j, k;
   i = 50;
   j = 124;
   k = i | j; /* OR bits of i and j */
   k = i & j; /* AND bits of i and j */
   k = i >> 2; /* shift right bits of i by 2 places */
   k = i << 3; /* shift left bits of i by 3 places *
}
```

6. **Access operators** These operators include the dot and -> operators for accessing fields of structures and unions by nonpointers and pointers, respectively. The brackets are used to access elements of an array, and the parentheses are utilized to access addresses.
7. **The** sizeof **operator** This function-like operator returns the size of a data type or a variable. The single argument of sizeof is either a data type or a variable name.
8. **Comma operator** This operator is mainly employed in delimiting expressions in the for loop.

Table 1.4 also shows the order of precedence for the various C operators.

Table 1.4 Operators in C

Arithmetic Operators		Arithmetic Assignment Operators	
C Operator	**Function**	**Assignment Operator**	**Equivalent Long Form**
+	Unary Plus	x += y	x = x + y
-	Unary Minus	x -= y	x = x - y
+	Add	x *= y	x = x * y
-	Subtract	x /= y	x = x / y
*	Multiply	x %= y	x = x % y
/	Divide		
%	Modulus		

Table 1.4 Operators in C *(continued)*

Relational Operators

Operator	Meaning
&&	AND
||	OR
!	NOT
N/A	XOR
<	
<=	
>	
>=	
==	=
!=	<>
?	:

Bit-manipulating Operator

Operator	Meaning
&	AND
|	OR
^	XOR
~	NOT
<<	SHL
>>	SHR

Bit-manipulating Assignment Operators

C Operator	Long Form
x |= y	x = x | y
x ^= y	x = x ^ y
x <<= y	x = x << y
x >>= y	x = x >> y

Operators in C with their precedence and evaluation direction

Category	Name	Symbol	Eval. Direction	Precedence
Selection	Parentheses	()	left to right	1
	Array indexing	[]	left to right	1
	Field reference	.	left to right	1
		->	left to right	1
Monadic	Post-increment	++	left to right	2
	Post-decrement	--	left to right	2
	Address	&	right to left	2
	Bitwise NOT	~	right to left	2
	Type cast	(type)	right to left	2
	Logical NOT	!	right to left	2
	Negation	-	right to left	2
	Plus sign	+	right to left	2
	Pre-increment	++	right to left	2
	Pre-decrement	--	right to left	2
	Type cast	(type)	right to left	2
	Size of data	sizeof	right to left	2
Multiplicative	Modulus	%	left to right	3
	Multiply	*	left to right	3
	Divide	/	left to right	3

Category	Name	Symbol	Eval. Direction	Precedence
Additive	Add	+	left to right	4
	Subtract	-	left to right	4
Bitwise Shift	Shift left	<<	left to right	5
	Shift right	<<	left to right	5
Relational	Less than	<	left to right	6
	Less or equal	<=	left to right	6
	Greater than	>	left to right	6
	Greater or equal	>=	left to right	6
	Equal to	==	left to right	7
	Not equal to	!=	left to right	7
Bitwise	AND	&	left to right	8
	XOR	^	left to right	9
	OR	|	left to right	10
Logical	AND	&&	left to right	11
	OR	||	left to right	12
Ternary	Cond. Express.	? :	right to left	13
Assignment	Arithmetic	=	right to left	14
		+=		
		-=		
		*=		
		/=		
		%=		
	Shift	>>=	right to left	14
		<<=	right to left	14
	Bitwise	&=	right to left	14
		|=		
		^=		
	Comma	,	left to right	15

EXPRESSIONS

C supports the following types of expressions.

1. **Expressions using operators** These are the most popular expressions that involve the different operators discussed in the last section.
2. **Array subscript expressions** These expressions are specialized in retrieving particular array elements. They come in two general forms:
   - Using an explicit index: <array>[<index>]
   - Using a pointer and an offset: *(<array_name> + <index>)

   Examples are:

```
#include <stdio.h>
main()
{
  int numbers[100], i, j, k, *ptr1;
  double table[10][10], x;
  double* *ptr2;
  ptr1 = numbers;
  i = 10;
  k = numbers[i];
  /* or */
  k = *(ptr1 + i);
  ptr2 = table;
  i = 5;
  j = 3;
  x = table[i][j];
  /* or */
  x = *( *(ptr2 + i) + j);
}
```

3. **Structure/Union member selection expressions** Variables that are structures or unions access any of their fields using the dot operator. Pointers to structures and unions use the -> operator instead. The following is an example for both access types:

```
#include <string.h>
struct pc_info_rec {
      char brand[31];
      unsigned int num_drive;
      unsigned int kram;
      double cost;
   };

typedef struct pc_info_rec pc_info;
```

```
main()
{
  pc_info my_pc, *ptr = &my_pc;
  /* assign values of first two fields using my_pc structure */
  strcpy("Hindi PC", &my_pc.brand[0]);
  my_pc.num_drive = 3;
  /* assign last two fields using pointer access */
  ptr->kram = 2000;
 ptr->cost = 5000.0;
}
```

4. **Typecast expressions** These expressions enable you to transform data from one type to another compatible type. When typecasting to types with a larger size, the expressions retain their information and sign if possible. In the following example, the information is passed from one type to another "upwardly compatible" type. The ASCII code of the letter A is stored in the integer and real variables:

```
main ()
{
  char c = 'A';
  int i;
  long j;
  double x;
  i = (int) c; /* i is assign 65 */
  j = (long) i; /* j is assigned 65, stored as a long integer */
  x = (double) j; /* x is assigned 65. */
}
```

DECISION-MAKING CONSTRUCTS

C supports the if and **if-else** statements. The general syntax for the **if** statement is:

```
if (tested expression is not zero)
    single statement | { sequence of C statements }
```

The general syntax for the **if-else** statement is:

```
if (tested expression is not zero)
    single statement | { sequence of C statements }
else
          single statement | { sequence of C statements }
```

Nested **if-else** statements are allowed in C and have the following general syntax:

```
if (tested expression #1 is not zero)
    single statement | { sequence of C statements }
```

```
else if (tested expression #2 is not zero)
    single statement | { sequence of C statements }
else if (tested expression #3 is not zero)
    single statement | { sequence of C statements }
..........
else if (tested expression #n is not zero)
    single statement | { sequence of C statements }
else
    single statement | { sequence of C statements }
```

The tested expressions of a nested **if-else** statement are evaluated in sequence until either one of them returns a nonzero value, or until the **else** clause is reached.

Other rules for using the if statement are:

1. The tested expression must be enclosed in parentheses.
2. The C language has no **then** keyword.
3. Block statements in C are enclosed in open and close braces. Each statement must end with a semicolon, including the last one in a block. The close brace must not be followed by a semicolon.

An example for using the if statement is shown below. The program toggles the case of letters of a string and converts all nonletter characters to the dot character:

```
#include <stdio.h>
main()
{
   char string[81];
   char *ptr;
   printf("Enter a string : ");
   gets(string);
   for (i = 0, ptr = string; *ptr != '\0'; ptr++)
      /* if lowercase convert to uppercase */
      if (*ptr >= 'a' && *ptr <='z')
         *ptr += 'A' - 'a';
      /* if uppercase convert to lowercase */
      else if (*ptr >= 'A' && *ptr <= 'Z')
         *ptr -= 'A' - 'a';
      else
         *ptr = '.'; /* assign a dot to non-letters */
   puts(name); /* display altered case version */
}
```

The C language supports the **switch** statement, which closely resembles a nested **if-else** statement. The general syntax is:

```
switch (variable) {
    case constant1:
   [case constant2:...]
        one or more statement;
        break;
    case constant3:
   [case constant4: ...]
        one or more statement;
        break;
    ......
    default:
        one or more statement;
        break;
}
```

The following must be observed when using a **switch** statement:

1. The **switch** value must be an integer-compatible value. You may use a variable, function, or expression to supply the **switch** value.
2. The **case** labels must contain constants (enclosed in optional parenetheses) only.
3. One **case** label is allowed for each constant value. C does not support ranges of values to be associated with a single **case** label.
4. The **break** statement must be used at the end of a case clause to force the program flow to resume after the end of the **switch** statement.
5. No braces are needed to contain statement blocks within each **case** clause.

The following example requests a day number and comments on the value entered.

```
#include <stdio.h>
main()
{
   enum days { Sunday = 1, Monday, Tuesday,
               Wednesday, Thursday, Friday, Saturday };
   enum days week_day;
   int day_num;
   do {
      printf("Enter a week day number (Sunday = 1) : ");
      scanf("%d", &day_num);
   } while (day_num < 1 || day_num > 7);
   week_day = day_num;
   switch (week_day) {
      case Sunday:
      case Saturday:
```

```
            printf("Enjoy the weekend\n");
            break;
        case Monday:
        case Tuesday:
        case Wednesday:
        case Thursday:
            printf("Working 9 to 5:30!\n");
            break;
        case Friday:
            printf("T.G.I.F.!\n");
            break;
    }
}
```

LOOP CONSTRUCTS

C supports a number of loop constructs.

1. The **for** loop has three parts: the initialization statement, loop continuation test, and increment/decrement statement. This is shown in the following general syntax:

```
for(list of value initialization statement;
    loop continuation test;
    list of increment statement)
```

The **for** loop in C is noted for the following:

a. Each part of the **for** loop is optional. Eliminating all three parts results in having an open **for** loop that will execute indefinitely without interruption.

b. The initialization and increment/decrement parts may contain multiple statements separated by commas. Thus, multiple loop control variables may be used in a **for** loop.

The following example initializes an array with values in descending order and sorts it ascending order. Both array access methods are used.

```
#include <stdio.h>
#define SIZE 100
main()
{
    int numbers[SIZE];
    int i, j, *ptr;
    /* assign descending values to array members */
    /* scroll through the array */
```

```
    for (i = 0, ptr = numbers; i < SIZE; i++, ptr++)
       *ptr = SIZE - i;
    ptr = numbers; /* reassign base-address of array to pointer */
    /* employ bubble sort to arrange the array in ascending order */
    for (i = 0; i < (SIZE - 1); i++) {
       for (j = i+1; j < SIZE; j++) {
          /* access elements in an imperfect sequential manner */
          if (*(ptr+i) > *(ptr+j)) {
                tempo = *(ptr+i);
                *(ptr+i) = *(ptr+j);
                *(ptr+j) = tempo;
          }
       }
    }
    /* display array in ascending order */
    for (i = 0; i < SIZE; i++, ptr++)
       printf("%d  ",numbers[i]);
    printf("\n\n\n");
}
```

2. The **do-while** reiterates the loop body as long as a tested expression is true (i.e., nonzero). The general syntax of the **do-while** loop is:

   ```
   do {
       sequence of statements
   } while (logical expression);
   ```

   An example of a **do-while** loop is the following code fragment that prompts for a Yes/No answer:

   ```
   do {
      printf("More calculations? Y/N ");
      answer = getche();
      printf("\n");
   } while (answer != 'Y' || answer != 'y' ||
            answer != 'N' || answer != 'n');
   ```

3. The **while** loop executes its statements as long as the tested condition is true (i.e., nonzero). The general syntax for the **while** loop is:

   ```
   while (logical expression)
       single statement | { sequence of statements }
   ```

Loops are exited using the **break** statement. The program resumes after the end of the loop where the **break** is placed. The **exit** statement is used to exit a loop and halt the program altogether.

An example for using the **while** loop is shown below. The program toggles the case of letters of a string and converts all nonletter characters to the dot character. The **while** loop is employed to examine every character of the input string:

```
#include <stdio.h>
main()
{
   char string[81];
   char *ptr string;
   int i = 0;
   printf("Enter a string : ");
   gets(string);
   while (*ptr != '\0') {
      /* if lowercase convert to uppercase */
      if (*ptr >= 'a' && *ptr <= 'z')
         *ptr += 'A' - 'a';
      /* if uppercase convert to lowercase */
      else if (*ptr >='A' && *ptr <= 'Z')
         *ptr -= 'A' - 'a';
   else
         *ptr = '.'; /* assign a dot to non-letters */
      ptr++;
   }
   puts(name); /* display altered case version */
}
```

Loop execution flow may be controlled using the **continue** or **exit** statements. The **break** statement is used to exit a loop and resumes right after its end. The **continue** statement, as the name suggests, bypasses the remainder of the loop and resumes at its beginning. It attempts to execute the next iteration.

CHAPTER

2

Functions

This chapter takes a brief look at the different types of user-definable functions in C. The following is a list of these functions:

1. Functions that return a result
   a. Return a predefined data type
   b. Return a user-defined data type
2. Functions that modify their arguments (may or may not return a result)
3. Functions that do not return a result or modify arguments

The general syntax for declaring a function following the ANSI standard is:

```
[data type] function name(list of typed arguments | void)
{
   <declarations of data objects>
   <statements>
   return <expression>; /* optional */
}
```

When the function's data type is omitted, the function is assumed to return a result of type **int**. The list of typed arguments contains the detailed declaration of the parameters; each parameter is preceded by its data type. If no parameter list is used, the void keyword must be placed in parentheses following the function's name. Every function may declare its own constants, types, and variables. All of these data objects are local to that function only. The return statement is normally used to transmit a result back to the calling routine.

Under the new ANSI standard, all functions whose data type are not **int** must be declared. This is called *prototyping* and it enables the compiler to detect any misapplication of a function. Function prototyping normally occurs outside any function to achieve a desired global effect.

FUNCTIONS THAT RETURN RESULTS

This category of functions follows the typical notion of a function: a routine that takes arguments by value and returns a single result. No argument modification is performed with the functions of this category, in which there are two classes of functions:

1. **Functions that return a predefined data type** This class of function represents the simplest functions in C. The following program illustrates how to prototype, utilize, and declare a set of functions. These functions also demonstrate the variations in this class of functions stemming from the different types of arguments:

```
#include <stdio.h>
#include "math.h"
struct point {
               double xcoord;
               double ycoord;
             };
#define ARRAY_SIZE 100
/* declare function prototype */
double get_pi(void);
double dbl_square(double);
long int_power(int, int);
double distance(struct point, struct point);
double mean(double*, int);
main()
{
      double y;
      long base, expon;
      struct point a = { 1.0L, 2.0L };
      struct point b = { 2.0L, 3.0L };
      double x[ARRAY_SIZE];
      int i, ndata = ARRAY_SIZE;
      char string[31] = "Hello World";
      /* test function get_pi() */
      printf("Pi is aprox. = %lf\n", get_pi());
      /* test function dbl_square */
      y = 5.0;
      printf("%lf squared = %lf\n", y, dbl_square(y));
      /* test function int_power */
```

```
        base = 2;
        expon = 4;
        printf("%ld^%ld = %ld\n", base, expon, int_power(base, expon));
        /* test function distance */
        printf("Distance between points a and b = %lf\n",distance(a, b));
        /* test function mean */
        for (i = 0; i < ndata; i++)
           x[i] = i * i - 1;
        printf("Mean value of array = %lf\n", mean(x, ndata));
        /* test function strlen */
        printf("There are %d characters in '%s'\n",
          my_strlen(string), string);
}
/* function with no arguments.  Works as a pseudo-constant */
double get_pi(void)
{
        return 355.0L / 113.0L;
}
/* function with a single argument */
double dbl_square(double x)
{
        return x * x;
}
/* function with two simple arguments */
long int_power(int base, int exponent)
{
        long power = 1;
        while (exponent-- > 0)
           power *= base;
        return power;
}
/* function that takes structured arguments */
double distance(struct point a, struct point b)
/* this function needs math.h to use the sqrt function */
{
        double x, y;
        x = b.xcoord - a.xcoord;
        y = b.ycoord - a.ycoord;
        return sqrt(x * x + y * y);
}
/* function that takes an array */
```

```
double mean(double x[], int ndata)
{
      double sumx, sum = ndata;
      while (ndata-- > 0)
         sumx += x[ndata];
      return sumx / sum;
}
/* function that takes a string-typed argument */
int my_strlen(char* string)
{
      int count = 0;
      char* ptr = string;
      while (*ptr != '\0') {
         ptr++;
         count++;
      }
      return count;
}
```

2. **Functions that return a user-defined data type** Enumerated types, structures, and unions may be used as function types. The following examples illustrate how functions may return structures.

```
/* function that calculates the centroid of a shape */
struct point centroid(struct point vertex[], int num_vertex)
{
      struct point result = { 0.0, 0.0 };
       int i;
      for (i = 0; i < num_vertex; i++) {
         result.xcoord += vertex[i].xcoord;
         result.ycoord += vertex[i].ycoord;
      }
      result.xcoord /= num_vertex;
      result.ycoord /= num_vertex;
      return result; /* return structure result */
   }
   struct string {
                  char str[256];
                  int strlen;
                };
   /* return the concatenation of two structured strings */
   struct string concat(struct string str1, struct string str2)
```

```
{
    struct string result;
    int i, j;
    /* initialize result */
    result.str[0] = '\0';
    result.strlen = 0;
    if (str1.strlen > 0) {
       /* copy characters of str1 to intermediate result */
       for (i = 0; i < str1.strlen; i++)
          result.str[i] = str1.str[i];
       result.strlen = str1.strlen; /* copy string length field */
    }
    if (str2.strlen > 0) {
       j = str1.strlen;
       /* concat characters of str2 to intermediate result */
       for (i = 0; i < str2.strlen; i++)
          result.str[i+j] = str2.str[i];
       result.strlen += str1.strlen;
    }
    return result;
}
```

Returning structures enables a C function to return multiple results that are logically related.

ARGUMENT-MODIFYING FUNCTIONS

This category of functions modifies its arguments and may or may not return a result. Frequently, these functions return results to primarily reflect the success or failure status of their tasks. The arguments, which as passed by reference, either receive data or are modified.

Functions may modify their scalar-typed arguments. These are either predefined or user-defined types. An example of a function whose arguments have their values modified is the function **swap_int**. Its takes two arguments and swaps their values:

```
/* function to swap two integers */
void swap_int(int *i, int *j)
{
    int tempo;
    tempo = *i;
    *i = *j;
    *j = tempo;
}
```

An example of a function with an argument that both receives and returns a value is the following **power** function:

```
int power(double base, double exponent, double *result);
{
    if (base == 0.0) {
        *result = 0.0;
        return 0; /* no-error code */
    }
    else if (base > 0.0) {
        /* function exp and log in math.h */
        *result = exp(exponent * log(base));
        return 0; /* no-error code */
    }
    else {
        *result = -1.0; /* dummy result */
        return -1; /* error code */
    }
}
```

If the exponentiation occurs without any error, the function returns a 0; otherwise, a -1 is returned.

Functions may modify their array-typed arguments. The following program creates, sorts, and displays a numeric array. The void-typed functions **initializearray** and **shellsort** alter the values of their arguments. The **initializearray** function simply fills its array-type argument with new values, overwriting any previous values (most likely random junk). The **shellsort** function alters the values of its array-type argument by putting the members of the array in ascending order:

```
/*
   Program will test the speed of sorting an integer array.
   It will create a sorted array (in descending order) and
   then sort it in the reverse order.
*/
#include <stdio.h>
#include "conio.h"
enum booleans { TRUE, FALSE };
typedef enum booleans boolean;
typedef unsigned char byte;
typedef unsigned int word;
/* define 'numbers' as an array-type identifier */
typedef word numbers[ARRAY_SIZE];
#define ARRAY_SIZE 1000
/* declare prototype of void functions used */
```

```
void initializearray(int*);
void swapthem(int*, int*);
void shellsort(int*);
void displayarray(int*);
main()
{
   char ch;
   numbers A;
   initializearray(A);
   printf("Beginning to sort press <cr>");
   ch = getche(); printf("\n");
   shellsort(A);
   puts("Finished sorting!");
   displayarray(A);
}
void initializearray(int *A)
/* routine to initialize array */
{
    int i;
    puts("Initializing integer array");
    for (i = 0 ; i < ARRAY_SIZE; i++)
        *(A++) = ARRAY_SIZE - i;
}
void swapthem(int *x, int *y)
/* routine that swaps elements x and y */
{
    int temporary = *x;
    *x = *y;
    *y = temporary;
}
void shellsort(int *A)
/* routine to perform a Shell-Metzner sorting */
{
    int offset, i, j;
    boolean sorted;
    offset = ARRAY_SIZE;
    while (offset > 1)  {
        offset /=  2;
        do {
            sorted = TRUE;
            for (j = 0; j < (ARRAY_SIZE - offset); j++)  {
```

```
                i = j + offset;
                if (*(A+i) < *(A+j))  {
                    swapthem((A+i),(A+j));
                    sorted = FALSE;
                }
            }
        } while (sorted == FALSE);
    }
}
void displayarray(int *A)
/* Display array members */
{
    int i;
    for (i = 0; i < ARRAY_SIZE; i++)
        printf("%4d", *(A+i));
    printf("\n");
}
```

PROCEDURE-ORIENTED FUNCTIONS

These functions are void-type functions that are similar to procedures in other structured languages, such as Pascal. They neither return a result nor modify arguments; instead, they perform a specific task. Examples of this class of function are the following routines used to perform basic screen and cursor control:

```
/* set of void functions (i.e. procedures) to perform screen
   management and waiting for a key to be pressed.
   The screen and cursor routines work with the ANSI.SYS driver.
*/
void clrscr(void)
{
   printf("\x1b[2J");
}
void gotoxy(int col,int row)
{
   printf("\x1b[%d;%dH", row, col);
}
void clreol(void)
{
   printf("\x1b[K");
}
void wait_key(void)
{
```

```
  char akey;
   printf("\n\npress any key to continue");
   akey = getch();
}
```

Among the above **void** functions, only **gotoxy** utilizes a parameter list. The rest of the routines do not require arguments.

RECURSIVE FUNCTIONS

C supports recursive functions. This enables C applications to handle data structures, such as lists and trees, using recursive algorithms. The following recursive function calculates factorials:

```
double factorial(int n)
/* recursive function that calculates factorials */
{
      if (n > 1)
         /* issue a recursive function call */
         return factorial(n-1) * (double) n;
      else
         return 1.0L;
}
```

FUNCTION POINTERS

A function name followed by an argument list leads to its evaluation, but a bare function name is a pointer to that function. Using pointers to functions, you are able to perform two basic types of tasks:

1. *Assign a function to a pointer and use the pointer as an indirect reference to the function.* This may sound like it is creating more work, but it can be used to reduce the code length. Consider the case of a program that has a library of similar functions (i.e., they have the same parameter list and return the same data type), of which only one is needed at a time. Without using pointers to functions you must use a **switch** statement every time one of these functions is invoked. As the number of calls increases, the code length also increases rapidly. In contrast, by using pointers to functions, the code length is controlled more effectively. A **switch** statement is used once to connect the pointer to the sought function. Any reference to a library function is carried out using the pointer.
2. *Pass functions as arguments to other functions.* This enables you to create an advanced function system where part of the function is another function selected from a library of routines.

The following is an example of using a pointer to a function to invoke the function. It displays the values of a function, accessed by a pointer, for the range of one to ten:

```
#include <stdio.h>
main()
{
   double x;
   const double delta = 1.0;
   const double first = 0.0;
   const double last = 10.0;
   /* declare function pointer */
   double (*fx)();
   /* declare prototype of sample function */
   double quad_poly(double);
   fx = quad_poly; /* assign function name to pointer */
   x = first;
   while (c <= last) {
      printf("f(%lf) = %lf\n", x, *(fx)(x));
      x += delta;
   }
}
double quad_poly(double x)
{
   double a = 1.0, b = -3.0, c = 5.0;
   return ((x * a) * x + b) * x + c;
}
```

The next example illustrates how an array of function pointers is declared and used. Three function pointers are declared. The first accesses the user-defined function, and the other two pointers are connected with function in file **math.h**. The program displays the values of each function, accessed by its pointer, for the range of one to ten:

```
#include <stdio.h>
#include <conio.h>
#include <math.h>
#define MAX 3
main()
{
   double x;
   const double delta = 1.0;
   const double first = 0.0;
   const double last = 10.0;
   /* declare array of function pointers */
   double (*fx[MAX])();
   int i;
   char ch;
```

```
   /* declare prototype of sample function */
   double quad_poly(double);
   fx[1] = quad_poly; /* assign function name to pointer */
   fx[2] = sqrt;
   fx[3] = log;
   for (i = 0; i < MAX; i++) {
      x = first;
      while (c <= last) {
         printf("f(%lf) = %lf\n", x, *(fx)(x));
         x += delta;
      }
      printf("press any key to continue ");
      ch = getche();
      clrscr();
}
double quad_poly(double x)
{
   double a = 1.0, b = -3.0, c = 5.0;
   return ((x * a) * x + b) * x + c;
}
```

The next example illustrates how a pointer to a function enables you to pass the function as a parameter to another function. It contains the **find_largest** function that looks for the function's largest value in a given range. The scanned function is passed as an argument to **find_largest** by using the function pointer **fx**.

```
#include <stdio.h>
main()
{
   double x;
   const double delta = 0.01;
   const double first = 0.0;
   const double last = 10.0;
   /* declare function pointer */
   double (*fx)();
   /* declare prototype of sample function */
   double quad_poly(double);
   double find_largest(double, double, double, double (*fx)());
   fx = quad_poly; /* assign function name to pointer */
   printf("The largest value in the range %lf -> %lf ", first, last);
   printf("is %lf\n", find_largest(first, last, delta, fx));
   }
}
```

```
double quad_poly(double x)
{
   double a = 1.0, b = -3.0, c = 5.0;
   return ((x * a) * x + b) * x + c;
}
double find_largest(double a, double b, double step, double (*fx)())
/* find the largest function value in the range [a,b], scanning in
   the step size.
*/
{
   double x = a, big = (*fx)(a);
   while (x <= b) {
      if (big < (*fx)(x) )
         big = (*fx)(x);
      x += step;
   {
   return big;
}
```

ACCESSING THE COMMAND LINE ARGUMENTS

A language like C, used to develop operating systems, is expected to provide a mechanism for accessing command line arguments. This enables you to fine-tune the way the program works. The general format is:

```
A> <program name> <argument 1> <argument 2> ... <argument n>
```

The number of command line arguments varies, depending on what the program does.

In C you resort to using a special parameter list for function **main**. The parameter list is:

```
main(int argc, char* argv[])
```

The first parameter, **argc**, returns a count for the number of command line arguments. The **argv** is an array of character pointers that accesses the arguments.

The following table maps the items pointed to by each element of **argv**.

i	Contents of argv[i]
0	program name (in DOS 3.0 and later)
1	argument #1
2	argument #2
argc-1	argument #(argc-1)

The following program demonstrates the access of command line arguments and their use to influence its (i.e., the program's) behavior. The program is similar to a simple four-function calculator that takes its input from the DOS command line. It is used following this general syntax:

```
       CALC <operand 1> <operator> <operand 2>
/* C program that uses command line arguments to
  perform one-line calculations.  Only the four basic
  operations are supported.
  For practical use make filename CALC.EXE, so that when
  you invoke it from DOS you type, for example:
    A> CALC  355 / 113
*/
#include <stdio.h>
#include "stdlib.h"
main(int argc, char* argv[])
{
    char opr;
    int error1, error2, error3;
    char strng[81];
    double result, first, second;
    if (argc < 4)   {
      printf("Proper arguments : <number> <operation> <number>");
      printf("\n\n");
      exit(0);
    }
    /* convert operands to double */
    first  = atof(argv[1]);
    second = atof(argv[3]);
    strcpy(strng,argv[2]);
    opr = strng[0];
    if (opr != '+' && opr != '-' && opr != '*' && opr != '/')
         error2 = 1;
    else
         error2 = 0;
    if (first == 0.0 || error2 == 1 || second == 0.0) {
         printf("bad number(s) or operator\n\n");
         exit(0);
    }
    switch (opr) {
         case '+' :
             result = first + second; break;
```

```
        case '-' :
           result = first - second; break;
        case '*' :
           result = first * second; break;
    case '/' :
       result = first / second; break;
    }
    printf("result = %lf\n\n", result);
}
```

FUNCTIONS WITH A VARIABLE NUMBER OF ARGUMENTS

C permits you to write functions that accept a variable number of arguments. The components you need to write functions with a variable number of arguments include data objects and routines imported from library **stdarg.h**. The following general steps must be followed:

1. Include file **stdarg.h** in your C code.
2. If the variable-argument function is not of type **int**, you prototype it using:

   ```
   <type> <function>(<list for the type of fixed arguments>,...);
   ```

   The above indicates that there must be at least one fixed argument in the function.
3. The function is declared:

   ```
   <type> <function>(<list of fixed parameters>,...);
   ```

4. The **va_list** pointer-type, imported from **stdarg.h**, is used to declare a pointer to the variable argument list:

   ```
   va_list <list pointer>;
   ```

5. The variable-list pointer is initialized by calling **va_start** (also imported from **stdarg.h**), using the following syntax:

   ```
   va_start(<list pointer>,<name of last fixed parameter>);
   ```

   This enables the list pointer to point to the first variable-argument.
6. Accessing the variable-arguments is carried out using the **var_arg** function, which takes two arguments. The first is the list pointer, previously initialized. The second is the name of the data type of the variable-argument. The result returned by the **va_arg** is the same as the latter data-type argument:

   ```
   <variable> = va_arg(<list pointer, <type casted>);
   ```

   To stop reading the variable-argument list, place an end-of-list element at the end of the list and check for its value. A **while** loop is well suited for that purpose, as shown in the next example.

The following C program uses a function with a variable number of arguments to detect the largest number in a numeric list. The list is the variable-sized argument list. The code is as follows:

```
/* C program that illustrates functions with a variable
   number of arguments
```

```
*/
#include <stdio.h>
#include <stdarg.h>
#define EOL -1
main()
{
   int big;
   void vmax(int*, char*, ...);
   vmax(&big, "The largest of 55, 67, 41 and 28 is ",
                              55, 67, 41, 28, EOL);
   printf("%d\n",big);
}
void vmax(int* large, char* message, ...)
{
   int num;
   va_list num_ptr;
   va_start(num_ptr, message);
   printf("%s",message);
   *large = -1;
   while ((num = va_arg(num_ptr, int)) != EOL)
     if (num > *(large))
         *(large) = num;
   va_end(num_ptr);
}
```

CREATING AND USING LIBRARIES

C is a small core language that relies extensively on function libraries. Every C compiler comes with a set of compiled libraries and the accompanying header filer (usually with a .H file extension name) to prototype the library functions, data types, constants, and any other declarations. Header files like **stdio.h**, **stdlib.h**, **string.h**, and **alloc.h**, to name just a few, are commonly used in programs.

There is some question concerning the creation and use of user-defined libraries. The process involves the following steps:

1. The primary step of creation of the library source code may take place in any of the following ways:
   - The code is written from scratch and tested as part of a main program.
   - The code is modified or adapted from an existing listing and then tested.
   - The code is copied or extracted from existing listings.
2. The code for the library is collected into a separate source file, call it **source.c**. This file should also contain the header files of the routines imported from other libraries (standard and/or user-defined).

3. A header file, **source.h**, is created to contain the function prototype, data types, and constants. If there are data types and/or constants in the header file, the **source.h** should also be inserted in the **source.c** file. In addition, the declarations of the data types and constants must be removed from the **source.c** file.
4. A project file is created for every application that employs user-defined libraries. The project file (with a .PRJ extension name) is a text file that lists the source files involved: the application filename as well as the user-defined libraries. Each filename is placed on one line, with no extended filenames. Suppose that an application stored in file **calc.c** uses the **source.c** library, the project file, call it **calc.prj**, looks like this:

```
calc
source
```

This project file informs the compiler of the files involved that are not part of the standard library.

If **source.c** were to employ the functions of another user-defined library, call it **smart.c**, then the **calc.prj** project file would contain the following:

```
calc
source
smart
```

The Project option must be invoked in either the Turbo C environment or the command-line version, and the project filename must be specified. Armed with this information, the Turbo C compiler is able to utilize the user-defined libraries.

TO USE THE LIBRARIES PRESENTED IN THE NEXT CHAPTERS, YOU WILL NEED TO CREATE AND USE PROJECT FILES.

CHAPTER

3

Basic Keyboard, Mouse, and Screen I/O

In this chapter you will learn the basics of keyboard, mouse, and screen I/O. The techniques developed here will be used extensively throughout the rest of the book, so it is important to study them carefully. The coverage of each I/O device is not meant to be exhaustive, but rather to show you just what you need to know to develop everyday applications. In particular, you will learn how to develop mouse- and keyboard-based pop-up window applications.

THE KEYBOARD

The first thing we'll learn is how to handle keystrokes in ways that go beyond the standard C **getch()**, **getche()** and **getchar()** functions. Keys obtained from these functions are routed through DOS. There are other places that you can tap to get keys in a more direct way. These other ways are often more convenient, particularly for windowed applications. To start off, you will learn how keystrokes are turned into the key codes used by your program.

There are basically two keyboard interrupts that handle keys: one is interrupt 0x09, the other is interrupt 0x16. Interrupt 0x09 is a hardware-generated interrupt that is activated whenever you press or release a key. This interrupt handles all the low-level communication with the keyboard, and translates the keystrokes into two-byte codes, which we will call *scan-ASCII codes*. These codes are then placed into a keyboard buffer, ready to be delivered to your application.

Table 3.1 shows the scan-ASCII code mappings of all the possible combinations of key presses. You will notice that the table does not show every conceivable key press combination. This is because BIOS does not translate them all. The table shows only those translated.

The high byte of the scan-ASCII code is called the *scan code* and represents a mapping of the actual key pressed. The scan code does not reflect the state of the shift, control, or alt keys, and as such is not unique. The low byte is known as the *ASCII code*, and if printed, will yield the appropriate printable character associated with that key. The ASCII code is also not unique; for instance, both the tab key and Ctrl-I yield the same ASCII code of 0x09, although their scan codes are different. Fortunately, the complete combination of scan code and ASCII code is unique, and we shall see later how to take advantage of this.

Whenever you get a key through DOS, it obtains it from the keyboard buffer, strips off the scan code, and returns just the ASCII code. Some keys, however, don't have an ASCII code, so DOS will return a null code, and place the scan code back in the keyboard buffer ready for the next read. Thus, if after receiving a null code you request another key, DOS gives the associated scan code. In this manner, you can check for certain control and function keys by first looking for a null, then doing another read to get the actual function code. However, this method may not be convenient, because it forces you to do a different number of reads for each key in a sequence. An easier way would be to simply read both codes in as an integer, and if you desire to store the key in a character string just mask off the scan code.

How can you do this? Well, as it turns out, there is another interrupt handler in BIOS that is used to extract keys from the keyboard buffer: interrupt 0x16. By sending the appropriate function code, you can invoke interrupt 0x16 to either look to see if a key is waiting to be read, or to actually obtain the key. Fortunately, you do not have to deal directly with any interrupts because Turbo C provides a built-in function called **bioskey()**, which does the low-level interface for us. It has the following parameters:

```
0  -  get the next key from the buffer, wait if necessary
1  -  just look to see if a key is ready in the buffer
2  -  get modifier status
```

The first two functions return the scan-ASCII code as an integer. Note that they do not echo the key that was entered. This gives you finer control over echoing characters to the screen, as in doing validated input and text editing.

For the last function, the current shift key status is returned as follows:

```
0x80  Insert Key toggled on
0x40  Caps Lock on
0x20  Num Lock on
0x10  Scroll Lock on
0x08  Alt pressed
0x04  Ctrl pressed
0x02  Left Shift down
0x01  Right Shift down
```

These codes are ORed together to give the value returned. Retrieving the shift status is useful in the following situation. Some key press combinations are not translated by BIOS, and as such no key is placed in the buffer for them; an example is ALT-ENTER. Many pop-up memory-resident programs use these "ghost" combinations to provide a hot key that does not conflict with normal keyboard use.

The shift status is also useful for converting the cursor keypad into a number keypad via the NUM LOCK status. Every time a key from the cursor pad is read, you can check the state of NUM LOCK to see whether to interpret the key as a cursor key or as a number. For instance, PGUP and 9 on the numeric keypad share the same scan-ASCII code. The interpretation of that code is up to you.

As an example of doing direct BIOS key access, the following program will wait for each key, and then print out its scan code, ASCII code, and attempt to print the character as well. It terminates on an escape key. Notice the useful macros provided to extract the individual bytes from the scan-ASCII code. The listing is as follows:

```
/*  Keyboard I/O example  (ioex1.c)  */
#include <stdio.h>
#include <bios.h>         /* Turbo C's BIOS routines header */
/* macros to retrieve low and high byte of an integer */
#define lo(f)   ((f) & 0xff)
#define hi(f)   (lo(f >> 8))
void main() {
  int key;
  do {
    key = bioskey(0);    /* wait for key */
    printf("0x%02x  0x%02x %c\n", hi(key), lo(key), lo(key));
  } while( key != 0x011b );
}
```

Instead of trying to remember each scan-ASCII code, the best thing to do is build a header file of useful mnenomic names for the codes. An example is given as part of Listing 3.5, which will be used later on in application programs. It is also helpful to keep Table 3.1 handy.

All in all, there are three basic ways you can obtain keys: trapping interrupt 0x09, calling interrupt 0x16, and through DOS via the standard I/O routines. Which is better? Unless you are going to write keyboard macro programs or pop-up memory-resident ones, it is rarely a good idea to trap interrupt 0x09. This is mainly because you would to have to translate the hardware key codes into scan-ASCII codes by yourself. You would also have to handle the fact that interrupt 0x09 is called both when a key is pressed and when it is released.

Using interrupt 0x16 turns out to be the convenient way to get keystrokes, since you can get the whole key code in one read. However, it does have one drawback: since you are not going through DOS to get the keys, using CTRL-BREAK or CTRL-C will not work to abort some programs (for instance the Turbo C environment), so when you are in the initial debugging stages, it is very easy to hang your computer should your program go into an infinite loop. In addition, using the standard I/O routines has the advantage of allowing you to use I/O redirection. The appropriate choice depends on the application. The following chapters use both BIOS and standard I/O calls. You will also write your own custom CTRL-C trapper that will be useful in pop-up window applications.

Table 3.1 Scan-ASCII Key Code Mappings

Key	Code	Name	Key	Code	Name	Key	Code	Name
1	0x0000	ctrl brk	41	0x1100	alt w	81	0x1c0a	ctrl enter
2	0x011b	esc	42	0x1265	e	82	0x1e61	a
3	0x0231	1	43	0x1245	E	83	0x1e41	A
4	0x0221	!	44	0x1205	ctrl e	84	0x1e01	ctrl a
5	0x0332	2	45	0x1200	alt e	85	0x1e00	alt a
6	0x0340	@	46	0x1372	r	86	0x1f73	s
7	0x0300	ctrl @	47	0x1352	R	87	0x1f53	S
8	0x0433	3	48	0x1312	ctrl r	88	0x1f13	ctrl s
9	0x0423	#	49	0x1300	alt r	89	0x1f00	alt s
10	0x0534	4	50	0x1474	t	90	0x2064	d
11	0x0524	$	51	0x1454	T	91	0x2044	D
12	0x0635	5	52	0x1414	ctrl t	92	0x2004	ctrl d
13	0x0625	%	53	0x1400	alt t	93	0x2000	alt d
14	0x0736	6	54	0x1579	y	94	0x2166	f
15	0x075e	^	55	0x1559	Y	95	0x2146	F
16	0x071e	ctrl ^	56	0x1519	ctrl y	96	0x2106	ctrl f
17	0x0837	7	57	0x1500	alt y	97	0x2100	alt f
18	0x0826	&	58	0x1675	u	98	0x2267	g
19	0x0938	8	59	0x1655	U	99	0x2247	G
20	0x092a	*	60	0x1615	ctrl u	100	0x2207	ctrl g
21	0x0a39	9	61	0x1600	alt u	101	0x2200	alt g
22	0x0a28	(	62	0x1769	i	102	0x2368	h
23	0x0b30	0	63	0x1749	I	103	0x2348	H
24	0x0b29	)	64	0x1709	ctrl i	104	0x2308	ctrl h
25	0x0c2d	-	65	0x1700	alt i	105	0x2300	alt h
26	0x0c5f	_	66	0x186f	o	106	0x246a	j
27	0x0c1f	ctrl -	67	0x184f	O	107	0x244a	J
28	0x0d3d	=	68	0x180f	ctrl o	108	0x240a	ctrl j
29	0x0d2b	+	69	0x1800	alt o	109	0x2400	alt j
30	0x0e08	bs	70	0x1970	p	110	0x256b	k
31	0x0e7f	ctrl bs	71	0x1950	P	111	0x254b	K
32	0x0f09	tab	72	0x1910	ctrl p	112	0x250b	ctrl k
33	0x0f00	bk tab	73	0x1900	alt p	113	0x2500	alt k
34	0x1071	q	74	0x1a5b	[	114	0x266c	l
35	0x1051	Q	75	0x1a7b	{	115	0x264c	L
36	0x1011	ctrl q	76	0x1a1b	ctrl [	116	0x260c	ctrl l
37	0x1000	alt q	77	0x1b5d	]	117	0x2600	alt l
38	0x1177	w	78	0x1b7d	}	118	0x273b	;
39	0x1157	W	79	0x1b1d	ctrl]	119	0x273a	:
40	0x1117	ctrl w	80	0x1c0d	enter	120	0x2827	'

Key	Code	Name
121	0x2822	"
122	0x2960	'
123	0x297e	~
124	0x2b5c	\
125	0x2b7c	|
126	0x2b1c	ctrl \
127	0x2c7a	z
128	0x2c5a	Z
129	0x2c1a	ctrl z
130	0x2c00	alt z
131	0x2d78	x
132	0x2d58	X
133	0x2d18	ctrl x
134	0x2d00	alt x
135	0x2e63	c
136	0x2e43	C
137	0x2e03	ctrl c
138	0x2e00	alt c
139	0x2f76	v
140	0x2f56	V
141	0x2f16	ctrl v
142	0x2f00	alt v
143	0x3062	b
144	0x3042	B
145	0x3002	ctrl b
146	0x3000	alt b
147	0x316e	n
148	0x314e	N
149	0x310e	ctrl n
150	0x3100	alt n
151	0x326d	m
152	0x324d	M
153	0x320d	ctrl m
154	0x3200	alt m
155	0x332c	,
156	0x333c	<
157	0x342e	.
158	0x343e	>
159	0x352f	/
160	0x353f	?
161	0x372a	grey *
162	0x3920	space
163	0x3b00	f1
164	0x3c00	f2
165	0x3d00	f3
166	0x3e00	f4
167	0x3f00	f5
168	0x4000	f6
169	0x4100	f7
170	0x4200	f8
171	0x4300	f9
172	0x4400	f10
173	0x4700	home
174	0x4737	shft home
175	0x4800	up arrow
176	0x4838	shft up
177	0x4900	pgup
178	0x4939	shft pgup
179	0x4a2d	grey -
180	0x4b00	left arrow
181	0x4b34	shft left arrow
182	0x4c35	num 5
183	0x4d00	right arrow
184	0x4d36	shft right arrow
185	0x4e2b	grey +
186	0x4f00	end
187	0x4f31	shft end
188	0x5000	down arrow
189	0x5032	shft down arrow
190	0x5100	pgdn
191	0x5133	shft pgdn
192	0x5200	ins
193	0x5230	0
194	0x5300	del
195	0x532e	shft del
196	0x5400	shft f1
197	0x5500	shft f2
198	0x5600	shft f3
199	0x5700	shft f4
200	0x5800	shft f5
201	0x5900	shft f6
202	0x5a00	shft f7
203	0x5b00	shft f8
204	0x5c00	shft f9
205	0x5d00	shft f10
206	0x5e00	ctrl f1
207	0x5f00	ctrl f2
208	0x6000	ctrl f3
209	0x6100	ctrl f4
210	0x6200	ctrl f5
211	0x6300	ctrl f6
212	0x6400	ctrl f7
213	0x6500	ctrl f8
214	0x6600	ctrl f9
215	0x6700	ctrl f10
216	0x6800	alt f1
217	0x6900	alt f2
218	0x6a00	alt f3
219	0x6b00	alt f4
220	0x6c00	alt f5
221	0x6d00	alt f6
222	0x6e00	alt f7
223	0x6f00	alt f8
224	0x7000	alt f9
225	0x7100	alt f10
226	0x7200	ctrl prt scrn
227	0x7300	ctrl left arrow
228	0x7400	ctrl right arrow
229	0x7500	ctrl end
230	0x7600	ctrl pgdn
231	0x7700	ctrl home
232	0x7800	alt 1
233	0x7900	alt 2
234	0x7a00	alt 3
235	0x7b00	alt 4
236	0x7c00	alt 5
237	0x7d00	alt 6
238	0x7e00	alt 7
239	0x7f00	alt 8
240	0x8000	alt 9
241	0x8100	alt 0
242	0x8200	alt -
243	0x8300	alt =
244	0x8400	ctrl pgup

BASIC TEXT OUTPUT

In addition to the standard C routines to print to the screen, (namely **printf()**, **putchar()**, and **puts()**), Turbo C provides other functions that are useful for windowed applications. The routines **cprintf()**, **cputs()**, and **putch()** mimic their standard I/O counterparts; in addition, they know about the current window in use and keep all output within its bound. Before showing how to use these functions, it is useful to see how the screen is accessed at the low level.

DIRECT VIDEO ACCESS

The screen is organized into an 80x25 grid of two-byte cells called *texels* (short for textcells), as shown in Figure 3.1. Each texel consists of a character code and an attribute. The character code is an extended ASCII code that includes various graphics characters. The attribute code controls the text foreground and background colors, as well as underlining and blinking. Figure 3.2 shows the background and foreground mapping of the attribute byte for monochrome displays, and Figure 3.3 shows the mapping for color displays. The values given are the defaults. The newer video cards (ie., EGA, VGA) have many more colors available, which you can use by changing the palette.

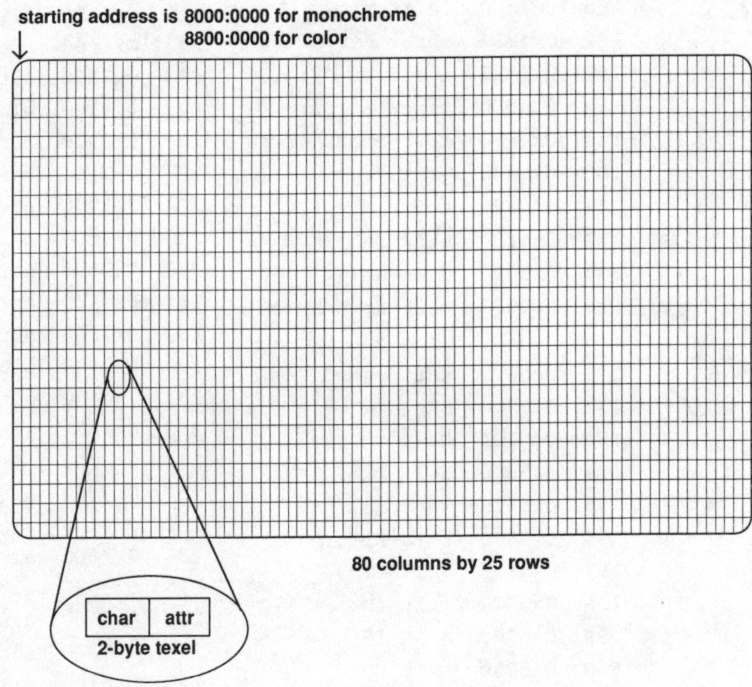

Figure 3.1 Screen organization in text mode

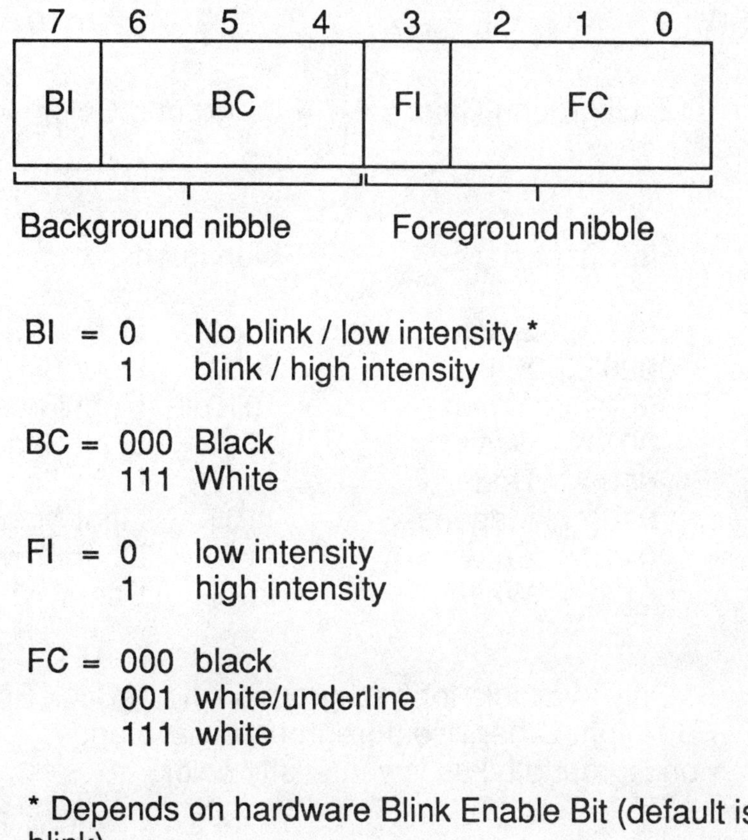

Figure 3.2 Attribute mapping for monochrome mode

Bit 7 of the attribute byte serves a dual purpose: it either controls the blinking of the foreground characters, or serves as a high-intensity bit for the background color. The mode used depends on the current state of the BLINK ENABLE BIT of your video card. When selecting a new text mode, BIOS sets the BLINK ENABLE BIT to one so that bit 7 of the attribute byte causes blinking. You must reset the BLINK ENABLE BIT if you wish to have high-intensity background colors. Refer to the technical reference manual of your video card for further details.

The grid of texels resides in the RAM on your video card and can be accessed like normal memory. The address depends on the card you are using. For monochrome graphics adapters, it starts at address 0xb000:0000, the first number is the segment address, the second is the offset. For CGA, EGA, and VGA cards, the normal starting address is 0xb800:0000. Some of these cards have multiple pages that have other addresses, but they are not dealt with here, since the high-level Turbo-C calls are used most of the time.

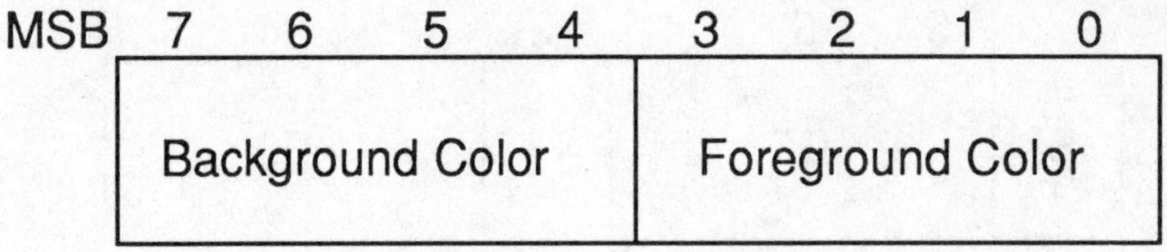

MSB 7 6 5 4	3 2 1 0
Background Color	Foreground Color

low intensity		high intensity *	
0000	Black	1000	Grey
0001	Blue	1001	Light Blue
0010	Green	1010	Light Green
0011	Cyan	1011	Light Cyan
0100	Red	1100	Light Red
0101	Magenta	1101	Light Magenta
0110	Brown	1110	Light Brown
0111	White	1111	Bright White

* Only available for background color if Blink Enable Bit is off. Otherwise, foreground blinks and background takes low intensity color.

Figure 3.3 Attribute mapping for color modes

As an example, you will see how to write a program to print the message "Hello, World" on the screen using direct access. To do so, it is useful to first create a structure that represents a texel:

```
typedef struct texel_struct {
  unsigned char ch;
  unsigned char attr;
} texel;
```

With this structure, you can define the texel grid itself, as follows. Note that the texels are stored by row.

```
typedef texel screen_array[25][80];
```

To access the screen, you can define a pointer and initialize it to the appropriate address. Since the screen will always reside outside any segment of your program, you should declare it as a far pointer. That way, the same code will work for any memory model.

```
/* for monochrome cards */
screen_array far *screen_ptr = (screen_array far *) 0xb0000000L;
/* for color cards */
screen_array far *screen_ptr = (screen_array far *) 0xb8000000L;
```

It's then useful to declare the following macro, after which you can access the screen as if it were an array:

```
#define screen (*screen_ptr)
```

For example, to write the character **A** at row 1, column 5, you could use:

```
screen[1][5].ch = 'A';
```

You could set its color to reverse video with:

```
screen[1][5].attr = 112;
```

Note that like all C arrays, the indices count from 0; thus, the top corner of the screen is screen[0][0].

To complete the example, here is the famous "Hello world" program written for color cards:

```
/*  Low level screen access example  (ioex2.c)   */
#include <string.h>
#include <conio.h>
#define screen (*screen_ptr)
typedef struct texel_struct {
   unsigned char ch;
   unsigned char attr;
} texel;
typedef texel screen_array[25][80];
screen_array far *screen_ptr = (screen_array far *)0xb8000000L;
char hello[] = "Hello world";
void main() {
  int i;
  /* write out the characters to row 10, col 0 */
  for (i = 0; i < strlen(hello); i++) {
      screen[10][i].ch = hello[i];
  }
  getch();  /* wait for key */
  /* Now, for fun, lets change its color to reverse video */
  for (i = 0; i < strlen(hello); i++) {
      screen[10][i].attr = 112;
  }
}
```

Did you notice snow when you ran this program? If you have one of the older graphics cards, writing directly to the video memory causes interference with the video tracing. Most commercial programs get around this by trapping a certain horizontal retrace interrupt generated by the graphics card, and then waiting for the appropriate time to write to the screen. You do not have to deal with that because Turbo C's screen routines do that for you. If you use functions **cprintf()**, **cputs()**, and **putch()**, they will write directly to RAM, but only at the appropriate times.

Although the **cprintf()**, **cputs()**, and **putch()** routines normally go directly to RAM, you can go through the BIOS instead by setting the global variable **direc tvideo** to 0. This is provided for computers that are BIOS compatible, but have noncompatible video hardware. Going through BIOS, however, is *slow*. As an experiment, when you type in the pop-up window code to be presented later, try setting the direct video bit to 0 at the start of the program. You will then see what I mean.

Even using the Turbo C functions in direct video mode is slower than writing directly to RAM, mainly because you access the screen through function calls rather than by simply writing to an array. Unless you have one of the slower computers, the trade-off is worth it because the snow is taken care of for you, and by using the high-level calls, your code may be much easier to port to future operating systems.

TURBO C WINDOWS

Turbo C provides a built-in function that allows you to define rectangular regions on the screen which scroll independently from other parts of the screen. This is the **window()** function. You use this function to make a region on the screen the *active* window. Once this is done, the routines **cprintf()**, **putch()**, and **puts()** will automatically print and scroll within this region. There are also routines to support clearing the window (**clrscr()**), and inserting and deleting lines (**insline()**, **delline()**) which can be used to do your own scrolling and editing functions.

Turbo C also provides functions for controlling the cursor relative to the current window and returning its status. These are **gotoxy()**, **wherex()**, and **wherey()**. There is also a function called **gettextinfo()**, which will return the current window coordinates, the current colors in use, and the current position of the cursor.

Starting off with a simple example, the following program will set up a window of 20 columns by 4 rows at the center of the screen, move the cursor to row 4, column 2, and then echo keys typed in by calling **putch()**. It clears the screen and quits when you press the escape key.

```
/*  Turbo C window example  (ioex3.c)   */
#include <conio.h>   /* include this whenever you use windows */
void main() {
  int c;
  window(30,10,49,13);  /* window at upper left (30,10), */
                        /* lower right (49,13)           */
  gotoxy(0,0);          /* x is column, y is row         */
  do {
    c = getch();
```

```
    putch(c);
  } while(c != 0x1b);
  window(1,1,80,25);
  clrscr();
}
```

What is missing from this example is a box around the window. Turbo C is not going to draw one for you. The routine **my_box()** in Listing 3.1 will. In fact, it will even let you select the type of border. Note how the window coordinates are INSIDE the box coordinates. Otherwise, the box outline would get written over too! You must also draw the box before setting the window, or else the characters would be written at positions relative to the window, and a garbled screen would result.

Listing 3.1 Drawing Boxed Windows (IOEX4.C)

```
/*  Drawing text boxes example  (ioex4.c)  */
#include <conio.h>
void my_box(int xul, int yul, int xlr, int ylr, int btype);
void main() {
  int c;
  my_box(29,9,50,14,2);  /* double line with reverse video */
  window(30,10,49,13);   /* window at upper left (30,10),  */
                         /* lower right (49,13)            */
  gotoxy(0,0);           /* x is column, y is row          */
  do {
    c = getch();
    putch(c);
  } while(c != 0x1b);
  window(1,1,80,25);
  clrscr();
}
void my_box(int xul, int yul, int xlr, int ylr, int btype)
/* Draws a box at the upper left (xul,yul) and lower right
   (xlr,ylr) coordinates.
   If btype = 0, no box is drawn.
   If btype = 1, a single line box is drawn.
   If btype = 2,  a double line box is drawn.
*/
{
   static int boxcar[2][6] = {   /* graphics characters for a box */
     {218,196,191,179,192,217},  /* single line box */
     {201,205,187,186,200,188}   /* double line box */
   };
```

```
   int i, hzchar, vtchar;
   if (btype) {
      hzchar = boxcar[btype-1][1];
      vtchar = boxcar[btype-1][3];
      /* draw top and bottom sides */
      gotoxy(xul,yul);
      for (i=xul; i<=xlr; i++) putch(hzchar);
      gotoxy(xul,ylr);
      for (i=xul; i<=xlr; i++) putch(hzchar);
      /* draw vertical sides */
      for (i=yul; i<=ylr; i++) {
         gotoxy(xul,i);
         putch(vtchar);
         gotoxy(xlr,i);
         putch(vtchar);
      }
      /* draw corners */
      gotoxy(xul,yul);  putch(boxcar[btype-1][0]);  /* upper left  */
      gotoxy(xlr,yul);  putch(boxcar[btype-1][2]);  /* upper right */
      gotoxy(xlr,ylr);  putch(boxcar[btype-1][5]);  /* lower right */
      gotoxy(xul,ylr);  putch(boxcar[btype-1][4]);  /* lower left  */
   }
}
```

TEXT COLORS

Turbo C provides support to change the color of the text written to the screen in the following functions:

```
textattr       - sets both background and foregound colors in
                 attribute byte
textbackground - sets only the background color
textcolor      - sets only the foreground color
highvideo      - sets high-intensity bit of foreground color
normvideo      - sets both foreground and background colors
                 back to what they were on program startup
lowvideo       - resets the high-intensity bit of foreground
                 color
```

In addition, if you have an EGA or VGA adapter, there are routines to set and retrieve the color palette information. See the Turbo C manual for discussion of these.

One thing that is missing from the set of functions provided by Turbo C is a direct way to set just the color of text on the screen without also rewriting the characters. In other words, something equivalent to using:

```
screen[0][0].attr = 112;
```

which sets the attribute byte of row 0, column 0 to reverse video without changing the character there. Such a feature is useful when highlighting menu bars, for instance, because you do not have to remember what characters are currently in the menu entry being highlighted. You can get around this problem (other than writing directly to the screen) by using two other functions provided by Turbo C: **gettext()** and **puttext()**.

The **gettext()** routine copies the memory image from a region on the screen into a user-supplied array. **Puttext()** goes the other way. You can simulate the effect of just changing the attribute byte in the following manner: suppose you wish to set column 5, row 4 to the color blue **(attr = 1)**. The following program fragment shows how:

```
texel t;
gettext(5,4,5,4, &t);   /* get one texel */
t.attr = 1;             /* set color     */
puttext(5,4,5,4, &t);   /* put back text */
```

Extending the window example to include text highlighting, the program given in Listing 3.2 allows you to move the cursor around with the arrows, and to toggle highlighting on or off with the INS key. This program uses keyboard I/O as discussed in the last section, and includes the box routine given earlier.

One thing you will probably note is how hard it is to keep track of which coordinate system is in use and to figure out the boundaries of the windows. The next chapter develops a set of pop-up window utilities that will ease the problem of keeping track of all these details.

CONTROLLING THE CURSOR SIZE

The BIOS contains a method for changing the shape of the cursor, anywhere from a single scan line to a 14-line box. You can even turn the cursor off completely. This is useful for things like menu bars, where having the cursor on distracts from the highlighted bar itself. Unfortunately, one thing you can not do is control the blinking. There is no way to shut it off, as it is built into the hardware. The default cursor is a blinking hyphen, which uses the bottom two lines of the character box.

To change the cursor shape, you call BIOS interrupt 0x10 with a function code of 0x01. You then pass two parameters in CH and CL, representing the starting and ending lines of the cursor, as the following code fragment shows:

```
regs.h.ah = 0x10;
regs.h.ch = startline;
regs.h.cl = endline;
int86(0x10, &reg, &regs);
```

Each character in text mode takes up 14 scan lines, and the lines are numbered from 0 at the top to 13 at the bottom. Thus, if you set CH = 0x00, and CL = 0x0d, a full-sized cursor will be displayed. Using CH = 0x0d and CL = 0x0d, the cursor becomes a flashing hyphen located at the bottom of the character cell. The following program allows you to experiment with different cursor shapes (just rerun it for each different shape) and shows how to make the appropriate BIOS call via Turbo C's **int86()** function:

```
/*  Changing cursor shape example  (ioex5.c)   */
#include <dos.h>
#include <stdio.h>
void cursor_size(int startline, int endline);
void main() {
  int s,e;
  printf("enter starting line and ending line: \n");
  scanf("%d %d", &s,&e);
  cursor_size(s,e);
  printf("Press return to exit\n");
  getch();
}
void cursor_size(int startline, int endline)
{
 union REGS regs;
 regs.h.ch = startline;      /* starting cursor line */
 regs.h.cl = endline;        /* ending cursor line */
 regs.h.ah = 1;              /* Call BIOS with the set cursor size */
 int86(0x10,&regs,&regs);    /* function code in ah  */
}
```

If you have an MCGA, EGA, or VGA adapter, you might have noticed something strange with this program. Even though the cursor size is 14 lines high on these adapters, you can only individually address 8 of them. This is for backwards compatability with older color adapters. The mapping used varies between these adapters, so the best thing to do is simply experiment with the values. Because of this problem, making a general routine for setting the cursor size can be difficult, as you need to know what adapter is being used and what mode it is in. Fortunately, Turbo C provides the **detectgraph()** function in its graphics package to help you out.

You can turn off the cursor by calling the same interrupt routine and by setting bit 5 of the CH register. The following function is a modified version of our **cursor_size()** function that allows the cursor to be turned off by passing a starting and ending code of zero.

```
void cursor_size(int startline, int endline)
{
 union REGS regs;
 /* erase cursor on (0,0) input, else set cursor size */
 if ((startline == 0) && (endline == 0)) {
    regs.h.ch = 0x20; /* set bit 5 of ch to erase cursor */
 }
 else  {
    regs.h.ch = startline;     /* starting cursor line */
    regs.h.cl = endline;       /* ending cursor line */
 }
```

```
 regs.h.ah = 1;               /* Call BIOS with the set cursor size */
 int86(0x10,&regs,&regs);     /* function code in ah  */
}
```

To turn the cursor on again, simply call **cursor_size()** with valid starting and ending lines.

Listing 3.2 The Highlighting Example (IOEX6.C)

```
/*  Text highlighting example  (ioex6.c)  */
#include <bios.h>
#include <conio.h>
#define UPKEY        0x4800
#define DOWNKEY      0x5000
#define LEFTKEY      0x4b00
#define RIGHTKEY     0x4d00
#define INSKEY       0x5200
#define ESCKEY       0x011b
typedef struct texel_struct {
  unsigned char ch;
  unsigned char attr;
} texel;
void my_box(int xul, int yul, int xlr, int ylr, int btype);
void main() {
  int highlite = 1;
  int x = 1, y = 1, k;
  texel t;
  my_box(29,9,50,14,2);
  window(30,10,49,13);
  cprintf("Here is some text\r\n");
  cprintf("for you to highlite\r\n");
  cprintf("Use the INS KEY to\r\n");
  cprintf("toggle highliting");
  do {
    gotoxy(x,y);
    if (highlite) {   /* these are absolute (full screen) coords !!! */
       gettext(x+29,y+9,x+29,y+9,&t);
       t.attr = 112;
       puttext(x+29,y+9,x+29,y+9,&t);
    }
    else {   /* back to normal */
       gettext(x+29,y+9,x+29,y+9,&t);
       t.attr = 7;
```

```
        puttext(x+29,y+9,x+29,y+9,&t);
      }
      k = bioskey(0);
      switch(k) {
        case UPKEY:               /* remember coords are relative to window */
          if (--y < 1) y = 1;
        break;
        case DOWNKEY:
          if (++y > 4) y = 4;
        break;
        case LEFTKEY:
          if (--x < 1) x = 1;
        break;
        case RIGHTKEY:
          if (++x > 20) x = 20;
        break;
        case INSKEY:
          highlite = !highlite;
        break;
        default: ;
      }
    } while (k != ESCKEY);
    window(1,1,80,25);
    clrscr();
}
void my_box(int xul, int yul, int xlr, int ylr, int btype)
/* Draws a box at the upper left (xul,yul) and lower right
   (xlr,ylr) coords with given attribute.  If btype = 0, no box is drawn,
   if btype = 1, a single line box is drawn, if btype = 2,  a double line
   box is drawn.
*/
{
   static int boxcar[2][6] = {   /* graphics characters for a box */
     {218,196,191,179,192,217},  /* single line box */
     {201,205,187,186,200,188}   /* double line box */
   };
   int i, hzchar, vtchar;
   if (btype) {
      hzchar = boxcar[btype-1][1];
      vtchar = boxcar[btype-1][3];
      /* draw top and bottom sides */
```

```
        gotoxy(xul,yul);
        for (i=xul; i<=xlr; i++) putch(hzchar);
        gotoxy(xul,ylr);
        for (i=xul; i<=xlr; i++) putch(hzchar);
        /* draw vertical sides */
        for (i=yul; i<=ylr; i++) {
           gotoxy(xul,i);
           putch(vtchar);
           gotoxy(xlr,i);
           putch(vtchar);
        }
        /* draw corners */
        gotoxy(xul,yul);  putch(boxcar[btype-1][0]);  /* upper left */
        gotoxy(xlr,yul);  putch(boxcar[btype-1][2]);  /* upper right */
        gotoxy(xlr,ylr);  putch(boxcar[btype-1][5]);  /* lower right */
        gotoxy(xul,ylr);  putch(boxcar[btype-1][4]);  /* lower left */
    }
}
```

USING THE MOUSE

The use of a mouse as an I/O device is becoming increasingly more common, particularly as computers like the Macintosh are driving the industry toward full use of them. For those of you with a Microsoft-compatible mouse, you will learn the basics of integrating it into your DOS applications. For those whose mouse is not Microsoft compatible, much of the code will still be useful, but the exact details are going to be different. The purpose of this chapter is not to give you an exhaustive treatment of all the possible functions for the mouse, but merely to show enough for everyday applications.

The mouse works in the following way: first, it must be properly installed as part of the system by loading the appropriate mouse driver. This is usually done at boot time via the **config.sys** file, or by executing a program in your **autoexec.bat** file. Both of these methods will install the mouse driver routine as a memory-resident program. (See your mouse handbook for details.) Your program communicates with the mouse via interrupt 0x33. With this interrupt, you can get the mouse coordinates, get the button status, change the mouse color and shape, make it visible and invisible, and perform many other functions.

BASIC MOUSE FUNCTIONS

Once you have installed the mouse driver and initialized it in your program, you can turn the mouse on, and the mouse driver then takes care of many details for you. For instance, you do not have to keep track of mouse movement and update the cursor, the driver does that for you. All you need to do is poll the driver for changes in mouse status. This can be accomplished by using the function codes listed in Table 3.2 and Table 3.3. These tables show the basic functions available in the Microsoft mouse driver, and the parameters needed for those functions. Only some of the available functions are listed, and those will be the main focus. There are many other functions available, so see your mouse technical reference manual for further details. For the code we will be developing, those listed will be sufficient.

Table 3.2 Mouse Function Codes and Parameters

Code	Function	Parameters
0	Mouse reset	m1 = 0 (input)
		m1 = mouse status (output)
		(-1 if installed,else 0)
		m2 = number of butons
1	Show cursor	m1 = 1 (input)
2	Hide cursor	m1 = 2 (input)
3	Button status	m1 = 3 (input)
		m2 = button status
		m3 = x cursor position
		m4 = y cursor position
4	Set cursor posn	m1 = 4 (input)
		m3 = new x position
		m4 = new y position
5	get button	m1 = 5 (input)
	press info	m1 = button status (output)
		m2 = (input) 0 = left button checked
		1 = right button checked
		m2 = number of button presses
		m3 = x position at last press
		m4 = y position at last press
6	get button	m1 = 6 (input)
	release info	m1 = button status (output)
		m2 = (input) 0 = left button checked
		1 = right button checked
		m3 = x position of last release
		m4 = y position of last release
7	set x bounds	m1 = 7 (input)
		m3 = minimum x position
		m4 = maximum x position
8	set y bounds	m1 = 8 (input)
		m3 = minimum y position
		m4 = maximum y position
9	set graphics	m1 = 9 (input)
	cursor	m2 = cursor hot spot (x posn)
		m3 = cursor hot spot (y posn)
		m4 = pointer to cursor masks

Code	Function	Parameters
10	set text cursor	m1 = 10 (input) m2 = (input) 0 for s/w cursor, 1 for h/w cursor m3 = screen mask if m2 = 0 = scan line start if m2 = 1 m4 = cursor mask if m2 = 0 = scan line stop if m2 = 1

Table 3.3 Mouse Button Status Codes

Value	0	1
Bit 0 |	Left button up	Left button down
1 |	Right button up	Right button down
* 2 |	Middle button up	Middle button down

* For Logitech 3 button mouse only

For the most commonly used functions, the four parameters m1, m2, m3, and m4 are always mapped to the registers ax, bx, cx, and dx, respectively. Thus, the interface to the driver is quite simple. Listing 3.3 shows how to use the Turbo C **int86()** function to talk directly to it. The **mouse()** function works by loading the appropriate registers with the parameters, calling the interrupt, and then loading the registers back into the parameters. For other functions, the register mapping may be different, so consult your manual for more details.

CHECKING FOR THE MOUSE DRIVER

At the beginning of your program, you should check to see that the mouse driver is loaded. This can be accomplished by the function **check_mouse_driver()** given in Listing 3.4. This function works by calling Turbo C's **getvect()** function to return the interrupt vector for the mouse (interrupt 0x33). It then checks for a NULL address or a IRET (0xcf) instruction. If either of these is found, it means no mouse driver is present; otherwise, it is assumed that the interrupt vector is valid and points to an actual mouse driver. (There's really no way to tell for sure.)

The parameter **need_mouse** is included so that you can make your applications transparent to whether or not a mouse is present. Basically, if the mouse driver is not found, and **need_mouse** = 1, then an error message is printed and the program is exited. If you wish to make the mouse optional, set **need_mouse** = 0. The function returns a 1 if the mouse driver is found, otherwise it returns a 0.

THE MOUSE TOOL KIT

The **mouse()** and **check_mouse_driver()** routines are all you need to communicate with the mouse. However, it is better to build a tool kit of higher level functions, as we shall do here. In particular, the following functions are given in Listings 3.5 and 3.6.

Function	Usage
check_mouse_driver	Checks for mouse being installed
init_mouse	Calls check_mouse_driver(), resets the mouse, turns on the mouse cursor, and initializes some internal variables
mouse	The low-level mouse interface
mouse_reset	Used to reset the mouse driver
move_mouse	Forces the mouse cursor to a new location
mouse_on	Conditionally turns the mouse cursor on
mouse_off	Conditionally turns the mouse cursor off
mouse_text_posn	Returns the mouse position in text coordinates
mouse_grph_posn	Returns the mouse position in graphics coordinates
mouse_in_box	Tests to see if the mouse is within a given rectangular region
button_release	Tests to see if a button has been released since last time called
button_press	Tests to see if a button has been pressed since last time called
button_state	Returns the up/down status of the buttons
mouse_trigger	Looks for either a key press or a mouse button press or release

Many of these routines follow directly from the functions listed in Table 3.2. However, they do perform other convenient actions. One is to maintain the following variables:

Identifier	Meaning
low_resolution	Flag used when in a low-resolution graphics mode (ie., 320 pixels horizontally)
mouse_text_x	X position of mouse in Turbo C text coordinates.
mouse_text_y	Y position of mouse in Turbo C text coordinates.
mouse_grph_x	X position of mouse in graphics coordinates.
mouse_grph_y	Y position of mouse in graphics coordinates.
mouse_intialized	Set to 1 if mouse_init() succeeded.
prev_cursor_state	Stores the previous visible/invisible state of the mouse cursor.

Also provided in the mouse header file (see Listing 3.5) are the following "key" codes for mouse button presses and releases. These codes are values that have no key assignments to them, so we can safely use them:

```
#define LEFT_MOUSE_PRESS     0xff01
#define RIGHT_MOUSE_PRESS    0xff02
#define LEFT_MOUSE_REL       0xff11
#define RIGHT_MOUSE_REL      0xff12
```

The mouse header file also has macros defined for the common mouse functions and, as a convenience, a set of definitions for common key codes. Basically, use this header file whenever you wish to do keyboard or mouse I/O.

The function **init_mouse()** is provided to initialize the mouse. It has the following prototype:

```
int init_mouse(int need_mouse, int graphdriver, int graphmode);
```

This function calls **check_mouse_driver()** to see if the mouse is installed. It passes the parameter **need_mouse** to **check_mouse_driver()** for error handling. This parameter can take on the following values as defined in the mouse header file:

Macro	Code	Meaning
MOUSE_OPTIONAL	0	Mouse is optional. Not an error if mouse driver not present.
MOUSE_NEEDED	1	Mouse required. Reports error and aborts program if mouse driver not present.

Also passed to **init_mouse()** are two parameters that indicate what screen mode is being used. We'll defer discussion of these parameters until the graphics chapter. For text mode applications, set these two to the constant MOUSE_TEXT_MODE, which is defined in the mouse header file as a zero.

Although many of the parameters held in the global variables are available at the return of the appropriate function called, some of these functions actually obtain more information than is returned in the parameter list. For example, the **button_status()** function gets the current mouse position as well as the up/down status of the buttons, so it stores the position for your convenience.

Most of the functions are quite straightforward and can be easily followed from the listings. However, a few comments are warranted. One is that all the functions check for the mouse being initialized. If it is not, they take the appropriate action that makes the mouse installation status as transparent as possible to your program.

It is important to realize the distinction between the functions **button_press()**, **button_release()**, and **button_state()**. The first two return values that indicate whether or not a button has been pressed (or released) since the last time the function was called. **Button_state()** returns a value that signals whether or not a button is currently pressed down.

Typically, you will use **button_press()** to start a mouse "dragging" session, check **button_state()** while the mouse is dragging, and **button_release()** to end the session. Why not just use **button_state()** all the time? It is possible that you will miss the button being pressed and released (the combination known as a *single click*) if you do not check the status at the right time. The **button_press()** and **button_release()** functions save their respective events until you do call them. They will even return how many times it has happened since the last call.

Note the coordinate translation taking place in the internal function **set_mouse_posn()**. Turbo C starts its text coordinates at (1,1). However, the mouse driver always returns coordinates in terms of pixels and starts at position (0,0). The **set_mouse_posn()** function assumes that there are 8 pixels to a texel (which is true for the standard 80x25 mode), so it multiplies the coordinate by 8 and adds 1 to adjust to Turbo C text coordinates.

One problem occurs when you are in low-resolution (320x200) graphics modes. The mouse driver assumes a screen width of 640 horizontal pixels for CGA, EGA, and VGA. (For Hercules graphics, it uses 720 pixels.) If you're in a low-resolution mode, the X coordinate needs to be corrected by dividing by two. This is accomplished by passing **init_mouse()** the appropriate **graphdriver** and **graphmode** values, as will be discussed in the graphics chapter.

THE MOUSE CURSOR

Another subtlety with the functions given has to do with the mouse cursor. You may wonder how it is drawn, since the regular cursor also (usually) appears as well as the mouse cursor. The regular cursor is implemented in the hardware of the graphics adapter and is maintained by DOS. The mouse cursor is implemented in software and is maintained by the mouse driver. The driver draws the cursor by writing directly to the video RAM. Every time the cursor moves, the text underneath is saved and then restored when the cursor leaves that position.

This all works fine unless you happen to overwrite what is on the cursor. The driver has no way of knowing that happened and will faithfully replace the texel with the previous contents when it moves off that position. The result is a garbled screen.

The way out of this dilemmna is to turn off the mouse cursor anytime you are about to write to the screen; afterwards, you can turn it back on. It's a little trickier than this, for you want to turn the cursor back on only if it was previously on. To make this easy to do, the functions **mouse_on()** and **mouse_off()** are provided, which can keep track of the previous state of the mouse cursor and allow you to conditionally turn the cursor back on, depending on its previous state. These functions have the following prototypes:

```
void mouse_on(int restoreflag);
void mouse_off(int tempflag);
```

The parameters have the following meanings:

```
restoreflag  = 0: Unconditionally turn mouse cursor on.
             = 1: Restore mouse cursor to previous state.
tempflag     = 0: Turn mouse cursor off, set previous state
                  to off.
```

```
= 1: Turn mouse cursor off only if it is on,
     set previous state to on.
     If mouse already off, set previous state
     to off.
```

The following shows an example of conditionally turning off the mouse cursor, updating the screen, and then conditionally turning the mouse cursor back on.

```
mouse_off(1);
cprintf("Hello World");
mouse_on(1);
```

If you call **mouse_off()** and **mouse_on()** with parameters of **0**, they will turn the mouse off or on regardless of the previous state. You must be careful when doing this though, because the mouse driver queues up successive mouse off commands. If you issue two requests to turn the mouse off, without an intervening mouse on command, it will take *two* successive mouse on commands to turn the mouse back on.

This particular feature can cause great confusion, so it is best to avoid it. If you use the **mouse_off**(1), **mouse_on**(1) sequence when you wish to temporarily turn off the mouse, you will never have this problem. The pop-up window code to be presented follows this method rigorously.

It is possible to tell the mouse driver to use the hardware cursor instead of the software one. Normally, though, you should reserve the hardware cursor for text input positioning and use the mouse cursor for mouse positioning. When you do have the mouse in the system, it works best to keep it the shape of a full-height box (it is possible to change its shape) and make the regular cursor a blinking hyphen. That way you will not get them confused. It is also possible to change the color of the mouse cursor. The default is to make the color inverted with respect to the text underneath it, and this is usually satisfactory.

MOUSE HIGHLIGHTING EXAMPLE

As an example to using the mouse, let's revisit our text highlighting example of the previous section and change it so that it operates via the mouse. The main program is given in Listing 3.7 and operates as follows: when you press the left mouse button, the highlight flag is toggled. If you then drag the mouse across the screen holding down the left button, the text will be lightened or darkened, depending on the state of the highlight toggle. Only text in the window is affected by the highlighting. Notice the check to see if the mouse has actually moved. This is done to prevent the mouse from flickering as it is turned on and off during the loop. Notice also that you *do* have to turn it off, even if you are just highlighting text, because the mouse cursor saves and restores both the character *and* the attribute when moving around. To exit the program, click the right button. If you happen to have a single-button mouse, you will have to modify the code to allow some other way of exiting. As an exercise, try changing the code so that it exits if you click the left button outside the window.

Now that you have explored the keyboard, low-level screen I/O, and mouse I/O, it is time to move on to more exotic applications, such as the pop-up windows presented in the next section.

Listing 3.3 The Mouse Interface Function

```
void mouse(int *m1, int *m2, int *m3, int *m4)
/*
   C to mouse driver interface via interrupt 0x33.
   Only supports functions 0-10.
   See your mouse technical reference manual for the
   interface to other functions.
*/
{
   union REGS inregs, outregs;
   inregs.x.ax = *m1;
   inregs.x.bx = *m2;
   inregs.x.cx = *m3;
   inregs.x.dx = *m4;
   int86(0x33,&inregs,&outregs);
   *m1 = outregs.x.ax;
   *m2 = outregs.x.bx;
   *m3 = outregs.x.cx;
   *m4 = outregs.x.dx;
}
```

Listing 3.4 The Check Mouse Driver Function

```
int check_mouse_driver(int need_mouse)
/*
 * If need_mouse = 1, then abort program if no mouse.
 * Otherwise, if no mouse return 0, else return 1.
*/
{
    void far *address;
    /* get mouse interrupt vector address */
    address = getvect(0x33);
    /* look for NULL address or IRET instruction */
    if ((address == NULL) || (*(unsigned char *)address == 0xcf)) {
        if (need_mouse) {
           printf("Mouse driver NOT installed\n");
      exit(1);
        }
        else return 0;
    }
    return 1;
}
```

Listing 3.5 Source Code for the Mouse Tool Kit Header File (MOUSE.H)

```
/*  Mouse toolkit header file  */
/* Macros to retrieve low and high byte of an integer */
#define lo(f)   ((f) & 0xff)
#define hi(f)   (lo(f >> 8))
/* Common scan-ascii codes */
#define CTRLC        0x2e03
#define CTRLH        0x2308
#define CTRLI        0x1709
#define CTRLL        0x260c
#define CTRLK        0x250b
#define CTRLJ        0x240a
#define CTRLU        0x1615
#define CTRLR        0x1312
#define CRKEY        0x1c0d
#define CTRLCRKEY    0x1c0a
#define UPKEY        0x4800
#define DOWNKEY      0x5000
#define LEFTKEY      0x4b00
#define RIGHTKEY     0x4d00
#define SHFTLEFT     0x4b34
#define SHFTRIGHT    0x4d36
#define DELKEY       0x5300
#define INSKEY       0x5200
#define BSKEY        0x0e08
#define SPACEBAR     0x3920
#define PGUPKEY      0x4900
#define PGDNKEY      0x5100
#define SHFTUPKEY    0x4838
#define SHFTDNKEY    0x5032
#define SHFTPGUPKEY 0x4939
#define SHFTPGDNKEY 0x5133
#define HOMEKEY      0x4700
#define ENDKEY       0x4f00
#define ESCKEY       0x011b
#define ALT_D        0x2000
#define ALT_E        0x1200
#define ALT_I        0x1700
#define ALT_R        0x1300
#define ALT_S        0x1f00
#define ALT_T        0x1400
```

```
#define ALT_X        0x2d00
#define F10KEY       0x4400
/* Mouse pseudo "key" codes */
#define LEFT_MOUSE_PRESS    0xff01
#define RIGHT_MOUSE_PRESS   0xff02
#define LEFT_MOUSE_REL      0xff11
#define RIGHT_MOUSE_REL     0xff12
/* Mouse driver function codes */
#define M_RESET                 0
#define M_SHOW_CURS      1
#define M_HIDE_CURS      2
#define M_GET_STATUS     3
#define M_SET_CURS       4
#define M_GET_PRESS      5
#define M_GET_REL       6
#define M_SET_X_BOUNDS  7
#define M_SET_Y_BOUNDS  8
#define M_SET_G_CURS     9
#define M_SET_T_CURS    10
/* define other constants */
#define MOUSE_NEEDED    1
#define MOUSE_OPTIONAL  0
#define MOUSE_TEXT_MODE 0
/* Mouse external variables */
extern int mouse_text_x;
extern int mouse_text_y;
extern int mouse_grph_x;
extern int mouse_grph_y;
extern int mouse_intialized;
/* Mouse function prototypes */
extern void mouse(int *m1, int *m2, int *m3, int *m4);
extern int check_mouse_driver(int need_mouse);
extern int init_mouse(int need_mouse, int gd, int gm);
extern int mouse_reset(void);
extern void move_mouse(int x, int y);
extern void mouse_on(int code);
extern void mouse_off(int code);
extern void mouse_grph_posn(int *x, int *y);
extern void mouse_txt_posn(int *x, int *y);
extern int mouse_in_box(int graphflag, int left, int right,
                        int top, int bottom);
```

```
extern int button_release(int b);
extern int button_press(int b);
extern int button_state(void);
extern int mouse_trigger(int button_dir);
```

Listing 3.6 The Mouse Tool Kit Source Code (MOUSE.C)

```
/************************************************************
 *   Mouse toolkit      (mouse.c)
 ************************************************************/
#include <bios.h>
#include <dos.h>
#include <conio.h>
#include <process.h>
#include <stdio.h>
#include "mouse.h"
/* <<<< Global variables >>>> */
int mouse_text_x;    /* X posn of mouse in Turbo C text coordinates */
int mouse_text_y;    /* Y posn of mouse in Turbo C text coordinates */
int mouse_grph_x;    /* X posn of mouse in graphics coordinates     */
int mouse_grph_y;    /* Y posn of mouse in graphics coordinates     */
int mouse_initialized = 0;  /* Set to 1 if mouse_init() succeeds   */
/* <<<< Internal variables >>>> */
/* Previous cursor state.                        */
/* 0 = mouse previously off, 1 means prev on. */
static int prev_cursor_state = 0;
/* Pointer to start of bios video data */
static char far *bios_video_area = (char far *)0x00400049L;
/* This variable i for graphics mode only.      */
/* low_resolution = 1 if using 320x200 graphics */
static int low_resolution = 0; /* Leave at 0 for text mode      */
static void set_mouse_posn(int *x, int *y);  /* internal function */
static int low_res_mode(int gd, int gm);     /* internal function */
void mouse(int *m1, int *m2, int *m3, int *m4)
/*
   C to mouse driver interface via interrupt 0x33.
   Only supports functions 0-10.
   See your mouse technical reference manual for the
   interface to other functions
*/
{
   union REGS inregs, outregs;
```

```
   inregs.x.ax = *m1;
   inregs.x.bx = *m2;
   inregs.x.cx = *m3;
   inregs.x.dx = *m4;
   int86(0x33,&inregs,&outregs);
   *m1 = outregs.x.ax;
   *m2 = outregs.x.bx;
   *m3 = outregs.x.cx;
   *m4 = outregs.x.dx;
}
int check_mouse_driver(int need_mouse)
/*
 * If need_mouse = 1, then abort program if no mouse.
 * Otherwise, if no mouse return 0, else return 1.
*/
{
    void far *address;
    /* get mouse interrupt vector address */
    address = getvect(0x33);
    /* look for NULL address or IRET instruction */
    if ((address == NULL) || (*(unsigned char *)address == 0xcf)) {
        if (need_mouse) {
    printf("Mouse driver NOT installed\n");
    exit(1);
        }
        else return 0;
    }
    return 1;
}
int init_mouse(int need_mouse, int gd, int gm)
/*
   Initializes the mouse.  If it can't, and need_mouse = 1,
   this routine exits the program.  Else, it returns
   mouse_initialized = 1.
   If using the mouse for graphics, there are two special cases:
      (1) If using Hercules graphics, we must let the mouse
          driver know we're really in graphics mode, cause it
          can't tell.
      (2) If using any graphics mode with 320 pixels horizontally,
          (ie. low resolution), we must make sure that the mouse
          coordinates are scaled properly.
```

```
  These cases are detected by the parameters gd (graphics driver),
  and parameters gm (graphics mode), as defined by Turbo C graphics.
  If you're just using text mode, set both to zero.
  When fixing up Hercules graphics, we're assuming page 0.  If using
  page 1, set *bios_video_area = 5.
*/
{
   int m1;
   mouse_initialized = 0;
   if (check_mouse_driver(need_mouse)) {
      if (gd == 7) *bios_video_area = 6;  /* Fix up Hercules mode */
      if (low_res_mode(gd,gm))
         low_resolution = 1;        /* Fix up low resolution mode   */
      m1 = mouse_reset();           /* Start mouse at ground zero   */
      if (m1) {
         mouse_initialized = 1;     /* Set mouse init flag          */
         move_mouse(0,0);           /* Set coords to top of screen  */
         mouse_on(0);               /* Turn mouse on for first time */
      }
      else {
        if (need_mouse) {
           printf("ERROR activating mouse ...\n");
           exit(1);
        }
      }
   }
   return mouse_initialized;
}
static int low_res_mode(int gd, int gm)
/* Returns 1 if in any graphics mode with 320 pixels horizontally
   Returns 0 otherwise
*/
{
   if (
        (gd == 1 || gd == 2 || gd == 8) && /* CGA, MCGA, ATT400 */
        (gm >= 0 && gm <= 3)  /* 320 hz mode */
      )
      return 1;
   return 0;
}
int mouse_reset(void)
```

```
/* If the mouse was on, it turns it off.
   Then, the mouse state is reset.
*/
{
   int x1, m1, m2, m3, m4;
   mouse_off(1);       /* Turn off only if it was on */
   m1 = M_RESET;
   mouse(&m1, &m2, &m3, &m4);
   set_mouse_posn(&m3,&m4);  /* Initialize coord's */
   return m1;
}
void move_mouse(int x, int y)
/* Move mouse cursor to text position (x,y) */
{
   int m1, m2, m3, m4;
   if (!mouse_initialized) return;
   m1 = M_SET_CURS;
   m3 = x*8; m4 = y*8;      /* convert to pixel coordinates */
   mouse(&m1,&m2,&m3,&m4);
   set_mouse_posn(&m3,&m4);
}
void mouse_on(int restoreflag)
/* restoreflag = 0 means you want the mouse on regardless of previous state.
   restoreflag = 1 means you want the mouse on only if it was on previously.
*/
{
   int m1, m2, m3, m4;
   if (mouse_initialized) {
      if (!restoreflag || prev_cursor_state) {
         m1 = M_SHOW_CURS;
         mouse(&m1,&m2,&m3,&m4);
         prev_cursor_state = 1;
      }
   }
}
void mouse_off(int tempflag)
/* If tempflag = 1, it means you want to turn the mouse off, and if
   it had been on, set previous state to on.
   If tempflag = 0, it means you want to turn mouse off, and regardless
   of whether it was on or not, set previous state to off.
*/
```

```
{
   int m1, m2, m3, m4;
   if (mouse_initialized) {
      if (prev_cursor_state) {  /* Turn it off only if it was on */
         m1 = M_HIDE_CURS;
         mouse(&m1,&m2,&m3,&m4);
         /* leave prev_cursor_state alone if just turning off temporarily */
         if (!tempflag) prev_cursor_state = 0;
      }
   }
}
void mouse_grph_posn(int *x, int *y)
/* Returns the mouse text coordinates if the mouse is
   initialized, else it returns (0,0).
*/
{
   int m1, m2;
   if (mouse_initialized) {
      m1 = M_GET_STATUS;
      mouse(&m1,&m2,x,y);
      set_mouse_posn(x,y);
   }
   else {
      *x = 0;  *y = 0;  /* default to left hand corner */
   }
   return;
}
void mouse_txt_posn(int *x, int *y)
/* Returns the mouse text coordinates if the mouse is
   initialized, else it returns (1,1).
*/
{
   mouse_grph_posn(x,y);
   *x = mouse_text_x;
   *y = mouse_text_y;
   return;
}
int mouse_in_box(int graphflag,int left, int top, int right, int bottom)
/* Returns 1 if the mouse is in the box given by the
   coordinates, 0 otherwise.  The type of coordinates is
   given by graphflag.  If graphflag = 1, the coordinates
```

```
   are assumed to be graphics coordinates, else they're
   text coordinates.  Either way they are absolute coordinates.
   In order for this routine to work properly you must first
   call mouse_txt_posn, mouse_grph_posn, or any of the
   mouse functions that set the global mouse position variables.
   If mouse not initialized, it returns 0;
*/
{
  int x, y;
  if (mouse_initialized) {
     if (graphflag) {
        x = mouse_grph_x;
        y = mouse_grph_y;
     }
     else {
        x = mouse_text_x;
        y = mouse_text_y;
     }
     if ((y >= top) && (y <= bottom) &&
         (x >= left) && (x <= right))  return 1;
  }
  return 0;
}
int button_release(int b)
/*
   Looks for a left (b=0) or right (b=1) mouse button release.
   Returns 1 if the button has been released since the last time
   called, else returns 0.  If no mouse installed, it returns 0.
*/
{
   int m1, m2, m3, m4;
   if (mouse_initialized) {
      m1 = M_GET_REL;
      m2 = b;  /* which button */
      mouse(&m1,&m2,&m3,&m4);
      set_mouse_posn(&m3,&m4);
      if (m2) return 1;
   }
   return 0;
}
int button_press(int b)
```

```
/*
   Looks for a left (b=0) or right (b=1) mouse button press.
   Returns 1 if the button has been pressed since the last time
   called, else returns 0.  If no mouse installed, it returns 0.
*/
{
   int m1, m2, m3, m4;
   if (mouse_initialized) {
      m1 = M_GET_PRESS;
      m2 = b;  /* which button */
      mouse(&m1,&m2,&m3,&m4);
      set_mouse_posn(&m3,&m4);
      if (m2) return 1;
   }
   return 0;
}
int button_state()
/*
   Returns up/down state of the mouse buttons.  A button is
   down if its corresponding bit = 1.
      Bit   2  Middle button  (Logitech mouse only)
            1  Right button
      LSB   0  Left button
    Returns 0x00 if no button down or no mouse installed.
    Also stores mouse position information.
*/
{
   int m1,m2,m3,m4;
   if (mouse_initialized) {
      m1 = M_GET_STATUS;
      mouse(&m1,&m2,&m3,&m4);
      set_mouse_posn(&m3,&m4);
      return m2;
   }
   return 0;
}
static void set_mouse_posn(int *x, int *y)
/* Sets the internal mouse position variables       */
/* Corrects for 320x200 low resolution modes        */
{
  if (low_resolution) *x >>= 1;  /* divide by two */
```

```
  mouse_grph_x = *x;
  mouse_grph_y = *y;
  mouse_text_x = *x/8 + 1;
  mouse_text_y = *y/8 + 1;
}
int mouse_trigger(int button_dir)
/* Looks for a key press, or a button release (if button_dir = 0)
   or press (if button_dir = 1).  Key presses have  priority over
   mouse buttons.  The left mouse button has priority over the
   right button.  If a key has been pressed, it is then removed
   from the keyboard buffer.
*/
{
   int k;
   if (bioskey(1)) {
      k = bioskey(0);
   }
   else {
     k = 0;
     if (button_dir) {
        if (button_press(0)) k = LEFT_MOUSE_PRESS;
           else if (button_press(1)) k = RIGHT_MOUSE_PRESS;
     }
     else {
        if (button_release(0)) k = LEFT_MOUSE_REL;
           else if (button_release(1)) k = RIGHT_MOUSE_REL;
     }
   }
   return k;
}
```

Listing 3.7 The Mouse Highlighting Example (IOEX7.C)

```
/*
   Text highlighting example with mouse  (ioex7.c)
   Must link with: mouse.obj
*/
#include <bios.h>
#include <conio.h>
#include "mouse.h"        /* mouse routines header file */
typedef struct texel_struct {
  unsigned char ch;
```

```
  unsigned char attr;
} texel;
void my_box(int xul, int yul, int xlr, int ylr, int btype);
void main() {
  int highlite = 0;
  int x = 1, y = 1;
  texel t;
  init_mouse(MOUSE_NEEDED, MOUSE_TEXT_MODE, MOUSE_TEXT_MODE);
  my_box(19,9,66,14,2);
  window(20,10,65,13);
  clrscr();
  mouse_off(1);  /* mouse off temporarily */
  cprintf("Here is some text for you to highlight\r\n");
  cprintf("Click left button to toggle highlighting\r\n");
  cprintf("Drag w/left button down to highlight\r\n");
  cprintf("Click right button to exit");
  mouse_on(1);  /* restore mouse cursor */
  do {
    if (button_press(1)) break;   /* right button pressed means exit */
    if (button_press(0)) /* left button pressed means toggle highlighting */
       highlite = !highlite;
    if (button_state() == 1) {  /* look for left button depressed */
       if (mouse_in_box(0,20,10,65,13)) { /* only highlite window text */
         /* only do if haven't been here before */
         if (x != mouse_text_x || y != mouse_text_y) {
            x = mouse_text_x;  y = mouse_text_y;
            mouse_off(1);       /* remember why ? */
            if (highlite) {   /* all coords here are absolute */
               gettext(x,y,x,y,&t);
       t.attr = 15; /* we'll use "bright" so we can see mouse */
               puttext(x,y,x,y,&t);
            }
            else { /* back to normal */
               gettext(x,y,x,y,&t);
               t.attr = 7;
              puttext(x,y,x,y,&t);
            }
            mouse_on(1);       /* Only back on if previously on */
                               /* (In this program, this is always true) */
         }
       }
```

```
    }
  } while (1);
  mouse_reset();  /* reset mouse, turn it off */
  window(1, 1, 80, 25);
  clrscr();
}
void my_box(int xul, int yul, int xlr, int ylr, int btype)
/* Draws a box at the upper left (xul,yul) and lower right
   (xlr,ylr) coords with given attribute.  If btype = 0, no box is drawn,
   if btype = 1, a single line box is drawn, if btype = 2,  a double line
   box is drawn.
*/
{
   static int boxcar[2][6] = {    /* graphics characters for a box */
     {218,196,191,179,192,217},   /* single line box */
     {201,205,187,186,200,188}    /* double line box */
   };
   int i, hzchar, vtchar;
   if (btype) {
      hzchar = boxcar[btype-1][1];
      vtchar = boxcar[btype-1][3];
      /* draw top and bottom sides */
      gotoxy(xul,yul);
      for (i=xul; i<=xlr; i++) putch(hzchar);
      gotoxy(xul,ylr);
      for (i=xul; i<=xlr; i++) putch(hzchar);
      /* draw vertical sides */
      for (i=yul; i<=ylr; i++) {
         gotoxy(xul,i);
         putch(vtchar);
         gotoxy(xlr,i);
         putch(vtchar);
      }
      /* draw corners */
      gotoxy(xul,yul);  putch(boxcar[btype-1][0]);  /* upper left */
      gotoxy(xlr,yul);  putch(boxcar[btype-1][2]);  /* upper right */
      gotoxy(xlr,ylr);  putch(boxcar[btype-1][5]);  /* lower right */
      gotoxy(xul,ylr);  putch(boxcar[btype-1][4]);  /* lower left */
   }
}
```

CHAPTER

4

Pop-up Windows and Error Reporting

Now that you have the basic tools under your belt, you can go on to build more exotic ones. A popular tool these days is support for pop-up windows. This section presents code for them by using only the Turbo C screen functions. As a result, the windows will not be as fast as they could be by going directly to video RAM, but the code may prove to be more portable to future machines. If you have a 8-Mhz or higher machine, the windows will be plenty fast. Listings 4.1 and 4.2 present the header file and the source code for the pop-up window package. They contain the following functions and global variables:

Pop-up window functions

Function	Task
`init_win()`	Initializes the windowing system
`draw_win()`	Draws a new window
`view_win()`	Makes a window visible or erases it
`slct_win()`	Makes a window the active one (a macro)
`rmv_win()`	Erases a window (a macro that calls)
`clr_win()`	Clears a window
`draw_box()`	Draws a box with different borders and colors
`centerstr()`	Prints a string centered within given coordinates
`mprintf()`	A high-level formatted print routine
`prtfstr()`	A formatted print routine that supports line fill and highlighting
`swap_image()`	Toggles a window from visible to invisible

Variable	Usage
base_win	The window representing the whole screen.
curr_win	The current active window.
defcolors	The current color set in use.
invcolors	Reverse video monochrome colors.
monocolors	Normal monochrome colors.
errcolors	Error message colors.
msgcolors	Normal message colors.
CTRWIN	A code to use when centered windows are desired.

The following is a simple example of using these routines. First, it initializes the window system, pops up a window in the center of the screen, prints hello, waits for a key, and then removes the window and exits:

```
/*
   Popup window example  (popex1.c)
   Must link with: popup.obj, mouse.obj
*/
#include <conio.h>
#include "popup.h"  /* pop-up header file                       */
#include "mouse.h"  /* need for key defs and mouse functions */
main() {
  windesc *w;     /* our window pointer */
  init_win();     /* always do first    */
  init_mouse(MOUSE_OPTIONAL, MOUSE_TEXT_MODE, MOUSE_TEXT_MODE);
  w = draw_win(CTRWIN, CTRWIN, 20, 3,
             "My Window",  popup, &defcolors);
  mprintf("Hello world");
  getch();
  rmv_win(w);     /* removes window */
  mouse_reset(); /* resets mouse */
}
```

Each of these functions will be explained in turn, but first, we will start off by defining just what a window is. For our purposes, a window is a rectangular region on the screen that is independent of the rest of the screen, both in terms of scrolling and by having its own text cursor. Also, there are two distinct types of windows: those that pop up temporarily, and those that are more or less permanent. We will call the first kind *pop-up* windows, and the second *tiled* windows. The reason for the latter is that tiled windows are not supposed to overlap; instead, they split the screen into separate "tiles."

THE WINDOW STRUCTURE

In order to do pop-up windows, you must have some way of restoring the screen to its original state after popping up and then removing the window. The window must save the image underneath it to do this. How do you keep track of that and keep track of the cursor as well? As it turns out, the best way to think of windows is as objects, in the object-oriented style that is becoming fashionable these days.

You can do this by defining a structure to hold parameters unique to a given window. Actually, several structures and types are defined, as is given in the pop-up package:

```
typedef struct wincolors_struct {
   char border_type;
   unsigned char border_color, text_color,
                 title_color, hilite_color;
} wincolors;
enum windowtype {popup,tile};
```

The first structure holds information about what colors to use in the window. This is a convenience that becomes more important when you start doing commercial-quality code, and you wish to allow the user to change the colors. By using this structure faithfully, it becomes much easier to do. Also stored here is the type of border to use, as was discussed in the previous chapter. There are five different color sets that are predefined in the package: one each for color graphics cards, one each for monochrome normal and reversed, one for error message, and one for normal messages. You can change these to suit your needs.

The second definition gives an enumerated type for the kind of windows you have in your system: pop-up and tiled. This type will play an important role later on when we discuss the pop-up window stack. With these preliminary types out of the way, the window structure can be defined as:

```
typedef struct winstruct {
  char *name;                   /* window title */
  void *image;                  /* ptr to image save area */
  struct winstruct *under,
                   *over;       /* ptrs to window below and
                                   above on pop-up stack  */
  wincolors wc;                 /* colors for the window */
  char xul,yul,xlr,ylr,wd,ht;   /* window coord's and sizes */
  char xsave,ysave;             /* saved cursor posn */
  enum windowtype wtype;        /* window type */
} windesc;
```

It contains all the information you need to write code in a generic manner that supports many types of window sizes, shapes, and colors. There are three important pointers present in the window structure. The first is a pointer to a save area where the image below the window will be stored before popping up the window. This save area is allocated dynamically. The last two pointers are for linking windows together.

THE POP-UP WINDOW STACK

Many times there will be more than one window on the screen, and you would like to be able to move back and forth among them. To do this, you must know which one is currently visible, and you must be able to revert to a previous window when it is popped off the screen. What you need, then, is some kind of stack. The one we'll use here is a doubly linked list, with the two pointers ***under** and ***over**. These link to the window "below" and the window "above." This linked list is shown in Figure 4.1.

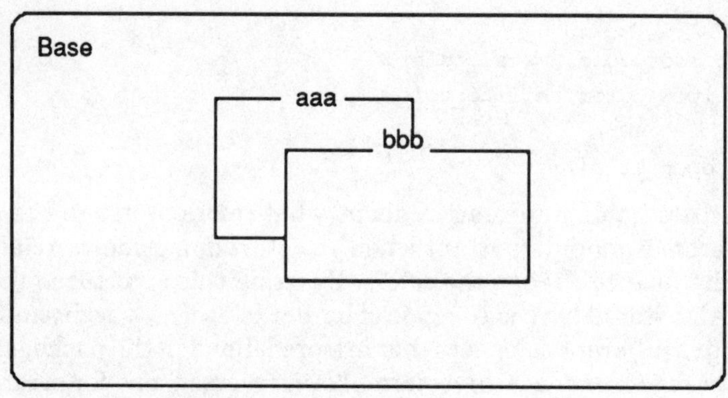

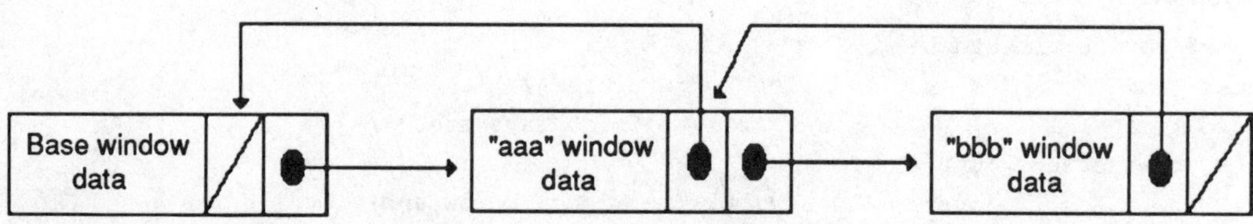

Figure 4.1 The doubly-linked pop-up window stack

What exactly is meant by "above" and "below"? Since each window saves the image underneath it (except for certain types of windows), you must keep track of the order in which the windows were popped up, so that when you remove them, the image underneath is restored properly. If you unpop the windows in the wrong order, your screen will become very garbled. "Above" and "below" refers to this type of ordering. "Above" does not necessarily mean that a window actually resides on top of another one, only that it was popped up (or has swapped images) after the one below it.

At the very bottom of the stack is the "window" that represents the screen before any windows were popped up. We shall call this window the *base window*. Before any pop-up windows are used, you must first initialize the stack to point to this window. This is performed by the function **init_win()**, which calls Turbo C's **gettextinfo()** function to get current information about the screen. It then makes the base window become the top of the window stack. The pointers **base_win** and **curr_win** are global ones to the base window and the current or active window.

The routine to pop-up windows is **draw_win()**. It takes parameters representing the desired coordinates of the window: the upper left-hand corner, and the width and height. You also pass to it the title character string, the type of window it is, and the color set to use. This routine does a lot of bookkeeping, such as checking for valid coordinates and storing parameters in the new window structure. It also saves the image underneath, draws a box around the window, and puts the window on the top of the stack.

There is an important disctinction in the window type which is passed as a parameter. If you tell **draw_win()** to make a pop-up window, then the image underneath the window is saved. If it is to be a tiled window, then the image underneath is *not* saved. This distinction is done mainly to conserve memory. If your window represents a large portion of the screen, and is never going to be unpopped, then there is no reason to take up memory for the saved image underneath. Tiled windows also behave differently when window selection is done.

MANIPULATING THE WINDOW STACK

The function **view_win()** is used to select and/or remove windows. Along with it are two associated macros **slct_win()** and **rmv_win()**. Their definitions are:

```
#define slct_win(w)   view_win(w,1)
#define rmv_win(w)    view_win(w,0)
void view_win(windesc *w, int select)
/*
     w      - Window to view/remove
     select - 0: remove window
              1: select window
*/
```

The function **view_win()** works by moving the window to be selected or removed to the top of the stack. The reason for doing this when selecting a new window is to prevent writing to a window that may be hidden. The window package is not sophisticated enough to know when one window is on top of another. Its only piece of knowledge is the "pop-up" order as explained earlier. Thus, any time you select a window, the window stack is modified so that the new window will be on top.

This is accomplished by first hiding any windows that are above the one to be viewed or removed, hiding the window itself, putting back all the windows above, changing the pointers in the window stack, and then putting back the window to be viewed. If the window is to be removed, this is not done, instead, it is deleted from the window stack, and the window below it (ie., the new top) is selected as the current window. In both cases, the internal function

chg_win() is then called to change the current window coordinates to the new window. The cursor position of the newly selected window is also restored.

The order in which the images are swapped is very important. The windows above the desired one are erased by swapping their saved images with what is currently on the screen. This is done by calling **swap_image()**. The images are swapped from the stack top down to the desired window. When putting the windows back, they are swapped in the reverse order. By doing this, screen integrity is maintained.

There are two other important things to mention about **view_win()**. One is that if the window to move is a tiled window, then no images are swapped. This is due to two reasons: one is that a tiled window has no saved image, so it should not be swapped. Second, if you are not going to swap it, then why bother swapping all the images above it, only to restore them right back where they were? The consequence of the first fact is that you should never select a tiled window if you know another window is even partially on top of it. If you write to the tiled window, you will most likely write over the pop-up window above, and garbage will ensue. The consequence of the second fact is that if you have only tiled windows in your system, hopping back and forth between them is fairly efficient, since no images are being swapped. This is most noticeable on slower machines. In summary, use each type of window in the manner suggested by their names. Tiled windows are semipermanent, pop-up windows are supposed to be temporary.

HIDING AND SHOWING WINDOWS

The function **swap_image()** uses the Turbo C functions **gettext()** and **puttext()** to alternately save and restore the image under a window. It is written as an *image toggle*. If you call it a number of times in succession, it will alternately hide and show the window. Thus, it is convenient if you wish to temporarily hide a window and then redraw it, without having to reconstruct all of the text inside it. Be warned, however, that you should only swap the top window on the stack, as was explained in the preceding paragraphs.

In order to do the swapping, **swap_image()** uses not only the image buffer stored with the window, but allocates additional memory of the same size to be used as a temporary buffer. This rather inefficient method is necessary unless one uses a more direct method to update the screen. As an exercise, see if you can use the direct-to-video technique explained in the last chapter to write a routine to swap images using only a one-texel buffer. If you do write one, remember to hide the mouse cursor while updating the screen. The function **swap_image()** does.

WINDOW I/O

Included in the pop-up window package are five routines for writing to windows: **mprintf()**, **prtfstr()**, **centerstr()**, **clr_win()**, and **draw_box()**. These perform higher-level operations than the Turbo C **cprintf()**, **putch()**, **cputs()**, and **clrscr()** functions. Like their Turbo C counterparts, the pop-up window print routines always write to the current window, but they hide the mouse during screen updates, which the Turbo C functions do not. That is why **mprintf()** is provided, which does the same thing as **cprintf()** (in fact it calls **cprintf()**). If you are using a mouse, you should always use **mprintf()** instead of **cprintf()**. The code for **mprintf()** and **prtfstr()** shows examples of using C's variable number of argument calling sequence, explained in Chapter two. Although they are not provided, you could write routines analogous to **mprintf()** for **cputs()** and **putch()** (i.e., ones that maintain the mouse cursor).

The **prtfstr()** routine can be used in a variety of ways; one use is for highlighting text. If you pass it a nonzero attribute, it will write the text out using the attribute as the new color. This is useful for doing highlighted menu bars, for example. If **attr = 0**, then it writes the text with whatever color is currently on the screen. The following call to **prtfstr()** prints all eleven characters of "Hello world" using a blue color, at screen column 10 and row 5.

```
prtfstr(10,5,"Hello world",1,11);
```

If you give it a width parameter larger than the string, the string length is used instead, unlesss it's truncated by the window.

```
prtfstr(10,5,"Hello world",1,80);
```

You can use 80 for the width whenever you do not want to bother computing the proper length; **prtfstr()** will do that for you. If the printing would cause the text to go past the window boundaries, then no scrolling takes place; the text is truncated instead. For example,

```
w = draw_win(1,1,20,6,"my win",popup,&defcolors);
prtfstr(15,1,"this text will be truncated",0,80);
```

would print only "this t" at column 15, row 1 of the window. Since the attribute is passed as 0, the color is not changed.

To do truncation without going directly to RAM requires some trickery. Because the Turbo C print functions always move the cursor, if you print a character at the last column in the window, the cursor is moved to the next line and the window is scrolled if necessary. This means you could not have windows that were one row high, because if you write to the last character on the row, the window scrolls and your text disappears. Because Turbo C does not provide any way of turning the scrolling off, the only alternative is to get the text image off the screen, make changes to it, and then put it back using **gettext()** and **puttext()**. These two routines do not affect the cursor, but they do slow down the printing. For ultimate speed, you might consider going directly to RAM.

If you pass the width as a negative parameter, and if the string length equals one, (i.e., a single character), then that tells **prtfstr()** to do a line fill. The following will print 25 c's (unless truncated):

```
prtfstr(1,5,"c",0,-25);
```

You can also do formatting by passing the string as a format string and passing the arguments to format after the wd parameter.

```
prtfstr(1,5,"The mouse is at %d %d",0,80,mouse_text_x,mouse_text_y);
```

One nice formatting trick can be used when printing highlighted menu bars. The following statement will highlight a bar 25 characters wide, left justifying the string inside it. It uses the **printf()** left justification code "%-*.*s" and passes the width and precision of the formatting field as parameters.

```
prtfstr(1,5,"%-*.*s",112,25,25,25,"Menu choice #1");
```

Note that the first "25" is the width parameter to the **prtfstr()** function itself. The other two are for the format string.

The routine **centerstr()** will automatically compute coordinates so that you can center some text both horizontally and vertically within a given rectangular region. It calls **prtfstr** to do the actual printing. Note that no provision is given for formatting with this function.

The routine **clr_win()** is used to clear the current window. It is just like **clrscr()** except it maintains the mouse cursor. Finally, **draw_box()** is an expanded version of the **my_box()** routine presented in a previous chapter. It allows you to pass a color for the border, and it maintains the mouse cursor, as well. Another important change from **my_box()** is that it draws the lower right corner using the **gettext()-puttext()** method. This is to keep the screen from scrolling should this corner be at the very bottom of the screen.

A SIMPLE MENU PROGRAM

Now that you have all these tools in your shop, you are ready to see some examples of them in use. The first example is a simple menu program given in Listing 4.3. This program pops up a menu and allows you to move around with the up and down arrows. You make a selection with the Return key. The selections are printed in a second window, and the process continues until an ESC key is pressed. Note that the windows are tiled. If they had been pop-up windows, then you would get annoying flicker each time a window was selected due to the windows being swapped. The window package is not smart enough to know that the windows do not overlap, and hence do not need to be swapped. As an exercise, you might try making it smarter. As a "work-around", here we make them tiled.

After you've understood the code as given (it uses a lot of the features discussed earlier), then try out the program in Listing 4.4. This is the same menu program except it is extended to work with the mouse. By pressing the left button on a menu entry, that entry is selected. If you press the right button, the program exits. Figure 4.2 shows a sample screen from the simple menu program.

This program shows how you to write code to use the mouse if it is there but ignore it if it is not. We've called **mouse_init()** and told it that a mouse is optional. It will not fail if there is no mouse installed, it just ignores the request. Also, the **mouse_trigger()** function was written to ignore the mouse if it was not installed and initialized. It will still return key codes.

MOVING WINDOWS PROGRAM

The next program, Listing 4.5, demonstrates how to move windows around on the screen. This program also shows how the windows are shuffled to the top of the stack when they are selected. It works as follows: if you press the number of a window given in its title, then that window is selected. If you use the arrow keys, you can then cause that window to move around. Any other keys are echoed in the current window. Pressing ESC exits the program. Figure 4.3 shows a sample screen from the moving windows program.

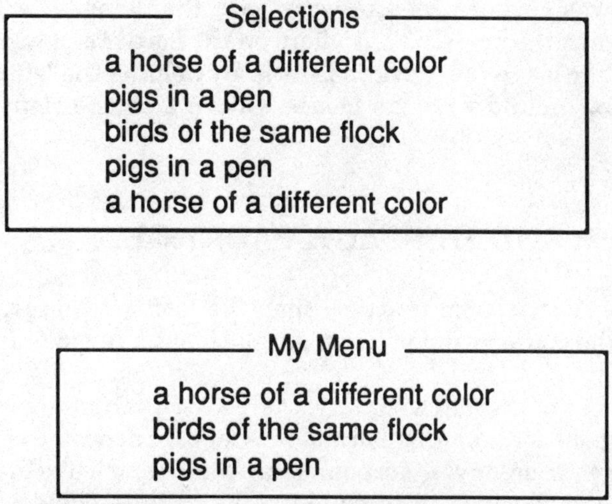

Selections

a horse of a different color
pigs in a pen
birds of the same flock
pigs in a pen
a horse of a different color

My Menu

a horse of a different color
birds of the same flock
pigs in a pen

Figure 4.2 Sample screen of the simple menu program

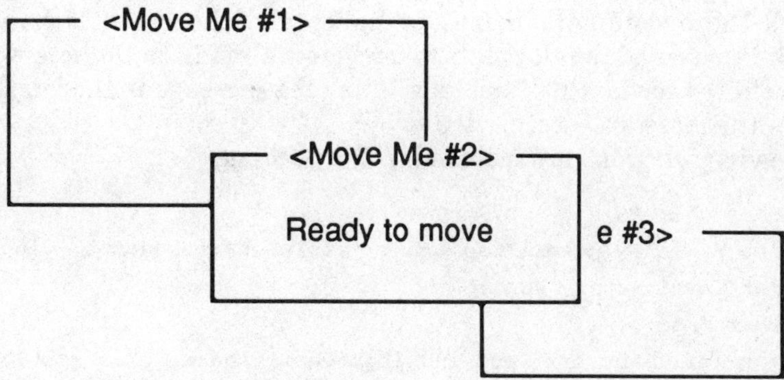

Figure 4.3 Sample output from the moving windows program

The program was also designed to work with the mouse if it is present. Pressing the left mouse button when the mouse is anywhere on the border of a window causes that window to be selected and shuffled to the top of the stack. By holding the left mouse button down, you can drag the window around with the mouse. Clicking on the right mouse button exits the program.

POP-UP ERROR AND MESSAGE PACKAGE

The next example is a little more practical than the last two. In fact, it is so useful that it is included as part of the pop-up window package, given in Listing 4.6. It is a system for handling error messages.

The system works in the following way: there are two windows involved, one for handling error messages, and one for handling normal messages. The windows can either be popped up on the fly as messages arise, or you can pop them up once and leave them for the duration of the program. Routines are provided to route messages to these windows as appropriate. These routines use the following globally defined window pointers:

```
int errx = CTRWIN;          /* Default to center of the screen */
int erry = CTRWIN;
windesc *errw = NULL;       /* Default to pop-up window */
int msgx = CTRWIN;          /* same for messages */
int msgy = CTRWIN;
windesc *msgw = NULL;
```

The window pointers default to NULL. If the candidate window is NULL at the time its corresponding message routine is called, then a window is popped up to display the message. The error window is popped up at the coordinates given by **(errx,erry)**, and the message window at **(msgx,msgy)**. These coordinates default to the center of the screen. If the window pointer is not NULL, then it is assumed that it points to a window already on the screen, and that window is temporarily selected to show the message. After the message is shown, the window that was current before the message is reselected.

The following functions are included in the package:

```
void numnewlines(char *s, int *n, int *w);
void popmsg(int x, int y, char *msg, char *title,char soundout, wincolors *wc);
void reperr(int level, char *msg);
void repmsg(char *msg);
void sayerr(int ferr, int errflag, int lno, char *pname, char *fmt,...);
void beep(void);
unsigned int getkey(void);
```

The last two will be explained first. The **beep()** function simply calls Turbo C's **sound()**, **delay()**, and **nosound()** functions to make a custom bell routine. You can change the parameters used to suit your taste.

The **getkey()** function is used to trap CTRL-C keys. It calls **bioskey(0)** to get the next key from the buffer. If that key is a CTRL-C, an abort window is popped up to see if the user wishes to abort. This routine can be used in place of **bioskey(0)**, if you wish to provide a way to abort the program. This is especially useful during debugging. Note that the Turbo C **ctrlbrk()** function will not do us much good. It only checks for CTRL-C when DOS calls are made. The functions **bioskey()**, **cprintf()**, **putch()**, and so on, do not call DOS, so the ctrl-break handler does not have much effect. Since these are the functions you would normally use when doing windows, some other way of trapping CTRL-C is needed. The **getkey()** function provides a way.

The **sayerr()** function is the high-level interface into the error-reporting system. The parameters for it are as follows:

Parameter	Meaning
ferr	1 means print out the last DOS error 0 means don't print it
errflag	0 means treat as message, 1 means warning, 2 means an error
lno,pname	If pname is not a null string, then it is assumed to be a file name, and lno the line number in that file. These together will be included in the message.
fmt, ...	A printf-style format string and its optional arguments

This function basically takes your formatted message and, depending on the parameters, may tack on the last DOS error message, as well as the line number and file name in which the error occurred. These last parameters are useful for debugging purposes. You can have it automatically load in the current line of the C source file where the error occurred. This is accomplished by using the C predefined macros __LINE__ and __FILE__. When __LINE__ is expanded during preprocessing, it gets replaced with the current line number being compiled. __FILE__ gets replaced with the full path name of the compiled file. In order to make it convenient to use, the following additional macros are defined for **sayerr()**:

```
/* Use these if you wish to include source file and line number */
  #define SWRNF  0,1,__LINE__,__FILE__
  #define SERRF  0,2,__LINE__,__FILE__
  #define SMSGF  0,0,__LINE__,__FILE__
  #define FWRNF  1,1,__LINE__,__FILE__
  #define FERRF  1,2,__LINE__,__FILE__
  #define FMSGF  1,0,__LINE__,__FILE__
  /* Otherwise, use these */
  #define SWRN  0,1,0,""
  #define SERR  0,2,0,""
  #define SMSG  0,0,0,""
  #define FWRN  1,1,0,""
  #define FERR  1,2,0,""
  #define FMSG  1,0,0,""
```

These macros make up the first four parameters of your **sayerr()** function call. In order to make them easy to remember, the macros' names are composed as follows. The "S" prefix is used when you do not wish to include the last DOS error message; the "F" prefix is used when you do. (The "F" stands for "File". Many of the DOS error messages are file related). Next comes the type of message: "WRN" for warnings, "ERR" for errors, and "MSG" for normal messages. The suffix "F" tacked on to the end indicates you wish to have the current line number and file included in the message. As an example, the following code fragment prints out the DOS "file not found" message, along with the place in the code the error occurred:

```
/* ... */
handle = open("nosuchfile",O_RDONLY)
if (handle == -1) sayerr(FERRF,"%s\r\n","nosuchfile");
/* ... */
```

The code for sayerr() is given as follows:

```
void sayerr(int ferr, int errflag, int lno,
            char *pname, char *fmt, ...)
{
   va_list arg_ptr;
   char t[255];   /* temp character buffer */
   int j;         /* temp character count */
   if (*pname) {
      j = sprintf(t,"On line %d in pgm %s\r\n",lno,pname);
   }
   else j = 0;
   if (ferr == 1) {
      /* add last dos error */
      j += sprintf(t+j,"%s: ",strerror(errno));
   }
   va_start(arg_ptr,fmt);        /* point to optional arguments  */
   vsprintf(t+j,fmt,arg_ptr);    /* add rest of formatted string */
   va_end(arg_ptr);
   switch(errflag) {
     case 1:
        reperr(0,t);       /* just a warning */
     break;
     case 2:
        reperr(1,t);       /* an error */
     break;
     default:
        repmsg(t);         /* or a plain old message */
   }
}
```

The code uses many features of C to build up the error message: variable number of arguments, internal formatting via **sprintf()**, and retrieving the last DOS error message via **strerror()**. Once the error message is created, it is passed along to the appropriate message-reporting routine, either **reperr()** or **repmsg()**. These routines check to see if the appropriate message window is defined. If it is, the message is routed to that window; otherwise, another routine is called to pop up the message **popmsg()**.

The function **popmsg()** takes an arbitrary string of characters and automatically sizes a window to print out the message contained therein. It does this by calling yet another function, **numnewlines()**, which counts the number of newline characters occuring in the string, and determines along the way the maximum length of any line in the message. After popping up a window, it waits for either a carriage return or an ESC key before unpopping the window. A parameter is passed to indicate whether or not you want the beeper to beep. The **popmsg()** routine is useful anytime you wish to display a multiple line-message without having to figure out the size of window needed. One restriction, however, is that the formatting cannot exceed 255 characters, so it is good only for short messages.

The program shown in Listing 4.7 is an example of how the error message reporting system works. It draws a tiled "main" window, and then shows a popup error window, complete with a DOS error message. It then draws a tiled error window and routes several error messages to it, changing the severity level from error to warning along the way. Finally, it pops up a general message window. Figures 4.4 and 4.5 show sample output from the program.

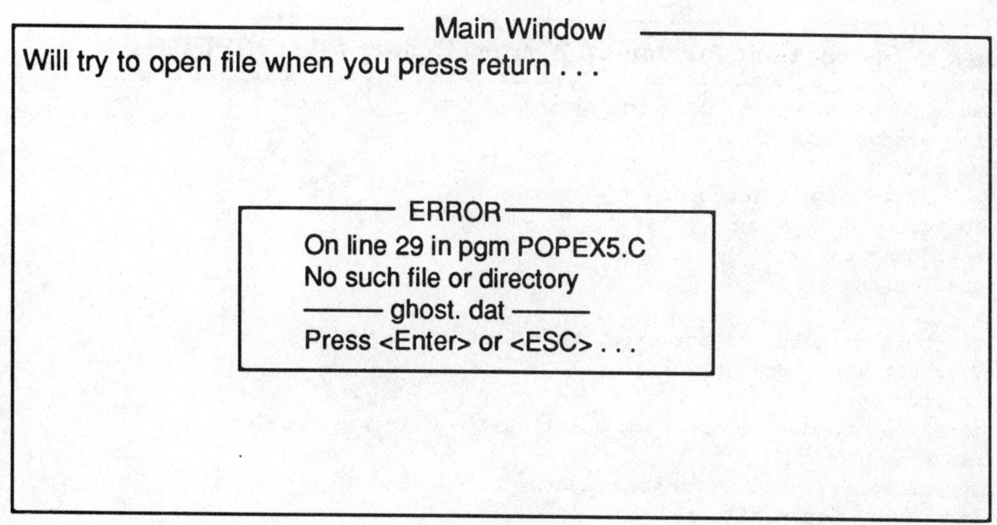

Figure 4.4 Sample pop-up error window

```
Main Window
Will try to open file when you press return . . .
Press return to construct static error window . . .
Ready to try opening again, press return . . .
Press return to see error message without line no and source file . . .
Press return to see it as a warning . . .

Error Wondow
ERROR: On line 42 in pgm POPEX5.C
No such file or directory
——— ghost. dat ———
ERROR: No such file or directory
——— ghost. dat ———
```

Figure 4.5 Sample static error window

Listing 4.1 Source Code for Pop-up Window Header File (POPUP.H)

```
/*  Text mode popup window package  (popup.h)  */
/* Center window code */
#define  CTRWIN  999
/* video ram text-cell structure */
typedef struct texel_struct {
  unsigned char ch;
  unsigned char attr;
} texel;
/* A structure to hold the box type, and a set of window colors */
typedef struct wincolors_struct {
  char border_type;
  unsigned char border_color, text_color, title_color, hilite_color;
} wincolors;
/* popupwindows save the image underneath, tiled windows don't */
enum windowtype {popup,tile};
/* A structure to hold information for each window */
typedef struct winstruct {
   char *name;                     /* window title */
   void *image;                    /* ptr to image save area */
```

```
    struct winstruct *under,*over;  /* ptrs to window below and above
                                       on popup stack  */
    wincolors wc;                   /* colors for the window */
    char xul,yul,xlr,ylr,wd,ht;     /* window coord's and sizes */
    char xsave,ysave;               /* saved cursor posn */
    enum windowtype wtype;          /* window type */
} windesc;
extern windesc *base_win;     /* can be used to access whole screen */
extern windesc *curr_win;     /* current window in use */
extern wincolors defcolors;   /* predefined color sets */
extern wincolors invcolors;
extern wincolors monocolors;
extern wincolors errcolors;
extern wincolors msgcolors;
/* macros for easy use in removing and selecting window */
#define rmv_win(w)  view_win(w,0)
#define slct_win(w) view_win(w,1)
/* Now the prototypes for the popup functions */
extern void init_win(void);
extern windesc *draw_win(int x, int y, int wd, int ht, char *title,
                        enum windowtype wt, wincolors *wc);
extern void view_win(windesc *this, int move_to_top);
extern void clr_win(void);
extern void draw_box(int xul,int yul,int xlr,int ylr,int btype,int attr);
extern void centerstr(int xul, int yul, int xlr, int ylr,
                      char *s, unsigned char a);
extern void mprintf(char *fmt,...);
extern void prtfstr(int x, int y, char *fmt, unsigned char attr, int wd,...);
extern void swap_image(windesc *w);
/* Includes for sayerr.c */
/* the first set of macros include line number and name of source file */
#define SWRNF  0,1,__LINE__,__FILE__
#define SERRF  0,2,__LINE__,__FILE__
#define SMSGF  0,0,__LINE__,__FILE__
#define FWRNF  1,1,__LINE__,__FILE__
#define FERRF  1,2,__LINE__,__FILE__
#define FMSGF  1,0,__LINE__,__FILE__
/* The second set do not */
#define SWRN  0,1,0,""
#define SERR  0,2,0,""
#define SMSG  0,0,0,""
#define FWRN  1,1,0,""
#define FERR  1,2,0,""
#define FMSG  1,0,0,""
extern int errx;        /* Default error coordinates */
extern int erry;
extern windesc *errw;   /* error window pointer         */
extern int msgx;        /* same for messages */
```

```
extern int msgy;
extern windesc *msgw;
extern void numnewlines(char *s, int *n, int *w);
extern void popmsg(int x, int y, char *msg, char *title,
                   char soundout, wincolors *wc);
extern void reperr(int level, char *msg);
extern void repmsg(char *msg);
extern void sayerr(int ferr, int errflag, int lno,
                   char *pname, char *fmt,...);
extern void beep(void);
extern unsigned int getkey(void);
```

Listing 4.2 Pop-up Window Source Code (POPUP.C)

```
/********************************************************************
 *   Popup window toolkit for Turbo C  (popup.c)
 ********************************************************************/
#include <stddef.h>
#include <stdarg.h>
#include <stdio.h>
#include <stdlib.h>
#include <alloc.h>
#include <conio.h>
#include <string.h>
#include <process.h>
#include "popup.h"
#include "mouse.h"
#define MAX(a,b)  ((a) > (b) ? (a) : (b))
#define MIN(a,b)  ((a) < (b) ? (a) : (b))
/*
 * Global data definitions
 */
windesc *base_win = NULL;     /* The "Base Window" pointer */
windesc *curr_win  = NULL;    /* The current window pointer */
/* Color sets for color monitors                                        */
/* {border_type, border_color, textcolor, title_color, hilite_color} */
wincolors defcolors   = {1,   23,   30,   27, 94  };
wincolors invcolors   = {1,  112,  112,  112, 15  };
wincolors monocolors  = {1,    7,   15,   15, 112 };
wincolors errcolors   = {1,   79,   79,   79, 4   };
wincolors msgcolors   = {1,   47,   47,   46, 112 };
/* variables internal to popup.c */
static windesc *top_win;    /* window stack pointer */
static void chg_win(windesc *this);
static windesc *make_window_node(void);
static windesc *push_window_node(void);
static void  dispose_window_node(windesc *w);
void init_win(void)
/*
```

```
  init_win initializes the internal variables for the popup windows
  package. This function creates a base window "base_win" which
  represents the entire screen.
  This function MUST be called before any popup routines are used.
*/
{
  struct text_info ti;                /* turbo-c predefined structure */

  base_win = make_window_node();      /* allocate a window node */
  gettextinfo(&ti);                   /* get base window coords */
  base_win->xul = ti.winleft - 1;     /* but our coords include border !!! */
  base_win->xlr = ti.winright + 1;
  base_win->yul = ti.wintop - 1;
  base_win->ylr = ti.winbottom + 1;
  base_win->wd  = ti.screenwidth + 2;
  base_win->ht  = ti.screenheight + 2;
  base_win->xsave = ti.curx;
  base_win->ysave = ti.cury;
  base_win->wc = monocolors;              /* default to monochrome colors */
  base_win->wc.text_color = ti.attribute; /* but use current window color */
  base_win->name = "base";                /* window has no title         */
  base_win->wtype = tile;                 /* no saved image underneath   */
  base_win->wc.border_type = 0;           /* has no border either        */
  top_win = base_win;                     /* set up window stack         */
  curr_win = base_win;
}
windesc *draw_win(int x, int y, int wd, int ht, char *title,
                  enum windowtype wt, wincolors *wc)
/*
   draw_win creates a new window at a designated screen location.
   All window coordinates include the border!!.  Note that the
   Turbo-C window function does not know about the border, and that
   its coordinates are actually "inside" the border.
   Besides the usual coordinates for (x,y), you can use the following
   codes:
        x = CTRWIN   (Center window in x direction)
        y = CTRWIN   (Center window in y direction)
*/
{
  windesc *w;
  int xsave, ysave;
  mouse_off(1);             /* hide mouse cursor during screen updates */
  w = push_window_node();   /* create and link up a window node */
  /* Check for valid window size */
  wd = MAX(wd,3);
  wd = MIN(wd,80);
  ht = MAX(ht,3);
  ht = MIN(ht,25);
  /* Check for centering coordinates and current coordinates.
```

```
   Reminder: these are absolute coordinates !!! */
if (x == CTRWIN) x = (80-wd) / 2;
if (y == CTRWIN) y = (25-ht) / 2;
/*
   Check for valid coordinates.  Coordinates (0,0) are valid only for
   borderless windows, (the actual window will start at (1,1)).
*/
if (wc->border_type) {
   x = MAX(x,1);
   y = MAX(y,1);
}
else {
   x = MAX(x,0);
   y = MAX(y,0);
}
if ((x+wd) > 80) x = 80-wd+1;
if ((y+ht) > 25) y = 25-ht+1;
/* Store the window parameters */
w->wd  = wd;                w->ht  = ht;
w->xul = x;                 w->yul = y;
w->xlr = x + w->wd - 1;     w->ylr = w->yul + w->ht - 1;
w->wc = *wc;    /* set up our set of colors */
w->xsave   = 1;             w->ysave    = 1;
w->wtype   = wt;            w->name     = strdup(title);
/* allocate and save image underneath if a popup window */
if (wt == popup) {
   w->image = calloc(wd*ht,2);
   swap_image(w);
}
/* Ready to draw box and title.  To do this we must be in base
   or "absolute" coords.  But we must be careful to save the
   base cursor coords cause draw box and centerstr will change
   them on us.
 */
if (curr_win == base_win) {
   xsave = wherex();
   ysave = wherey();
}
else {
  xsave = base_win->xsave;
  ysave = base_win->ysave;
}
chg_win(base_win);
draw_box(w->xul,w->yul,w->xlr,w->ylr,w->wc.border_type,w->wc.border_color);
centerstr(w->xul,w->yul,w->xlr,w->yul,w->name,w->wc.title_color);
gotoxy(xsave,ysave);         /* restore base window cursor coords */
chg_win(w);                  /* Now select new window             */
clr_win();                   /* and clear it                      */
mouse_on(1);                 /* restore mouse state               */
```

```
  return w;                      /* return new window pointer          */
}
void view_win(windesc *this, int select)
/* If select = 1, then view_win moves "this" window to the
   top of the stack and makes it the active window.
   If select = 0, then the window is removed from the stack and erased.
   Note that no moves take place if already at the top.
   If this is merely a tiled window, then it is just selected.
*/
{
   windesc *p;
   if (select && this == top_win) return;
   mouse_off(1);    /* make sure mouse hidden */
   /* if this is a popup window, move its image to the top */
   if (this->wtype == popup) {
      p = top_win;
      while(p != this) {     /* hide all window above */
        swap_image(p);
        p = p->under;
      }
      swap_image(this);      /* and then this window */
      p = this;              /* then put rest of windows back */
      while(p != top_win) {
        p = p->over;
        swap_image(p);
      }
   }
   /* link up window underneath this one, with the window above it */
   if (this == top_win) {        /* if this == top_win here, then it is also */
      this->under->over = NULL; /* true that we're removing it for good    */
      top_win = this->under;
   }
   else {
     this->under->over = this->over;
     this->over->under = this->under;
   }
   if (select) {
      top_win->over = this; /* move window to the top */
      this->under = top_win;
      top_win = this;
      swap_image(this);     /* put back it's image. Does nothing if tiled */
      chg_win(this);        /* change window */
   }
   else {
     chg_win(top_win);           /* might as well select top window */
     dispose_window_node(this); /* but do before free old window   */
   }
   mouse_on(1);        /* restore mouse state */
}
```

```
static void chg_win(windesc *this)
/* Internal routine to select a window */
{
  curr_win->xsave = wherex();
  curr_win->ysave = wherey();
  window(this->xul+1, this->yul+1, this->xlr-1, this->ylr-1);
  textattr(this->wc.text_color);   /* restore window color and cursor */
  gotoxy(this->xsave, this->ysave);
  curr_win = this;                 /* selected window is active */
}
void swap_image(windesc *w)
/*
   This routines swaps the image buffer of a window with what is
   on the screen.  If the window is not a popup window, then
   nothing happens.
*/
{
  int xstart, ystart, xfin, yfin;
  char *temp_image;
  unsigned int nbytes;
  if (w->wtype == popup) {
     xstart = w->xul;  ystart = w->yul;
     xfin   = w->xlr;  yfin   = w->ylr;
     if (!w->wc.border_type) {
        /* don't swap border area if no border */
        xstart++; ystart++;
        xfin--; yfin--;
     }
     nbytes = (xfin-xstart+1)*(yfin-ystart+1)*2;
     mouse_off(1);   /* hide mouse cursor during screen update */
     temp_image = malloc(nbytes);
     gettext(xstart, ystart, xfin, yfin, temp_image);
     puttext(xstart, ystart, xfin, yfin, (void *)w->image);
     memcpy(w->image, temp_image, nbytes);
     free(temp_image);
     mouse_on(1);    /* restore mouse cursor */
  }
}
void clr_win(void)
/*
 * High level clear window. Supports the mouse cursor, and uses
 * the text_color of the current window when clearing it.
 */
{
   mouse_off(1);
   textattr(curr_win->wc.text_color);
   clrscr();
   mouse_on(1);
}
```

```
void mprintf(char *fmt,...)
/*
   mprintf is a high level printf-like function that calls cprintf
   (so it knows about the current window), but also takes care of
   the mouse.
   NOTE:  The formatting must not exceed 255 characters !
*/
{
  va_list arg_ptr;
  char t[255];
  va_start(arg_ptr,wd);
  vsprintf(t,fmt,arg_ptr); /* internal format function */
  mouse_off(1);            /* hide mouse cursor during screen update */
  cprintf("%s", t);        /* print the string with scrolling supported */
  mouse_on(1);             /* restore mouse cursor */
  va_end(arg_ptr);
}
void prtfstr(int x, int y, char *fmt, unsigned char attr, int wd,...)
/*
   prtfstr prints a formatted string in the current window. prtfstr is
   similar cprintf except that it doesn't support wrap-around, in fact,
   it goes to great lengths to get around it.  If the string is too long
   to fit in the window, it will be truncated.
   If attr != 0, the string will be printed with that color, otherwise
   the color will be left alone.
   If wd < 0 and the length of the formatted string = 1, then prtfstr
   will print the one-character string abs(wd) times.  This is useful
   for filling a line with a character.
   NOTE:  The formatting must not exceed 255 characters !
*/
{
  va_list arg_ptr;
  char t[255];
  int len, i, n, xa, ya, fillflag;
  static texel line[80];      /* text image buffer */
  va_start(arg_ptr,wd);
  vsprintf(t, fmt,arg_ptr);   /* internal format function */
  va_end(arg_ptr);
  n = abs(wd);                /* compute and bounds check desired width */
  n = MIN(n, curr_win->wd-x-1);
  xa = curr_win->xul + x;      /* get absolute coordinates */
  ya = curr_win->yul + y;
  len = MIN(strlen(t), n);    /* keep string inside the window */
  t[len] = 0;                 /* by truncating if necessary    */
  if (len) {  /* only do non-null strings */
     if (wd < 0 && (strlen(t) == 1)) {
        fillflag = 1;
        len = n;
     }
```

```
    else {
      fillflag = 0;
    }
    mouse_off(1);                          /* remember to hide mouse */
    gettext(xa, ya, xa+len-1, ya, line);   /* extract text image */
    for (i=0; i<len; i++) {                /* change it */
        if (fillflag) line[i].ch = *t;
          else line[i].ch = t[i];
        if (attr) line[i].attr = attr;
    }
    puttext(xa, ya, xa+len-1, ya, line);   /* put it back */
    mouse_on(1);                           /* restore mouse on */
    if (x+len == curr_win->wd-1) x--;      /* Keep cursor in window */
    gotoxy(x+len, y);                      /* then move it to end of string */
  }
  else { /* for null strings, just move cursor */
    gotoxy(x,y);
  }
}
void centerstr(int xul, int yul, int xlr, int ylr,
               char *s, unsigned char a)
/*
  centerstr prints a string centered between the relative coord's
  (xul,yul) and (xlr,ylr), with attribute a.
*/
{
  int xs,ys,wd;
  if (*s != 0) {
     mouse_off(1);
     wd = xlr-xul+1;
     if ((xs = (wd-strlen(s)) / 2 + xul) < xul) xs = xul;
     if ((ys = (ylr-yul+1) / 2 + yul) < yul) ys = yul;
     prtfstr(xs, ys, s, a, wd);
     mouse_on(1);
  }
}
void draw_box(int xul, int yul, int xlr, int ylr, int btype, int attr)
/* Draws a box at the upper left (xul,yul) and lower right
   (xlr,ylr) coords with given attribute.  If btype = 0, no box is drawn,
   if btype = 1, a single line box is drawn, if btype = 2,  a double line
   box is drawn.
*/
{
   static int boxcar[2][6] = {
     /* graphics characters for boxes                                  */
     /* { topleft, hz, topright, vt, bottomleft, bottomright } */
     {218,196,191,179,192,217},   /* single line box */
     {201,205,187,186,200,188}    /* double line box */
   };
```

```
   int i, hzchar, vtchar, oldattr;
   texel t;
   struct text_info ti;
   if (btype) {
      mouse_off(1);
      gettextinfo(&ti);          /* save old text attribute */
      oldattr = ti.attribute;
      textattr(attr);            /* set new one */
      hzchar = boxcar[btype-1][1];
      vtchar = boxcar[btype-1][3];
      /* draw top and bottom sides */
      gotoxy(xul+1,yul);
      for (i=xul+1; i<xlr; i++) putch(hzchar);
      gotoxy(xul+1,ylr);
      for (i=xul+1; i<xlr; i++) putch(hzchar);
      /* draw vertical sides */
      for (i=yul+1; i<ylr; i++) {
         gotoxy(xul,i);
         putch(vtchar);
         gotoxy(xlr,i);
         putch(vtchar);
      }
      /* draw corners */
      gotoxy(xul,yul);  putch(boxcar[btype-1][0]);  /* upper left */
      gotoxy(xlr,yul);  putch(boxcar[btype-1][2]);  /* upper right */
      gotoxy(xul,ylr);  putch(boxcar[btype-1][4]);  /* lower left */
      /* can't write lower right corner via putch, due to possible
         scroll problems, so must do it a roundabout way */
      gettext(xlr,ylr,xlr,ylr,&t);
      t.ch = boxcar[btype-1][5];  t.attr = attr;
      puttext(xlr,ylr,xlr,ylr,&t);
      textattr(oldattr);  /* restore old attribute */
      mouse_on(1);
   }
}
static windesc *make_window_node(void)
{
/*
  Make_window_node allocates room for a new window structure,
  and initializes it's links to NULL.
*/
  windesc *q;
  q = (windesc *)malloc(sizeof(windesc));
  q->image = NULL; q->under = NULL; q->over = NULL;
  return q;
}
static windesc *push_window_node(void)
{
/*
```

```
  Push_window_node "pushes" the window w onto the window stack.
*/
   windesc *q;
   q = make_window_node();      /* allocate a window node */
   top_win->over = q;           /* link top of stack to new node */
   q->under = top_win;          /* link new node to top of stack */
   top_win = q;                 /* set top of stack to new node  */
   return q;
}
static void dispose_window_node(windesc *w)
{
/*
  Dispose_window_node frees up the image save area of the window,
  and the window structure itself.
*/
  if (w != NULL) {     /* safety test for base window   */
    if (w->wtype == popup) free(w->image);
    free(w->name);     /* free up window title          */
    free(w);           /* and then the structure itself */
  }
}
```

Listing 4.3 Source Code For A Simple Menu Program (POPEX2.C)

```
/*
   Popup menu example  (popex2.c)
   Must link with: popup.obj, mouse.obj
*/
#include <bios.h>
#include <conio.h>
#include "popup.h"     /* popup function prototypes */
#include "mouse.h"     /* to get key definitions    */
char *menu_entries[] = {
  "a horse of a different color",
  "birds of the same flock",
  "pigs in a pen"
};
void disp_entry(windesc *w, char *entry[], int entryno, int hilite);
void main() {
  windesc *w1, *w2;
  int entryno = 1, i, key;
  init_win();     /* always do this first */
  w1 = draw_win(CTRWIN,CTRWIN,30,5," My Menu ",tile,&monocolors);
  w2 = draw_win(CTRWIN,1,50,7," Selections ",tile,&monocolors);
  /* display menu choices */
  slct_win(w1);
  for(i=0; i<3; i++) prtfstr(1,i+1,menu_entries[i],0,80);
  do {  /* loop until esc key pressed */
     do { /* make selection */
```

```
      disp_entry(w1,menu_entries,entryno,1); /* hilite bar */
      key = bioskey(0);
      disp_entry(w1,menu_entries,entryno,0); /* back to normal */
      switch(key) {
        case UPKEY:
          if (--entryno < 1) entryno = 3;  /* support wrap-around */
        break;
        case DOWNKEY:
          if (++entryno > 3) entryno = 1;
        break;
        default: ;
      }
    } while ((key != CRKEY) && (key != ESCKEY));
    if (key == CRKEY) {
      slct_win(w2);
      mprintf("\r\n%s",menu_entries[entryno-1]);
      slct_win(w1);
    }
  } while(key != ESCKEY);
  rmv_win(w2);  /* free up window memory, (they stay on screen */
  rmv_win(w1);  /* cause they're tiled                        */
  clrscr();     /* so erase 'em this way */
}
void disp_entry(windesc *w, char *entry[], int entryno, int hilite)
/*
   Displays menu entry number entryno in window w.
   If hilite = 1, then the entry is highlited.  The highliting
   takes place the width of the window.
*/
{
   int bar_color;
   if (hilite) bar_color = w->wc.hilite_color;
      else     bar_color = w->wc.text_color;
   /* bar gets highlighted all the way across window by left justified
      formatting trick.
   */
   prtfstr(1,entryno,"%-*.*s",bar_color,80,
           w->wd-2,w->wd-2,entry[entryno-1]);
}
```

Listing 4.4 A Simple Mouse Driven Menu Program (POPEX3.C)

```
/*
   Popup menus with mouse support example  (popex3.c)
   Must link with: popup.obj, mouse.obj
*/
#include <bios.h>
#include <conio.h>
#include "popup.h"     /* popup function prototypes */
```

```
#include "mouse.h"     /* to get key definitions    */
char *menu_entries[] = {
  "a horse of a different color",
  "birds of the same flock",
  "pigs in a pen"
};
void disp_entry(windesc *w, char *entry[], int entryno, int hilite);
void main() {
  windesc *w1, *w2;
  int entryno = 1, i, key;
  init_win();   /* always do this first */
  init_mouse(MOUSE_OPTIONAL, MOUSE_TEXT_MODE, MOUSE_TEXT_MODE);
  defcolors = monocolors;   /*  use if you have monochrome card */
  w1 = draw_win(CTRWIN,CTRWIN,30,5," My Menu ",tile,&defcolors);
  w2 = draw_win(CTRWIN,1,50,7," Selections ",tile,&defcolors);
  /* display menu choices */
  slct_win(w1);
  for(i=0; i<3; i++) prtfstr(1,i+1,menu_entries[i],0,80);
  do {  /* loop until esc key pressed */
     do { /* make selection */
       disp_entry(w1,menu_entries,entryno,1); /* hilite bar */
       while(!(key = mouse_trigger(1)));  /* wait for key or mouse event */
       disp_entry(w1,menu_entries,entryno,0); /* back to normal */
       switch(key) {
         case UPKEY:
           if (--entryno < 1) entryno = 3;  /* support wrap-around */
         break;
         case DOWNKEY:
           if (++entryno > 3) entryno = 1;
         break;
         case LEFT_MOUSE_PRESS:
           for (i = 1; i<=3; i++) { /* check for mouse on entry */
               if (mouse_in_box(0,w1->xul+1,w1->yul+i,
                                w1->xlr-1,w1->yul+i)) {
                  entryno = i;
                  key = CRKEY;  /* fake key for selection */
               }
           }
         break;
         case RIGHT_MOUSE_PRESS:
           key = ESCKEY;          /* fake key for exit code */
         break;
         default: ;
       }
    } while ((key != CRKEY) && (key != ESCKEY));
    if (key == CRKEY) {
       slct_win(w2);
   mprintf("\r\n%s",menu_entries[entryno-1]);
       slct_win(w1);
```

```
    }
  } while(key != ESCKEY);
  rmv_win(w2);  /* free up window memory.  (They stay on screen */
  rmv_win(w1);  /* cause they're tiled                          */
  mouse_reset();
  clrscr();
}
void disp_entry(windesc *w, char *entry[], int entryno, int hilite)
/*
   Displays menu entry number entryno in window w.
   If hilite = 1, then the entry is highlited.  The highliting
   takes place the width of the window.
*/
{
   int bar_color;
   if (hilite) bar_color = w->wc.hilite_color;
      else     bar_color = w->wc.text_color;
   /* bar gets highlighted all the way across window by left justified
      formatting trick.
   */
   prtfstr(1,entryno,"%-*.*s",bar_color,80,
           w->wd-2,w->wd-2,entry[entryno-1]);
}
```

Listing 4.5 Moving Windows Program (POPEX4.C)

```
/*
   Moving text window example   (popex4.c)
   Must link with: popup.obj, mouse.obj
*/
#include <conio.h>
#include <bios.h>
#include "popup.h"
#include "mouse.h"
#define MAX(a,b)   ((a) > (b) ? (a) : (b))
#define MIN(a,b)   ((a) < (b) ? (a) : (b))
char msg[] = "Ready to move";
int mouse_on_border(windesc **w, int *i, int *xofs, int *yofs);
void move_curr_win(int x, int y);
void main() {
 windesc *w[3];
 int x, y, xofs, yofs, i;
 unsigned int k;
 init_win();
 init_mouse(MOUSE_OPTIONAL, MOUSE_TEXT_MODE, MOUSE_TEXT_MODE);
 w[0] = draw_win(5,6,20,5,"\x11""Move Me #1\x10",popup,&monocolors);
 w[1] = draw_win(7,9,20,6,"\x11""Move Me #2\x10",popup,&monocolors);
 w[2] = draw_win(9,11,20,5,"\x11""Move Me #3\x10",popup,&monocolors);
 mprintf(msg); /* print ready message in current window */
```

```
do {
   while (!(k = mouse_trigger(1)));      /* get event trigger */
   if (k == LEFT_MOUSE_PRESS) {
      if (mouse_on_border(w, &i, &xofs, &yofs)) {
    clrscr();                          /* clear old window */
    slct_win(w[i]);                    /* select new one    */
    mprintf(msg);
    while(button_state()) {  /* move till button release    */
       mouse_txt_posn(&x,&y);
       move_curr_win(x-xofs,y-yofs);
         }
     }
   }
   else {                     /* possible keyboard press           */
     xofs = 0; yofs = 0;      /* reset mouse/window corner offsets */
     x = curr_win->xul;       /* default to current position       */
     y = curr_win->yul;
     switch(k) {
       case UPKEY:
         y--;
         move_curr_win(x,y); /* move_curr_win will do bounds checking */
       break;
       case DOWNKEY:
         y++;
         move_curr_win(x,y);
       break;
       case LEFTKEY:
         x--;
         move_curr_win(x,y);
       break;
       case RIGHTKEY:
         x++;
         move_curr_win(x,y);
       break;
   case 0x0231:        /* the "1" key */
     clrscr();         /* clear old window */
     slct_win(w[0]);   /* select new one */
     mprintf(msg);
       break;
   case 0x0332:        /* the "2" key */
     clrscr();
         slct_win(w[1]);
     mprintf(msg);
       break;
   case 0x0433:        /* the "3" key */
     clrscr();
         slct_win(w[2]);
     mprintf(msg);
       break;
       default:                  /*send character to current window */
```

```
        if (k != RIGHT_MOUSE_PRESS) mprintf("%c",lo(k));
     }
   }
 } while (k != ESCKEY && k != RIGHT_MOUSE_PRESS);
 rmv_win(w[2]);
 rmv_win(w[1]);
 rmv_win(w[0]);
 mouse_reset();
}
int mouse_on_border(windesc **w, int *i, int *xofs, int *yofs)
{
  int x, y, j;
  mouse_txt_posn(&x,&y);
  for (j = 0; j<3; j++) {
      if ((x >= (w[j])->xul && x <= (w[j])->xlr &&
           y >= (w[j])->yul && y <= (w[j])->ylr) &&
          (x == (w[j])->xul || x == (w[j])->xlr ||
           y == (w[j])->yul || y == (w[j])->ylr)) {
         *xofs = x - (w[j])->xul;  *yofs = y - (w[j])->yul;
         *i = j;
         return 1;
      }
  }
  return 0;
}
void move_curr_win(int x, int y)
/*
   Moves the current window. If coordinates haven't changed,
   then nothing happens.  Does bounds checking on the new position.
*/
{
  int xsave, ysave;
  if (x != curr_win->xul || y != curr_win->yul) {
     xsave = wherex();
     ysave = wherey();
     swap_image(curr_win);  /* hide window */
     curr_win->xul = x;
     curr_win->yul = y;
     curr_win->xul = MAX(curr_win->xul,1);
     curr_win->xul = MIN(curr_win->xul,81 - curr_win->wd);
     curr_win->yul = MAX(curr_win->yul,1);
     curr_win->yul = MIN(curr_win->yul,26 - curr_win->ht);
     curr_win->xlr = curr_win->xul + curr_win->wd - 1;
     curr_win->ylr = curr_win->yul + curr_win->ht - 1;
     swap_image(curr_win); /* show window */
     /* change window coordinates */
     window(curr_win->xul+1,curr_win->yul+1,curr_win->xlr-1,curr_win->ylr-1);
     gotoxy(xsave, ysave);
  }
}
```

Listing 4.6 A Pop-up Error Message Package (SAYERR.C)

```
/****************************************************************
 *  Popup error reporting package  (sayerr.c)
 ****************************************************************/
#include <stdio.h>
#include <stdarg.h>
#include <conio.h>
#include <bios.h>
#include <string.h>
#include <dos.h>
#include <process.h>
#include <errno.h>
#include "popup.h"
#include "mouse.h"
static char *level_msg[] = {"WARNING","ERROR"};
static char *pmsg = "Press <Enter> or <ESC> ...";
/*
   The way the error/trace windows work:  If errw/msgw is NULL, then
   a error/trace message is popped up at errx/msgx, erry/msgy.
   Else, the window errw/msgw (which should have been already
   popped up) will be used.  If errw/msgw is already defined, then
   the errx/msgx and erry/msgy coordinates are ignored.
*/
int errx = CTRWIN;                  /* Default to center of the screen */
int erry = CTRWIN;
windesc *errw = NULL;               /* Default to popup window */
int msgx = CTRWIN;                  /* same for messages */
int msgy = CTRWIN;
windesc *msgw = NULL;
void numnewlines(char *s, int *n, int *w)
/* Count number of newlines in the string s, also, return
   maximum width of the lines of the message
*/
{
   int j,k;
   for (*n=0,j = 0,*w=0,k=0; (s[j] != 0); j++,k++) {
     if (s[j] == '\n') {
        (*n)++;
         if (k > *w) *w = k;  k = 0;
      }
     if (k > *w) *w = k;
   }
}
void popmsg(int x, int y, char *msg, char *title,
            char soundout, wincolors *wc)
/*
   Pops up the message msg at (x,y)-(absolute coordinates),
```

```
   with title as the window header.   if soundout != 0, then the
   alarm will sound.   It will then wait for a key press before
   unpopping then window.
   The message can contain newlines, which are accounted for in
   the size of the window. Note: it SHOULD usually contain a new
   line at the end, or your message might scroll off the screen.
   The (x,y) cursor pos'ns use the same codes as for popup windows.
*/
{
   int wd,ht,c,k;
   windesc *w;
   /* Compute height and width of window */
   numnewlines(msg,&ht,&wd);
   /* add in border, and prompt message to size computations */
   ht += 3;
   if (wd < (strlen(pmsg)+1)) wd = strlen(pmsg)+3; else wd += 3;
   w = draw_win(x, y, wd, ht, title, popup, wc);
   mouse_off(1);
   cprintf(msg);
   cprintf(pmsg);
   mouse_on(1);
   if (soundout) beep();
   do {
      while(!(k = mouse_trigger(0)));
      if (k == CTRLC) exit(0);                /* control c aborts */
      if (k != CRKEY && k != ESCKEY) beep(); /* only cr or esc allowed */
   } while(k != CRKEY && k != ESCKEY);
   rmv_win(w);
}
void reperr(int level, char *msg)
/* Reports the error in the error window.
   Level = 0 means warning, level = 1 means error.
 */
{
    windesc *wsave;
    if (errw == NULL) { /* popup up error window */
       popmsg(errx, erry, msg, level_msg[level], 1, &errcolors);
    }
    else {  /* else route to existing error window */
      wsave = curr_win;
      slct_win(errw);
      mprintf("%s: %s", level_msg[level], msg);
      slct_win(wsave);
    }
}
void repmsg(char *msg)
/* Reports the message in the message window. */
{
    windesc *wsave;
```

```
    if (msgw == NULL) {  /* popup message window */
       popmsg(msgx, msgy, msg," Msg ", 0, &msgcolors);
    }
    else {  /* else route to existing message window */
      wsave = curr_win;
      slct_win(msgw);
      mprintf("Msg: %s", msg);
      slct_win(wsave);
    }
}
void sayerr(int ferr, int errflag, int lno,
            char *pname, char *fmt,...)
/*
     The parameters work as follows:
     ferr       if 1, then the last DOS error message is printed
     errflag    if 1, treat as warning, 2 treat as error, else
                just treat as a message
     lno,pname if pname = "", they're ignored, else
                they're treated as a line number and source file name.
     fmt,...    a format string followed by optional arguments
                NOTE: formatting should not exceed 255 characters
*/
{
   va_list arg_ptr;
   char t[255];
   int j;
   if (*pname) {
      j = sprintf(t, "On line %d in pgm %s\r\n", lno, pname);
   }
   else j = 0;
   if (ferr == 1) {
      j += sprintf(t+j, "%s\r", strerror(errno));  /* add last dos error */
   }
   va_start(arg_ptr,fmt);          /* point to optional arguments  */
   vsprintf(t+j, fmt, arg_ptr);  /* add rest of formatted string */
   va_end(arg_ptr);
   switch(errflag) {
     case 1:
        reperr(0,t);       /* just a warning */
     break;
     case 2:
        reperr(1,t);       /* an error */
     break;
     default:
        repmsg(t);         /* or a plain old message */
   }
}
unsigned int getkey(void)
/*
```

```
   Waits for and returns the scan-ascii code of the next key available.
   Does not echo. Pops up an abort window on ctrl-c.
*/
{
   windesc *w;
   int k;
   while(1) {  /* loop until non-ctrl-c key, or abort */
     k = bioskey(0);
     if (k == CTRLC) {
        w = draw_win(CTRWIN, CTRWIN, 25, 3, "", popup, &errcolors);
        mprintf("Abort program (Y/N) ?");
        k = bioskey(0);
        rmv_win(w);
        if ((k == 0x1559) || (k == 0x1579)) {  /* "Y" or "y" */
           mouse_reset();  /* don't forget to reset the mouse !! */
           exit(1);
        }
     } else break;
   }
   return k;
}
void beep(void)
/* sounds the bell */
{
   sound(50);
   delay(25);
   nosound();
}
```

Listing 4.7 Using the Pop-up Error Message Package (POPEX5.C)

```
/*
   Popup error message reporting example  (popex5.c)
   Must link with: popup.obj, mouse.obj, sayerr.obj
 */
#include <conio.h>
#include <fcntl.h>
#include <io.h>
#include "popup.h"
#include "mouse.h"
char myfile[] = "ghost.dat";
void main() {
   int fh;
   windesc *mainw;
   init_win();  /* always, always, always do this */
   mainw = draw_win(1,1,80,17," Main Window ",tile, &defcolors);
   /* error messages default to popup windows */
   mprintf("Will try to open file when you press return ...");
   getch();
```

```
   if ((fh = open(myfile,O_RDONLY)) == -1)
      sayerr(FERRF,"--- %s ---\r\n", myfile);
   /* but you can reroute them */
   mprintf("\r\nPress return to construct static error window ...");
   getch();
   errw = draw_win(1,17,80,9," Error window ", tile, &errcolors);
   slct_win(mainw);
   mprintf("\r\nReady to try opening again, press return ...");
   getch();
   if ((fh = open(myfile,O_RDONLY)) == -1)
      sayerr(FERRF,"--- %s ---\r\n", myfile);
   mprintf("\r\nPress return to see error message without"
        " line no and source file ...");
   getch();
   /* example of printing without line no and source file */
   if ((fh = open(myfile,O_RDONLY)) == -1)
      sayerr(FERR,"--- %s ---\r\n", myfile);
   mprintf("\r\nPress return to see it as a warning ...");
   getch();
   /* example of printing just as a warning */
   if ((fh = open(myfile,O_RDONLY)) == -1)
       sayerr(FWRN,"--- %s ---\r\n", myfile);
   mprintf("\r\nPress return for a wise saying ...\r\n");
   getch();
   /* example of printing a formatted message */
   sayerr(SMSG,"The cows jumped over the %s\r\nand landed on %s\r\n",
      "moon", "mars");
   rmv_win(errw);
   rmv_win(mainw);
   clrscr();
}
```

CHAPTER

5

File I/O

Probably the most confusing part of Turbo C is file I/O. As with most C compilers, Turbo C provides two different methods of file access and has many file access functions. The Turbo C manuals do not help the confusion because they say very little about the fact that there are two different methods, even though these methods should not, in general, be mixed. In fact, the manuals say very little about file I/O at all. Due to the large number of file I/O functions, you can get lost trying to figure out which ones to use. This chapter should clear up some of this confusion.

The two categories of file access are standard I/O and system level I/O. The standard I/O routines represent the normal method of file access in C, being more complete and somewhat easier to use. They are sometimes referred to as *stream I / O routines*, since the most common use of them is for access to files as streams of characters. The standard I/O routines provide buffered access to files and are at a higher level than what the operating system provides, making them fairly independent of it. The system-level I/O routines, on the other hand, are at a lower level, and some make direct calls to the operating system. Since they are more direct, they tend to run faster and take less memory. However, they are not quite as easy to use, since fewer functions are provided for them, most notably, automatic buffering and formatting. Table 5.1 shows the functions available for standard (i.e., stream) I/O, and the corresponding system-level functions.

Table 5.1 Standard versus System-Level Functions

Standard I/O	System-Level I/O	Standard I/O	System-Level I/O
—	chsize	fcloseall	—
clearerr	—	fdopen	—
—	dup	feof	eof
—	dup2	ferror	—
fclose	close	fflush	—
—	_close	fgetc	—

Table 5.1 Standard versus System-Level Functions *(continued)*

Standard I/O	System-Level I/O	Standard I/O	System-Level I/O
fgetchar	—	freopen	—
fgetpos	—	fscanf	—
fgets	—	fseek	lseek
fileno	—	fsetpos	—
flushall	—	fstat	fstat
fopen	open	ftell	—
—	_open	fwrite	write
—	_creat		_write
—	creat	rewind	—
—	creatnew	setbuf	—
—	creattemp	setvbuf	—
fprintf	—	stat	stat
fputc	—	ungetc	—
fputs	—	vfprintf	—
fread	read	vfscanf	—
	_read		

The standard I/O routines are sometimes mistakenly thought of as providing only stream-level I/O, that is, reading and writing files as a sequence or stream of characters. Although that is the most common use of them, they do provide much more than that. For instance, you can do formatted input and output, perform random access I/O on files, and perform block or record I/O. Standard I/O is commonly associated with text file access, whereas system level I/O is usually associated with binary file access. It should be pointed out, however, that there is no reason you can not do binary file access with the standard I/O routines.

One importance difference between the two methods is that standard I/O provides built-in buffering of files, making it more efficient because of fewer disk accesses. The system-level routines have no such buffering. However, since the system-level routines make direct calls to the operating system, they can be faster because there is less overhead. Which method to use depends on the preference of the programmer, and the type of application involved. We will concentrate mainly on standard I/O, since it provides more features and is the commonly used method.

TEXT VERSUS BINARY FILES

To further add to the confusion, there are two different modes of file access that come into play in both standard and system-level I/O. These are the text and binary modes. In the text mode, a carriage return-line feed pair is translated into a single newline character upon reading, and newlines are translated back into carriage return-line feed pairs upon writing. Binary mode access does no such translation.

The reason for the text mode access is historical. The C language was developed on Unix® systems, where the end-of-line character for text files is simply a single newline character.

However, DOS text files use a carriage return-line feed combination. In order to make it easy to port programs from the Unix world over to DOS, the text mode of access was invented.

There is a global variable, **_fmode**, which can be set to specify the translation mode for all file accesses. The **_fmode** variable can take on the following values:

```
O_BINARY     -  No CRLF translation
O_TEXT       -  CRLF pairs translated into a newline character
```

The default value of _fmode is O_TEXT. It is possible to override the translation mode at the time a file is opened, as you shall soon see.

FILE POINTERS VERSUS FILE HANDLES

The way you refer to a file once it is opened depends on whether it was opened for standard I/O or system level I/O. For a standard I/O file, Turbo C maintains some information about the file in a structure that is defined in the header file **stdio.h**:

```
typedef struct  {
   short            level;         /* Fill/Empty level of buffer */
   unsigned         flags;         /* File status flags          */
   char             fd;            /* File descriptor (handle)   */
   unsigned char    hold;          /* Ungetc char holder         */
   short            bsize;         /* Buffer size                */
   unsigned char    *buffer;       /* File buffer pointer        */
   unsigned char    *curp;         /* Current active pointer     */
   unsigned         istemp;        /* Temp file flag             */
   short            token;         /* Validity marker            */
} FILE;
```

Whenever you open a file for standard I/O access, a FILE structure is created and a pointer to this structure (known as the stream pointer) is returned. For all other file operations, this pointer is used to refer to the opened file. You should never access any of the fields in the FILE structure directly, as they are meant for internal use only. They are shown here merely to give you an idea of what is maintained by Turbo C. Other compilers may use a completely different structure, although they too define the type FILE.

The **fd** field of the FILE structure is known as the *file handle*. The file handle is a unique number for each open file which is returned by DOS when a file is opened. For system-level files, this number is used to refer to the file for all other operations, rather than a stream pointer. Files opened at the system level have no associated FILE structure.

The following code fragments contrast the two methods for opening and referring to a file. In both, the file is opened for reading only access:

```
/* standard I/O method */
#include <stdio.h>
FILE *f;
     main() {
```

```
  f = fopen("myfile.dat","r");  /* open for read only */
  fclose(f);                    /* then close it */
}
/* System level I/O method */
#include "fcntl.h"
#include "io.h"
int fhandle;
main() {
  fhandle = open("myfile.dat", O_RDONLY); /* open for read only */
  close(f);                               /* then close it */
}
```

In general, it is not wise to mix these two forms of file access. This is because standard I/O operations are buffered, and should you do a read/write or seek using a system-level call, the buffers may no longer correspond with the data that is supposed to be in the file. However, some functions work only with file handles, so Turbo C provides the macro **fileno()** to retrieve the file handle for a stream file. As you might have guessed, this macro simply returns the **fd** field of the FILE structure and is defined in **stdio.h** as:

```
#define fileno(f)        ((f)->fd)
```

It is best to use this macro, rather than accessing **fd** directly, since there is no guarantee the FILE structure will not change in the future. Also, as we have noted earlier, other compiler vendors may use an entirely different FILE structure.

There is a way to attach a FILE structure to a file already opened at the system level, via the **fdopen()** function. This allows you to do buffering and formatting on such a file, and mix the two forms of access. You must be very careful if you decide to use this feature.

DOS FILE INFORMATION

DOS itself keeps an internal table for each open file, usually enough for 20 files. The actual number is set by the FILES parameter of your config.sys file. Some of the information available about a open file can be obtained by examining the stat structure included in the header file <sys\stat.h>:

```
struct stat {
short st_dev;                 /* drive or device number        */
short st_ino;                 /* not used in DOS, for UNIX     */
   short st_mode;          /* read/write mode and access bits */
   short st_nlink;         /* set to 1                        */
   int   st_uid;           /* Unix user ID, not used in DOS   */
int   st_gid;          /* Unix group ID, not used in DOS  */
short st_rdev;         /* same as st_dev                  */
long  st_size;         /* size of the open file           */
long  st_atime;        /* time of most recent update      */
```

```
long  st_mtime;        /* for DOS, same as st_atime       */
long  st_ctime;        /* for DOS, same as st_atime       */
};
```

For files opened for standard I/O, this information is available in addition to that provided in the FILE structure.

Most of the fields in this structure are provided for Unix compatability, and not all are actually used by DOS. This structure can be obtained by the TURBO C functions **stat()** and **fstat()**. The first takes a filename of an open file and returns its information, the latter takes a file handle. If your file is a stream file, here is a case for using the **fileno()** macro, so that you can call **fstat()** with the proper file handle.

It would appear at this point that everything you need to know about an open file is available, either from the FILE structure or the stat structure; unfortunately, that is not the case. Once you have opened a file, there is no place where the NAME of file is kept. DOS knows only the file handle. This makes it difficult for doing user-friendly error reporting. Suppose you write a generic routine to read bytes from a file, and you wish it to print out an error message if an error occurs. You must somehow keep track of the name, so that you can print out a message like, "Error reading file myfile.dat", instead of "Error reading file #2". The former is bound have more meaning to the user. A sample file I/O package developed later in this chapter is devoted to handling such problems.

PREDEFINED STREAMS AND HANDLES

There are five predefined streams which are automatically assigned when your program executes:

Stream	Handle
stdin	0
stdout	1
stderr	2
stdaux	3
stdprn	4

These streams are defined in **stdio.h**, and refer to the standard input, standard output, standard error, standard auxiliary, and standard print streams. These symbolic names are stream pointers, so you can use them anywhere a standard I/O file reference can be used. The streams also have the predefined handles shown. You can access the streams at the system level using these handles.

By default, **stdin**, **stdout**, and **stderr** refer to the user's console. The assignment of the **stdaux** and **stdprn** streams depends on your particular machine. They are usually associated with an auxiliary port and a printer.

You can redefine any of these streams so that they refer to a disk file or a different device by using the **freopen()** function. This function closes the file currently associated with a stream, and reassigns it to a new file. If the stream were attached to a device, then the close operation does nothing. You can also use the two functions **dup()** and **dup2()** to do essentially the same thing.

Now that we have covered the basics about files in Turbo C, we will first examine how to do standard I/O and then system-level I/O. The end of this chapter provides a package of routines that uses the standard I/O functions.

STANDARD I/O

The routines for doing standard I/O can be classified into six groups:

- Opening/closing/flushing buffers
- Returning file status
- Moving the current read/write position
- Doing byte-level reading/writing
- Doing string-level reading/writing
- Doing record, or block-level, reading/writing.

Tables 5.2 through 5.7 show the functions associated with each category. Some of these routines have already been mentioned, but in this section we will take a closer look at them.

Opening and Closing Standard I/O Files

Table 5.2 shows the most common routines that are available for opening and closing files for standard I/O: **fclose()**, **fcloseall()**, **fdopen()**, **fopen()**, and **freopen()**.

Table 5.2 Opening, Closing, and Flushing Stream File Buffers

Function	Use
`int fclose(File *stream)`	Closes a stream
`int fcloseall(void)`	Closes all stream files
`FILE *fdopen(int handle, char *type)`	Attaches a stream file to a system-level file
`int fflush(FILE *stream)`	Flushes a stream file buffer
`int flushall(void)`	Flushes all stream file buffers
`FILE *fopen(char *filename, char *type)`	Opens a file for stream access
`FILE *freopen(char *filename, char *type, FILE *stream)`	Reopens a stream to a different device or file
`void setbuf(FILE *stream, char *buf)`	Turns buffering on/off
`int setvbuf(FILE *stream, char *buf, int type, unsigned size)`	Turns on buffering with arbitrary-sized buffer

Although there are three different functions with which you can open a standard I/O file, the **fopen()** is the one most commonly used. You first pass to it the name of the file to open and then a character string specifying the type of file access. These types are as follows:

Types of File Access

Type	Description
"r"	The file is opened for read-only access. It is an error if the file does not exist.
"w"	The file is opened for write-only access. If the file exists, its contents are destroyed; otherwise, the file is created.
"a"	The file is opened for writing at the end of the file (i.e., appending). If the file does not exist, it is created.
"r+"	The file is opened for reading and writing. It is an error if the file does not exist.
"w+"	The file is opened for reading and writing. If the file exists, its contents are destroyed; otherwise, the file is created.
"a+"	The file can be read at any position, but writing always occurs at the end of the file (i.e., only appending is allowed). If the file does not exist, it is created.

Basically, if you wish to create a file, you can use any type that begins with a "w" or an "a". For "w" type accesses, if the file exists, then the contents of it are overwritten. The "a" type accesses allow you to append to an existing file without overwriting previous contents. If you wish to access an existing file but also want to return an error if it is not there, then use the "r" type accesses.

Files opened with the access types "r+", "w+", or "a+" are said to be opened for updating, with both reading and writing allowed. However, you must be careful when mixing reads and writes. Every time you switch from one to the other, you must first do an intervening **fseek()** or **rewind()**. This is so the file pointer (i.e., the current position in the file) is updated properly. The file I/O package developed at the end of the chapter will conveniently do this for us.

Files opened for appending behave in the following manner: although you can use **fseek()** or **rewind()** to move the file pointer anywhere in the file, every time a write is performed, it is done at the end of the file. This means that existing data cannot be overwritten with append mode.

The following shows an example of opening an existing file for updating. If the file is successfully opened, then **fopen()** returns a FILE pointer. If an error occurs, then a NULL is returned. This example also shows how to close the file:

```
/* Standard I/O file example  (filex1.c) */
#include <stdio.h>
main() {
  FILE *f;   /* this is how we refer to the file */
  if ((f = fopen("c:\\mydir\\myfile.dat","r+")) == NULL) {
     printf("Error opening file, probably no such path\n");
  }
  else {
    printf("File successfully opened for updating.\n");
```

```
      fclose(f);
      printf("And is now closed.\n");
   }
}
```

Note the "\\" string in the pathname. It is a common mistake when specifying pathnames on DOS systems to try to say something like "mydir\myfile." The backslash (which goes the other way on Unix systems) is actually an escape character, so you must include it twice. Many hours of frustation have probably been caused by this, as you can spend a lot of time trying to figure out why your program will not open a file that you are sure is there.

When specifying the access type, you can also indicate whether the file is to be opened for text mode or binary mode. This is accomplished by attaching a "t" to the end of the access type for text mode, and a "b" for binary mode. The following example is changed so that the file is opened for binary update mode.

```
/* Binary file access example  (filex2.c)    */
#include <stdio.h>
main() {
   FILE *f;    /* this is how we refer to the file */
   /* Note the "b" in "r+b" */
   if ((f = fopen("c:\\mydir\\myfile.dat","r+b")) == NULL) {
printf("Error opening file, probably no such path\n");
   }
   else {
      printf("File opened for updating in binary mode.\n");
      fclose(f);
      printf("And is now closed.\n");
   }
}
```

As mentioned before, the default mode is specified in the **_fmode** variable, which itself defaults to text mode. It is much better just to explicitly state the mode, as is done here. That way, there can be no confusion about which mode is being used. However, if you are porting programs over from Unix (or plan to do so), it might be more convenient to set the **_fmode** variable, otherwise you would have to modify every **fopen()** call when porting the program.

The other two open routines, **fdopen()** and **freopen()**, take similar arguments, as shown in the Turbo C manual.

Obtaining File Status

Table 5.3 shows the functions that are available for obtaining status about an open file. The **stat()** and **fstat()** functions have already been described. The **feof()** function returns a nonzero value if an end-of-file indicator was detected during the last I/O operation. The **ferror()** function returns a non-zero if any error occurred on the stream during reading and writing. Both of these

Table 5.3 File Status for Stream Files

Function	Use
`void clearerr(FILE *stream)`	Clears errors associated with a stream
`int feof(FILE *stream)`	Returns end-of-file status
`int ferror(FILE *stream)`	Returns last read/write error on stream
`int fstat(char *handle, struct stat *buff)`	Returns file status for a given file handle
`int stat(char *pathname, struct stat *buff)`	Returns file status for a given file-name

states remain set until a call to **clearerr()**, **fseek()**, **rewind()**, or **fsetpos()** is made. All of these functions clear the end-of-file indicator, but only **rewind()** and **clearerr()** clear the other error status indicator.

When a file error occurs, DOS maintains the error status as well. The Turbo C functions **strerror()** and **perror()** allow you to print out the most recent DOS error message. Two global variables, **errno** and **_doserrno**, keep track of the most recent error. The errno variable is a Unix-compatible error indicator and is the one used by **perror()** and **strerror()**. The **_doserrno** variable is set to the actual DOS error code. Although these two indicators sometimes have equivalent codes, in general they do not. The code mappings are given in the *Turbo C Reference Guide.*

The **errno** and **_doserrno** indicators reflect the error value of the last call that set them. Many of the Turbo C I/O functions set these flags, but you should check the documentation on the specific functions to make sure. Be sure to use these indicators before the next function that might set them is called, so that the appropriate error condition is obtained.

Controlling File Buffering

Turbo C provides four routines that allow you to control the buffering of standard I/O files: **fflush()**, **flushall()**, **setbuf()** and **setvbuf()**. When a standard I/O file is opened, a buffer is automatically allocated for it by the system. This buffer is used for both reading and writing. A file read operation actually causes a whole block of file bytes to be read, rather than just the number specified. During a file write, bytes are actually written to the file buffer first. When the buffer is full, it is flushed to the disk. If the buffer is sized properly, file access can be performed very efficiently. Turbo C provides ways to control the buffering, so you can optimize file access to your particular application.

There can be problems caused by buffering. If you should happen to abort the program before a file buffer is flushed, data may be lost. Also, there is a problem when switching from reading to writing, as the buffer contents may get confused. This is why Turbo C requires you to reposition the file pointer via **fseek()** or **rewind()** before switching I/O directions. These operations effectively flush the buffer before moving to the new file position. It should be noted that Turbo C will automatically flush the buffer when the file is closed. Also, if you exit the program via the **exit()** function or by normal termination, all buffers will be flushed and all files closed. However, it is always best to close the file explicitly when you are finished. This is to free the limited space in the internal file tables so that other files can be opened.

You can also cause the buffer to be flushed at any time via the routine **fflush()**.There is also a routine to flush all open streams, **flushall()**. These routines can be used to maintain file integrity. It is a good idea to flush the buffer after writing critical data to a file in case the program should be improperly aborted; otherwise, data may be lost. We will see examples of this in the chapter on variable length record file I/O.

Turbo C allows you to turn off buffering completely or to change the size of the buffer via two routines: **setbuf()** and **setvbuf()**. The **setbuf()** routine is used if you wish to use your own buffer, or wish to turn off buffering. If you use this routine to specify your own buffer, it must be of a fixed size, as specified by the BUFSIZ macro in **stdio.h**, which is set to 512 bytes. You should use **setbuf()** only immediately after opening a file, or after flushing the file buffer; otherwise, the buffer contents may get confused. The following program fragment shows some examples of using **setbuf()**:

```
#include <stdio.h>
char mybuff[BUFSIZ];  /* must have BUFSIZ bytes in the buffer */
main() {
  FILE *f, *g, *h;
  f = fopen("file1.dat","r+");
  g = fopen("file2.dat","r+");
  h = fopen("file3.dat","r+");
  setbuf(g,NULL);    /* this is how you turn buffering off */
  setbuf(h,mybuff); /* this is how you specify your own buffering */
  /* ... */
}
```

After the **setbuf()** calls, file **f** uses the buffer allocated for it by the system, file **g** uses no buffering, and file **h** employs a user-defined buffer.

Turbo C also allows you to control the size of the buffer as well. To do this, use the function **setvbuf()**. Its arguments are a pointer to the buffer to be used, the type of buffering, and the size of the buffer. The type parameter must be one of the following:

```
_IONBF        Use this to turn off buffering, regardless of the other parameters,
                which are ignored in this case.
_IOLBF        The file is "line buffered". Anytime a newline is written, the buffer
                is automatically flushed. Read operations are still fully buffered.
_IOFBF        Use this for full buffering (the normal mode).
```

Some examples of using **setvbuf()** include the following:

```
#include <stdio.h>
char mybuff[8192];  /* We'll set buffer to 8k */
main() {
  FILE *f, *g, *h;
  f = fopen("file1.dat","r+");
  g = fopen("file2.dat","r+");
  h = fopen("file3.dat","r+");
```

```
 setvbuf(f,NULL,_IONBF,0);
  setvbuf(g,mybuff,_IOFBF,sizeof(mybuff));
    setvbuf(h,NULL,_IOFBF,1024);
    /* ... */
  }
```

After the **setvbuf()** calls, file **f** will have no buffering. Note that the other parameters to the call are ignored. File **g** will use the 8K buffer mybuff. File **h** will use a 1K buffer, which is allocated using an indirect call to **malloc()**. Be careful using this feature, as there is no provision to free the memory allocated this way other than by calling **fclose()**. The indirect call to **malloc** sets a flag bit so that **fclose** will properly free the buffer.

Another thing to watch out for is using a buffer that is a local variable to a function (i.e., one that is on the run-time stack). If that function is exited before the file is closed, further file operations will still continue to use this stack location, even though it is no longer allocated for that buffer. The result will most likely be a system crash. For this reason, it is best to always declare file buffers outside function definitions or to declare them as static variables.

There are some cases when stream files do not have automatic buffering. For instance, the stdin and stdout streams are not normally buffered, because they are usually connected to the console device (i.e., the screen and keyboard), where buffering makes no sense. If these streams are redirected to "real" files, then buffering is provided automatically.

In summary, the buffer control routines are good examples of the versatility provided in C. For most C operations, you have fine control on how C performs those operations. This ability to customize and optimize the basic functions is one reason why C is regarded as an "efficient" language. It is also one reason it can be difficult to learn, as there are many options to consider.

RANDOM ACCESS TO FILES

Table 5.4 shows the routines that can be used for moving the file pointer to any location within the file. The ones most commonly used are **fseek()** and **rewind()**. The **rewind()** function moves the file pointer to the beginning of the file, and the **fseek()** function moves it to the specified offset. The origin of offset is passed as a parameter and should have one of the following values:

```
SEEK_SET      offset from beginning of file
SEEK_CUR      offset from current position
SEEK_END      offset backwards from end of file
```

The one most commonly used is probably SEEK_SET, since that moves the file pointer in "absolute" terms, represented by the number of bytes offset from the beginning of the file. The following program opens a file for updating, clears it if it already exists, and then moves to byte 100 and writes out some text:

```
/*  File seek example  (filex3.c)  */
#include <stdio.h>
void main() {
  FILE *f;
```

```
    /* Open file for text mode, overwrite it if it already exists */
    if ((f = fopen("myfile.dat","w+t")) != NULL) {
       fseek(f,100,SEEK_SET);         /* Go to byte 100 */
       fprintf(f,"Hello world\n");    /* Write some bytes to it */
       fclose(f);
  printf("myfile.dat successfully written to\n"
        "There'll be garbage in first 100 bytes\n"
        "So only inspect file with hex dump pgm\n");
    }
    else {
       printf("Error opening file: myfile.dat\n");
    }
  }
```

This example shows that it is perfectly legal to seek beyond the end of the file and then write to it, effectively allowing you to expand the size of the file. Note, however, that the bytes in the expanded portion are uninitialized, so you may wish to write something sensible to them. Also, even though you can write past the end of the file, an error is returned should you try to read beyond the end of the file.

The function **ftell()** allows you to obtain the current position of the file pointer relative to the beginning of the file. This position is returned as a long type rather than an integer, so that files greater than 64K can be used.

There are subtle problems with using **ftell()**, such as when a file is opened for appending. In this case, **ftell()** returns the current file position determined by the last I/O operation, which may not necessarily be where the next write will occur. This is because you can seek to any position in append mode, but writes always occur at the end of the file. So be careful.

Another problem is using **ftell()** (and **fseek()** as well) in text mode. Because of carriage return-line feed translations, the value returned by **ftell()** may not represent the true byte offset from the beginning of the file. You can, however, use **ftell()** in conjunction with **fseek()** to remember and then return to a file location, and it will work correctly.

Table 5.4 Random Access Functions for Stream Files

Function	Use
`int fgetpos(FILE *stream,fpos_t *pos)`	Gets the curret file position for later restoration
`int fseek(FILE *stream, long offset, int origin)`	Moves to a new file position
`int fsetpos(FILE *stream, const fpos_t *pos)`	Sets the file position to that obtained by an earlier call to **fgetpos**
`long ftell(FILE *stream)`	Gets the current file position.
`int rewind(FILE *stream)`	Moves the file position back to the beginning

You can also save and return to file positions using the functions **fgetpos()** and **fsetpos()**. These functions are part of the new ANSI C standard. The **fgetpos()** function gets the current file position and stores it in an object of type **fpos_t**, defined in **stdio.h**. The function **fsetpos()** can then take this object and restore the file pointer sometime later in the program. The stored object is meant for internal use only and should not be tampered with otherwise. In Turbo C, type **fpos_t** is defined as being type long, which is what is used by **ftell()**. However, it is not guaranteed to be of this type across all systems. The **fgetpos()** and **fsetpos()** functions are provided as the new ANSI C standard way of saving and restoring the file position.

Both **fsetpos()** and **ftell()** undo any prior calls to **ungetc()** on that stream, so be careful. Also remember that the random access functions only make sense on real files. Streams attached to devices (such as the console) are not capable of random access.

Reading and Writing to Standard I/O Files

Turbo C provides three types of reading and writing to standard I/O files: you can write at the character-level, the string-level, and the block-level, as shown in Tables 5.5, 5.6, and 5.7.

Table 5.5 Functions for Single-Character Access

Function	Use
`int fgetc(FILE *stream)`	Gets the next character from a file
`int fgetchar(void)`	Gets the next character from stdin
`int fputc(int ch, FILE *stream)`	Puts a character in a file
`int ungetc(char *c, FILE *stream)`	Puts back a character that was read

Table 5.6 Functions for String-Level Access

Function	Use
`char *fgets(char *string, int n, FILE *stream)`	Reads the next line from a file into a string
`int fprintf(FILE *stream, char *fmt,...)`	Does a formatted print to a file
`int fputs(char *string, FILE *Stream)`	Does an unformatted print to a file
`int fscanf(FILE *stream, char *fmt, ...)`	Does a formatted read from a file
`int vfprintf(FILE *stream, char *fmt, va_list param)`	Same as printf, but provides hooks for the variable number of argument calling convention
`int vfscanf(FILE *stream, char *fmt, va_list argp)`	Sames as fscanf, but provides hooks for the variable number of argument calling convention

Character-Level and String-Level Access

With some minor exceptions, the character and string functions for file I/O work just like their console I/O counterparts. Therefore, they will not be discussed in much detail here. We will be concentrating mainly on block-level access.

One string-level function does need to be mentioned. The **fgets()** function works basically like its **gets()** counterpart, reading a character string from a file. However, unlike **gets()**, **fgets()** retains any newline character read. This can trip you up if your program was originally written for console I/O and you extend it to handle file I/O by changing **gets()** with **fgets()**. Watch out for this one.

Record-Level Access

The **fread()** and **fwrite()** functions, shown in Table 5.7, allow you to perform block- or record-level I/O on stream files. A *record*, as defined here, is nothing more than a block of unformatted bytes. There are two types of records, fixed-length and variable length. Only fixed-length records are discussed here. Variable-length records will be presented as an extension to the file system in a later chapter. It is worth pointing out that they, too, use **fread()** and **fwrite()**.

Table 5.7 Functions for Block-Level Access

Function	Use
`int fread(void *ptr, int size, int nitems, FILE *stream)`	Reads a series of bytes from a stream file
`int fwrite(void *ptr, int size, int  nitems,FILE *stream)`	Writes a series of bytes to a stream file

First, what do we mean by record I/O? It is simply the ability to read a file as though it were a collection of multiple-byte records, rather than as a series of characters. The records are stored in their internal representation and no textual formatting is performed. An example of record I/O is storing parts in an inventory file. Typically, the parts are defined as a structure, as shown in the following example. This program stores the part as the sixth record in the file by seeking the appropriate byte location. Note the proper typecasting on the offset variable. Although not strictly necessary here, it is included to remind you that the offset is of type long:

```
/*  Record I/O example   (filex4.c)   */
#include <stdio.h>
typedef struct my_parts_struct {
   int part_code;
   int quantity;
   float price;
} part;
```

```
main() {
  FILE *f;
  int nb;
  part mypart = {
     15,   /* part code */
     300,  /* quantity  */
     1.25  /* price     */
  };
  if ((f = fopen("myfile.dat","w+b")) != NULL) {
     fseek(f,(long)(sizeof(part)*6),SEEK_SET);
     nb  = fwrite(&mypart,sizeof(part),1,f);
     printf("The number of records written is %d\n",nb);
     fclose(f);
  }
  else {
    printf("Error opening file ...\n");
  }
}
```

The **fwrite()** function works by writing the record data pointed to by the first parameter to the file. The second parameter tells us the size of the record, and the third parameter tells how many such records to write out. Therefore, the buffer to be written should contain at least **size_of_rec * num_of_rec bytes**. Here, the size of the record is the size of the parts structure. Although you can calculate this size yourself by adding up the size of each field in the parts structure, the **sizeof()** function is a much better method. In fact, it is highly recommended that you do use it, as you will now see.

Structure Packing

On many C compilers, structures have padding in them, usually to align them to word boundaries. A typical packing scheme on the IBM PC is on integer boundaries. The default in Turbo C is for the tightest packing, (byte boundaries), but other compilers may be different. Rather than risk making mistakes (and preventing much confusion), you should let the compiler figure the size for you by using **sizeof()**.

If you wish to have integer alignment for fields in a structure, Turbo C provides the "-a" compiler option. With this option on, the following will take place:

1. The structure will always start on a even address in memory.
2. Any non-character fields in the structure will start on an even offset from the beginning of the structure.
3. The structure is padded to ensure it contains an even number of bytes.

Using this type of padding can lead to more efficient code, which is why it is included as an option.

The consequence of this structure alignment is that a program written by another compiler may not be able to read a binary file created by Turbo C without taking the structure padding into account. Even for Turbo C files, you must ensure that if you used the "-a" option for one program that accesses a file, then all programs accessing that file must use the same option. Unless you are trying to access data written with another compiler, it is a good idea to just use the Turbo C default. Your data will be packed as small as possible that way, and you will not have to remember to set the "-a" option (a difficult thing to do in a large project).

SYSTEM-LEVEL FILE I/O

In this section we will learn how to do system-level file I/O. This type of I/O is useful when storing binary data, and since it makes DOS calls directly, it can be more efficient than standard I/O. Since standard I/O is more commonly used, we will only briefly sketch the system-level routines.

The functions available are:

System-Level Functions

Function	Use
dup	Allows two file handles to point to same open file. The next available file handle is used
dup2	Similar to **dup()**, except new file handle can be user-specified
close	Closes the file
_close	DOS-level file close
eof	Returns end-of-file status
open	A Unix-like file open/create function
_open	A DOS specific form of **open()**
creat	A Unix-like file creation function
_creat	Similar to **creat()**, except DOS specific
creatnew	Creates a file. It is an error if the file exists
creattemp	Creates a file with a Turbo C-created unique filename
read	Reads file bytes using the specified text/binary translation mode
_read	Direct call to DOS system read. No translation performed
lseek	Moves the file pointer to a new position
fstat	Returns status of the file (also works for standard I/O files)
write	Writes bytes to the file using the specified text/binary translation mode
_write	Direct call to DOS system write. No translation is performed
stat	Returns status of the file (also works for standard I/O files)

The five basic functions are **open()**, **close()**, **read()**, **write()**, and **lseek()**, which are the ones on which we will focus. These routines are little more than interfaces to low-level DOS functions.

Opening Files for Random Access

The prototypes for the basic system-level functions are:

```
int  open(char *pathname, int access, [,int permiss]);
int  close(int handle);
int  read(int handle, void *buf, int nbyte);
int  write(int handle, void *buf, int nbyte);
long lseek(int handle, long offset, int origin);
```

When you open a file at the DOS level, DOS returns an integer code that represents a "handle" to the file, which is used from then on for referencing that file. If there is an error in opening, a -1 is returned. As an example:

```
/*   System level file I/O   (filex5.c)   */
#include <fcntl.h>      /* contains control flag definitions      */
#include <io.h>         /* function prototypes                    */
#include <sys\stat.h>   /* needed for permission flag definitions */
#include <stdio.h>      /* for printf function prototype          */
int fhandle;
char buffer[] = "some data";
main() {
   if ((fhandle=
    open("myfile.dat",O_CREAT|O_WRONLY|O_BINARY)) == -1)
   {
      printf("Error opening file\n");
   }
   else {
         write(fhandle, buffer, sizeof(buffer));
    close(fhandle)
      printf("Data successfully written to myfile.dat\n");
   }
}
```

Notice the flags O_CREAT, O_WRONLY and O_BINARY. These are just two of a possible set of flags which can be OR'd together to control how the file is opened. The most common ones are:

Flag	Use
O_RDONLY	Open file for read only
O_WRONLY	Open file for write only
O_RDWR	Open file for read/write
O_APPEND	Open file for appending
O_CREAT	Create the file
O_TRUNC	Erase contents of existing file, start over
O_BINARY	Raw data mode
O_TEXT	Translates CRLF pairs to the newline (0x0a) character

Given these flags, you have probably noticed that you can also use **open()** to create a file or to rewrite an existing one. If you use the O_CREAT flag, then the **open()** function can take an extra argument set from the following symbolic constants, which set the permissions for the new file:

```
S_IWRITE      Permission to write
S_IREAD       Permission to read
```

These can be OR'd together to provide read/write permission, the default. Note that the Turbo C manual fails to tell you that you must include the header file **<sys\stat.h>** if you wish to use these constants.

Turbo C also provides the functions **creat()**, **_creat()**, **creatnew()**, and **creattemp()** which can also be used to create a file. See the Turbo C manual for details.

Reading and Writing System-Level Files

The **lseek()** function moves the file position to the desired location. It has exactly the same parameters as **fseek()**, except the first parameter is a file handle instead of a FILE pointer. The same offset origins SEEK_SET, SEEK_CUR, and SEEK_END can be used.

Once you have moved to the desired position, you can use the functions **read()** and **write()** to move bytes in and out of the file. These two functions return the number of bytes actually read/written, which is convenient for error-checking purposes. For example, the following code opens a file, moves to byte location 5, and tries to read in 357 bytes into a buffer:

```
/*  System level seek example  (filex6.c)  */
#include <fcntl.h>
#include <io.h>
#include <stdio.h>
char buffer[400];
main() {
  int fh;
  int nb;
  if ((fh = open("myfile.dat",O_RDONLY)) != -1)
   lseek(fh,5L,SEEK_SET);      /* go to posn 5          */
   nb = read(fh,buffer,357);  /* try to read 357 bytes */
   printf("%d bytes read\n",nb);  /* probably couldn't */
   close(fh);
   }
   else
    printf("Error opening myfile.dat\n");
   }
}
```

Notice that if the file is opened for text mode, then the actual number of bytes read or written may not agree with the number returned by **read()** or **write()**. This is due to possible newline translations. Turbo C provides even lower-level functions in **_read()** and **_write()**, which are direct calls to DOS functions and perform no such translation, even for text files.

AN EXAMPLE FILE I/O PACKAGE

In this section we will build on the standard I/O routines, and create a package that simplifies some of the details of file access. This package also provides convenient error handling and reporting, and is a good example of using many of the standard I/O routines. It also gives examples of using the popup window and error-reporting routines developed in an earlier chapter. This package is given in Listings 5.1 and 5.2, and contains the following external functions:

Function	Use
`init_files()`	Initializes the internal file table
`get_file_data()`	Returns information from the internal table
`openfile()`	Opens/creates files
`closefile()`	Closes a file
`movepos()`	Moves the file position
`iobytes()`	Reads/writes to file
`inbytes()`	Macro that calls iobytes to do reads
`outbytes()`	Macro that calls outbytes to do writes
`rdstr()`	Reads in an unformatted string
`wrtstr()`	Writes out an unformated string
`rdfstr()`	Reads in a formatted string
`wrtfstr()`	Writes out a formatted string

This package basically does two things: it handles the reporting of errors that occur during file access, and it allows us to conveniently do record I/O. This is accomplished by maintaining an internal table which stores the stream file pointer, the filename, and the record size of each open file. The table is first initialized by a call to **init_files()**. Then, whenever **openfile()** is called, parameters for the newly opened file are added to the table. A call to **closefile()** closes the file and removes its information from the table. These functions have the following prototypes:

```
void init_files(void);
int  openfile(char *fname, char *access_type, int recsize);
int  closefile(int h);
```

It is important not to mix these routines with **fopen()** and **fclose()**, since the internal table will not be updated properly.

When initializing the file table, **init_files()** adds the following predefined streams:

File/Device	Index	Name	Record Size
stdin	0	"stdin"	1 byte
stdout	1	"stdout"	1 byte
stderr	2	"stderr"	1 byte
stdaux	3	"stdaux"	1 byte
stdprn	4	"stdprn"	1 byte

Since these streams are normally associated with devices, they are given a record size of 1 byte, which means "character/string level access."

When a file is opened with **openfile()**, the record size for the file is specified. This value is then used by all the other file access routines to allow record-level access to the file. The record size is also used as a multiplier when determining the number of bytes to actually read or write.

Even though the files opened and created by this package are standard I/O files, they are referenced by an integer number rather than by a stream pointer. This number is the index of the file in the file table and is very similar to, but should not be confused with, the DOS file handle.

With all of the functions contained in this package, the file operation performed is checked for errors. The **sayerr()** function described in Chapter 4 is called to report the error. Using **sayerr()** means you have the flexibility of routing error messages to a special error window, or allowing the error message to be popped up. Included in the error message is the name of the file, such as:

```
"File not found: myfile.dat".
```

The **movepos()** function is used to do file seeks and works much like **fseek()**, except the position is interpreted as a record offset and all errors are reported. Its function prototype is:

```
long movepos(int h, long recno, int origin);
```

As with **fseek()**, you can specify the offset origin as either SEEK_SET, SEEK_CUR, or SEEK_END.

Reading or writing to a file is accomplished with the **iobytes()** function and its associated macros **inbytes()** and **outbytes()**. They are defined as follows:

```
#define inbytes( h, r, d, n)  iobytes(h, r, d, n, 0)
#define outbytes(h, r, d, n)  iobytes(h, r, d, n, 1)
int iobytes(int handle, long recno, unsigned char *data, int numrecs, int iodir);
```

The **iobytes()** function combines seeking, reading, and writing into one function. Along with the file handle, you give it which record to read/write, the buffer to use for reading/writing, the number of records to read/write, and the direction of the I/O (i.e., reading or writing). The **inbytes()** and **outbytes()** macros set the I/O direction for you, resulting in one less parameter and fewer mistakes.

If you give a record position of -1L, then **iobytes()** interprets that to mean "use the current record"; otherwise, it is always interpreted as a record offset from the beginning of the file. Even if you specify the current record, **iobytes()** will do a seek so that the file buffer is maintained properly, as discussed earlier.

The **iobytes()** function returns the number of records read or written, or a -1 if an error occurred. If an error does occur during an **iobytes()** operation, it reports not only the file name and DOS error involved, but also the record position.

The following is an example given earlier, rewritten to use the file I/O package instead:

```
/*
    Record I/O example with file toolkit  (filex7.c)
 Must link with: popup.obj, mouse.obj, sayerr.obj,
           fileio.obj
*/
#include <stdio.h>
#include "popup.h"   /* Must have this to initialize windows */
#include "fileio.h"  /* High level file I/O header           */
typedef struct my_parts_struct {
   int part_code;
   int quantity;
   float price;
} part;
main() {
  int f;
  int nr;
  part mypart = {
     15,   /* part code */
     300,  /* quantity  */
     1.25  /* price     */
  };
  init_win();    /* Must always do this first */
  init_files(); /* Then remember to initialize the file table */
  /* For record I/O you should always open for binary access,
     (note the "b") */
  if ((f = openfile("myfile.dat","w+b",sizeof(part))) != -1) {
     /* Write the part out to record 6 */
     nr = outbytes(f, 6, (unsigned char *)&mypart, 1);
   mprintf("The number of records written is %d\r\n",nr);
     closefile(f);
  }
}
```

Whenever you use the file I/O package, you must first initialize the window package (in case error messages are printed) and then the internal file table by calling **init_files()**. It should be done in the order shown. The size of the table defaults to 20 files, but this can be changed by setting the constant MAXFILES given in the **fileio.h** header file (and recompiling **fileio.c**). This constant should not be confused with the FILES parameter of **config.sys**. That parameter is used by DOS to allocate space for its own file table. It probably is a good idea to use the same number for both.

Note that there is an error check in the previous example so that operations are not attempted on a file that is not open. The **openfile()** function, however, handles all error reporting for us. The file package uses -1 consistently for returning error indications, the same that the Turbo C file routines use.

The functions **rdstr()**, **wrtstr()**, **rdfstr()**, and **wrtfstr()** are provided to do character- and string-level access. They call the Turbo C routines **fgets()**, **fputs()**, **vfscanf()** and **vfprintf()**, respectively, and allow for both unformatted and formatted string access. Their prototypes are:

```
int rdstr(char *str, int n, int h);
int wrtstr(char *str, int h);
int rdfstr(int h, char *format, ...);
int wrtfstr(int h, char *format, ...);
```

When using these routines, you should open the file with a record size of one byte to indicate character–string-level access. Also, if it is really a text file, be sure to use the "t" indicator in the file access mode parameter. Unlike their Turbo C counterparts, these routines first do a seek to the current position for the same reason that **iobytes()** does.

The **rdstr()** function returns 0 on success, or -1 if an error occurs. The **wrtstr()** function returns the last character read, like its **fputs()** counterpart, or it returns -1 if an error occurred. Like its **vfscanf()** counterpart, **rdfstr()** returns the number of fields scanned, or a -1 if there is an error. The **wrtfstr()** function returns the number of bytes written, or a -1 if there is an error, also like its **vfprintf()** counterpart.

In the following example, a file is created and a formatted message is printed to it:

```
/*
    Formatted file I/O using file toolkit  (filex8.
Must link with: popup.obj, mouse.obj, sayerr.obj, fileio.obj
*/

#include <stdio.h>
#include "popup.h"   /* Must have this to initialize windows */
#include "fileio.h"  /* High level file I/O header           */
main() {
  int f, nb, age = 30;

  init_win();    /* Must always do this first */
  init_files(); /* Then remember to initialize the file table */
  /* Note that we are opening for text file access */
  if ((f = openfile("myfile.dat","w+t",sizeof(char))) != -1) {
```

```
    nb = wrtfstr(f, "Sally is %d years old\n", age);
    mprintf("The number of characters written is %d\r\n",nb);
    closefile(f);
  }
}
```

Listing 5.1 Source code for the header file "fileio.h"

```
/*  File I/O toolkit header file  (fileio.h)  */
#define inbytes(port,rec,d,nr)   iobytes(port,rec,d,nr,0)
#define outbytes(port,rec,d,nr)  iobytes(port,rec,d,nr,1)
#define MAXFILES 20
typedef struct fh_struct {
   FILE *fp;
   char *name;
   int  recsize;
} file_entry;
extern file_entry ft[]; /* our record and error reporting file table */
extern void init_files(void);
extern int get_file_data(int h, FILE **f, char **fname, int *recsize);
extern int openfile(char *fname, char *access_type, int recsize);
extern int closefile(int h);
extern long movepos(int h, long recno, int smode);
extern int iobytes(int h, long recno, unsigned char *d, int nr, int iodir);
extern int rdstr(char *str, int n, int h);
extern int wrtstr(char *str, int h);
extern int rdfstr(int h, char *format, ...);
extern int wrtfstr(int h, char *format, ...);
```

Listing 5.2 Source code for the file "fileio.c"

```
/*******************************************************************
 *   File I/O toolkit   (fileio.c)
 *******************************************************************/
#include <string.h>
#include <alloc.h>
#include <stdio.h>
#include "popup.h"
#include "fileio.h"
file_entry ft[MAXFILES]; /* our record and error reporting file table */
static char unknownfile[] = "unknown file"; /* use in error messages */
static char iowstr[] = "writing";
static char iorstr[] = "reading";
/* internal functions */
static int add_file(FILE *f, char *n, int recsize);
static void rmv_file(int h);
static int valid_index(int h);
```

```
void init_files(void)
/* Initializes file table for high level file i/o. */
{
   int h;
   for (h=0; h<MAXFILES; h++) {
       ft[h].fp = NULL;             /* initialize file entry      */
       ft[h].name = NULL;
   }
   add_file(stdin, "stdin", 1);   /* set up default file handles */
   add_file(stdout,"stdout",1);   /* for character level access  */
   add_file(stderr,"stderr",1);
   add_file(stdaux,"stdaux",1);
   add_file(stdprn,"stdprn",1);
}
static int add_file(FILE *f, char *n, int recsize)
/*  Searches for an open entry in the file table and stores
    the FILE pointer along with the file name and record size.
    Reports an error if not enough room in the table, and returns -1.
    If no error, the position in the file table is returned.
 */
{
   int h;
   /* search for open entry */
   for (h=0; (h<MAXFILES) && (ft[h].fp != NULL); h++);
   if (h == MAXFILES) {
      sayerr(SERR,"File table full\r\n");
      return -1;
   }
   ft[h].fp = f;            /* set FILE pointer              */
   ft[h].name = strdup(n);  /* allocate and copy file name   */
   ft[h].recsize = recsize; /* set the record size           */
   return h;
}
static void rmv_file(int h)
/*  Removes entry h from the file table by setting the file handle
    to NULL, and freeing up the space allocated for the name. The
    recsize is also set to zero.
 */
{
   ft[h].fp = NULL;
   free(ft[h].name);
   ft[h].recsize = 0;
}
static int valid_index(int h)
/* Returns 1 if h points to an existing file entry, else returns 0. */
{
  if ((h >= 0) && (h < MAXFILES) && (ft[h].fp != NULL)) {
     return 1;
  }
```

```
  else {
    sayerr(SERR,"Illegal file index %d\r\n",h);
    return 0;
  }
}
int get_file_data(int h, FILE **f, char **fname, int *recsize)
/* Sees if handle h is an opened file.  If so, the FILE pointer,
   the file name, and record size are returned. If the entry is
   empty, the file pointer is set to NULL, the file name is set to
   "unknown", and the recsize to zero. A -1 is returned as an
   error indicator, else a zero is.
*/
{
   if (!valid_index(h)) return -1;
   if ((*f = ft[h].fp) == NULL) {
      *fname = unknownfile;
      *recsize = 0;
      return -1;
   }
   else {
      *fname = ft[h].name;
      *recsize = ft[h].recsize;
      return 0;
   }
}
int openfile(char *fname, char *access_type, int recsize)
/*
   Opens/creates a file with given access type and record size.
   The FILE pointer, filename, and record size are stored internally
   for convenient error handling and record I/O purposes.
   Returns the new table entry position, or -1 if an error occurs.
*/
{
     FILE *f;
     if ((f = fopen(fname, access_type)) == NULL) {
        sayerr(FERR,"%s\r\n",fname);
        return -1;
     }
     else {
        return add_file(f, fname, recsize);
     }
}
int closefile(int h)
/*
   Closes file h (as indexed by the file table), and removes it from
   the file table.  Returns -1 if an error occurred, else 0.

   If h is out of bounds, an error is reported, and a -1 is returned.
*/
```

```
{
   if (!valid_index(h)) return -1;
   if (fclose(ft[h].fp) == -1) {
      sayerr(FERR,"%d - %s\r\n",ft[h].fp,ft[h].name);
      return -1;
   }
   rmv_file(h);
   return 0;
}
long movepos(int h, long recno, int smode)
/*
   Moves the file pointer to the record offset recno, using seek mode
   smode, (which should be either SEEK_SET, SEEK_CUR, or SEEK_END).
   Returns -1 and reports if there's an error, else it returns
   the new record position.
   The recno is multiplied by the record size to get the true byte
   position in the file, (ignoring any newline translations in text
   mode).
*/
{
    long newpos;
    if (!valid_index(h)) return -1;
    newpos = recno * ft[h].recsize;
    if ((newpos = fseek(ft[h].fp,newpos,smode)) == -1) {
       sayerr(FERR,"file: %s\r\nrecord %ld\r\n",ft[h].name,recno);
       return -1;
    }
    return newpos / ft[h].recsize;
}
int iobytes(int h, long recno, unsigned char *d, int nr, int iodir)
/*
    Reads/writes nr records in/out of buffer d at record recno of file h.
    if iodir = 1, it does a write, else, it does a read.
    If recno = -1, it means to read/write from the current position.
    Returns -1 if error, else number of bytes actually moved.
    The recno offset is always from the beginning of the file, (unless
    its -1, which means current position).
*/
{
    unsigned int recsmoved;
    char *iodirstr;
    long savepos;
    if (!valid_index(h)) return -1;
    /* Always do a seek, so that fread() and fwrite() work properly. */
    /* Either seek to current record, or to specified one. */
    if (recno == -1) {
       if (movepos(h, 0L, SEEK_CUR) == -1L) return -1;
    }
```

```
    else {
       if (movepos(h, recno, SEEK_SET) == -1L) return -1;
    }
    /*
       Use the following as a part of a work around for a bug in
       some older versions of Turbo C.  Must save the current
       position so we can use it as a reference.
       savepos = ftell(ft[h].fp);
    */
    if (iodir == 1) {
       recsmoved = fwrite(d,ft[h].recsize,nr,ft[h].fp);
    }
    else {
       recsmoved = fread(d,ft[h].recsize,nr,ft[h].fp);
    }
    if (recsmoved == -1) {
       if (iodir == 1)  iodirstr = iowstr; else iodirstr = iorstr;
       sayerr(FERR,"%s %s\r\npos'n %ld\r\n", iodirstr,ft[h].name, recno);
       return -1;
    }
    else {
      /*
         Use the following as a work around for a bug in some older
         versions of Turbo C.  Must move the stream pointer to
         proper position.
         savepos += recsmoved * ft[h].recsize;
         if (movepos(h, savepos, SEEK_SET) == -1L) return -1;
      */
    }
    return recsmoved;
}
int rdstr(char *str, int n, int h)
/* Reads a string from file h by calling fgets(). Unlike fgets()
   it does a seek to the current position first to properly
   maintain the file buffer. Returns 0 if successful, otherwise a -1.
 */
{
   if (!valid_index(h)) return -1;
   /* Seek to current position so buffer is maintained properly.
      NOTE: For some versions of Turbo C 1.5 and older this does
      not work correctly.  Contact Borland for update.
   */
   if (movepos(h, 0, SEEK_CUR) == -1L) return -1;
   if (fgets(str, n, ft[h].fp) == NULL) return -1;
   return 0; /* successful */
}
int wrtstr(char *str, int h)
/* Writes a string to file h by calling fputs(). Unlike fputs()
```

```
   it does a seek to the current position first to properly
   maintain the file buffer. Returns the last character written
   if successful, otherwise a -1.
 */
{
   int c;
   if (!valid_index(h)) return -1;
   /* Seek to current position so buffer is maintained properly.
      NOTE: For some versions of Turbo C 1.5 and older this does
      not work correctly.  Contact Borland for update.
   */
   if (movepos(h, 0, SEEK_CUR) == -1L) return -1;
   if ((c = fputs(str, ft[h].fp)) == EOF) return -1;

   return c; /* successful */
}
int rdfstr(int h, char *format, ...)
/* Reads a formatted string from file h at current posn.
 * If an error occurs a -1 is returned, else the number of fields
 * scanned is returned.
 */
{
   va_list arg_ptr;
   int e;
   if (!valid_index(h)) return -1;
   /* Seek to current position so buffer is maintained properly.
      NOTE: For some versions of Turbo C 1.5 and older this does
      not work correctly.  Contact Borland for update.
   */
   if (movepos(h, 0, SEEK_CUR) == -1L) return -1;
   va_start(arg_ptr,format);
   e = vfscanf(ft[h].fp, format, arg_ptr);
   va_end(arg_ptr);
   if (ferror(ft[h].fp) || feof(ft[h].fp)) {
      sayerr(FERR,"scanning %s\r\n", ft[h].name);
      clearerr(ft[h].fp);
      return -1;
   }
   return e;
}
int wrtfstr(int h, char *format, ...)
/* Writes a formatted string from file h at current position.
 * If an error occurs a -1 is returned, else the number of bytes
 * printed is returned.
 */
{
   va_list arg_ptr;
   int e;
   if (!valid_index(h)) return -1;
```

```
    /* Seek to current position so buffer is maintained properly.
       NOTE: For some versions of Turbo C 1.5 and older this does
       not work correctly.  Contact Borland for update.
    */
    if (movepos(h, 0, SEEK_CUR) == -1L) return -1;
    va_start(arg_ptr,format);
    e = vfprintf(ft[h].fp, format, arg_ptr);
    va_end(arg_ptr);
    if (ferror(ft[h].fp) || feof(ft[h].fp)) {
       sayerr(FERR,"printing to %s\r\n", ft[h].name);
       clearerr(ft[h].fp);
       return -1;
    }
    return e;
}
```

CHAPTER

6

String Function Libraries

This chapter presents two libraries that contain additional string functions. These functions supplement the versatile list if Turbo C string functions. The reason for presenting two somewhat similar libraries is the ability to manipulate strings using either pointers or a combination of pointers and character indices. In the first case, the pointers used are most likely separately declared pointers that access substrings. In the second case, the pointer employed can very well be the string identifier itself, which points to the index zero. The character index provides the offset to access any string character. Converting between either access method is easy. To obtain the pointer address, given the string identifier and the offset, you use:

```
ptr = str + index;
```

To obtain the character index, given a pointer and the string identifier name, you use:

```
index = (unsigned int) (ptr - str);
```

LIBRARY stropsl.c

Listings 6.1 and 6.2 show the first string library containing routines that are written using the same approach of the Turbo C string functions. These strings assume that the string pointer contains the address of a valid string location.

The first function is **pt_insert**, which inserts a substring into a string. It is declared as:

```
void pt_insert(char* ptr, char* substr)
```

The string pointer parameter contains the address of the string character where the substring is inserted. It may be regarded as the pseudostring's base address. Assuming that a valid string pointer is used, the operation can therefore be regarded as inserting the substring at the beginning of the pseudostring. This reduces the task of the code to moving a number of characters to higher indices and then copying the inserted substring. Two calls to **memmove** are used to swiftly carry out the insertion. To illustrate how **pt_insert** works, consider the following code:

```
/* program to demonstrate string insertion
   using pt_insert() in library "strops1.h" */
#include <stdio.h>
#include <string.h>
#include <strops1.h>
#include "conio.h"
main()
{
  char str1[41], str2[41];
  int index, len;
  clrscr();
  printf("                  01234567890123456789012345678901234567890\n");
  printf("                            1         2         3         4\n");
  printf("Enter a string -> ");
  gets(str1);
  printf("\nEnter string to be inserted -> ");
  gets(str2);
  len = strlen(str1);
  do {
     printf("\nEnter location : ");
     scanf "%d", &index);
     printf("\n");
  } while (index >= len);
  pt_insert(str1 + index, str2);
  printf("\nThe string is now '%s'", str1);
}
```

The **pt_overwrite** function overwrites a string with a substring. If the overwriting substring goes beyond the string delimiter, the string is expanded to accommodate the extra characters. The function is declared as:

```
void pt_overwrite(char* ptr, char* substr)
```

Using a pointer to the string, the problem is reduced to overwriting a pseudostring with a substring. To illustrate how **pt_overwrite** works, consider the following code:

```
/* program to demonstrate overwriting string characters
   using pt_overwrite() in library "strops1.h" */
#include <stdio.h>
#include <string.h>
#include <strops1.h>
#include "conio.h"
main()
{
```

```
  char str1[41], str2[41];
  int index, len;
  clrscr();
  printf("                    0123456789012345678901234567890123456789 0\n");
  printf("                              1         2         3         4\n");
  printf("Enter a string -> ");
  gets(str1);
  printf("\nEnter overwriting string -> ");
  gets(str2);
  len = strlen(str1);
  do {
     printf("\nEnter location : ");
     scanf("%d", &index);
     printf("\n");
  } while (index >= len);
  pt_overwrite(str1 + index, str2);
  printf("\nThe string is now '%s'", str1);
}
```

The **pt_delete** function removes a specified number of characters, starting at the character indicated by the string pointer. The function is declared as:

```
void pt_delete(char* ptr,  unsigned int count)
```

If the count for the deleted characters is greater than or equal to the length of the pseudostring, the string is simply truncated. Otherwise, characters from the tail portion of the string are copied to overwrite the deleted portion. To demonstrate how **pt_delete** works, consider the following code:

```
/* program to demonstrate deleting string characters
   using pt_delete() in library "strops1.h" */
#include <stdio.h>
#include <string.h>
#include <strops1.h>
#include "conio.h"
main()
{
  char str1[41];
  int count, index, len;
  clrscr();
  printf("                    01234567890123456789012345678901234567890\n");
  printf("                              1         2         3         4\n");
  printf("Enter a string -> ");
  gets(str1);
```

```
  printf("\nEnter the number of characters to delete : ");
  scanf("%d", &count);
  len = strlen(str1);
  do {
     printf("\nEnter location : ");
     scanf("%d", &index);
     printf("\n");
  } while (index >= len);
  pt_delete(str1 + index, count);
  printf("\nThe string is now '%s'", str1);
}
```

The **pt_replace_str** function scans a string and replaces the occurrences of a specified substring with another. The function is declared as:

```
int pt_replace_str(char* ptr,
                   char* find,
                   char* replace,
                   unsigned int freq)
```

The maximum number of text translation frequencies is also specified. The string pointer is used to indicate where the string translation begins. In most cases, the entire string is scanned, and consequently the string identifier is used as the string pointer argument. This **pt_replace_str** invokes the **pt_insert**, and **pt_delete** functions previously discussed, as well as the Turbo C **strstr** string function. The function returns -1 when either one or both the main and matching strings are null strings. To demonstrate how **pt_replace_str** works, consider the following code:

```
/* program to demonstrate translating string characters
   using pt_replace_str() in library "strops1.h" */
#include <stdio.h>
#include <string.h>
#include <strops1.h>
#include "conio.h"
main()
{
  char str1[41], find[41], replace[41];
  int count = 1;
  clrscr();
  printf("Enter a string -> ");
  gets(str1);
  printf("\nEnter the string to find -> ");
  gets(find);
  printf("\nEnter the string to replace -> ");
```

```
  gets(replace);
  pt_replace_str(str1,find,replace,count);
  printf("\nThe string is now '%s'", str1);
}
```

The **repeat_str** is used to create a string by the repeated concatenation of a pattern string. The function is declared as:

```
void repeat_str(char* str, char* pattern, int num)
```

The following listing contains a short and simple program that illustrates string insertion, deletion, and translation, using the above functions:

```
#include <stdio.h>
#include <string.h>
#include "strops1.h"
main()
{
   char str[81] = "Ada Byron";
   void pt_insert(char*, char*);
   void pt_delete(char*,  unsigned int);
   puts("0123456789|123456789|123456789|");
   puts(str);
   pt_insert(str+3," Augusta");
   puts(str);
   pt_replace_str(str,"Ada","Lady",1);
   puts(str);
   pt_delete(str+5,strlen("Augusta "));
   puts(str);
}
```

When the program is run, the following text appears on the screen:

```
0123456789|123456789|123456789|
Ada Byron
Ada Augusta Byron
Lady Augusta Byron
Lady Byron
```

LIBRARY strops2.c

The second string library is shown in listings 6.3 and 6.4. It contains more string functions, all of which employ the indexing of string characters. This means that the functions in this library have an additional argument that should be examined for valid values.

The first string function is **pos_str**, which searches for the first location of a substring within a string, starting with a given character index. The function is declared as:

```
int pos_str(char* str, char* substr, unsigned int start_index)
```

If no match is found, a -1 is returned. The coding of this function does not rely on any other string function, except **strlen**. The function can be used with both near and far pointers. To illustrate how **pos_str** works, consider the following code:

```
/* program to demonstrate locating substrings
   using pos_str() in library "strops2.h" */
#include <stdio.h>
#include <string.h>
#include <strops2.h>
#include "conio.h"
main()
{
  char str1[41], find[41];
  int start, len;
  clrscr();
  printf("                         01234567890123456789012345678901234567890\n");
  printf("                                   1         2         3         4\n");
  printf("Enter a string -> ");
  gets(str1);
  printf("\nEnter the string to find -> ");
  gets(find);
  len = strlen(str1);
  do {
     printf("\nEnter number of characters to skip : ");
     scanf("%d", &start);
  } while (start < 1 || start >= len);
  printf("\nThe substring matches at char %d",
     pos_str(str1, find, start));
}
```

The function **pos_str2** performs the same task as **pos_str**, but uses the **strstr** string function in the Turbo C library. The function is declared as:

```
int pos_str2(char* str, char* substr, unsigned int start_index)
```

The **strstr** function returns the pointer to the matching string location (or NULL if none is found). The function verifies whether or not a NULL pointer is returned and, if not, returns the difference between the non-Null pointer address and the string argument.

The **pos_char** function scans a string, starting at a specified index, looking for the first occurrence of a specific character. The function is declared as:

```
int pos_char(char* str, char ch, int start_index)
```

The heart of the function is a **for** loop that keeps on iterating until either the character is found or the end of the string is reached. If no match is found, a -1 is returned. To illustrate how **pos_char** works, consider the following code:

```
/* program to demonstrate locating characters
   using pos_char() in library "strops2.h" */
#include <stdio.h>
#include <string.h>
#include <strops2.h>
#include "conio.h"
main()
{
  char str1[41], find;
  int start, len;
  clrscr();
  printf("                         01234567890123456789012345678901234567890\n");
  printf("                                    1         2         3         4\n");
  printf("Enter a string -> ");
  gets(str1);
  printf("\nEnter the character to find -> ");
  find = getche();
  len = strlen(str1);
  printf("\n");
  do {
     printf("\nEnter number of characters to skip : ");
     scanf("d", &start);
  } while (start < 1 || start >= len);
  printf("\nThe character matches at string char %d",
     pos_har(str1, find, start));
}
```

The **in_insert** function inserts a substring in a string at a specified location. Compared with the **pt_insert** function, **in_insert** has an additional argument, namely, the insertion index. The function is declared as:

```
void in_insert(char* str, char* substr, unsigned int index)
```

This function handles two insertion cases:

1. The value of the index corresponds to a valid string character (i.e., before the null string delimiter). The substring is inserted at the location indicated by index.
2. The value of the index points to the null string delimiter or any character beyond it. In this case, the value of index is ignored and the substring is merely appended at the end of the string. To demonstrate how **in_insert** works, consider the following code:

```
/* program to demonstrate string insertion
   using in_insert() in library "strops2.h" */
#include <stdio.h>
#include <string.h>
#include <strops2.h>
#include "conio.h"
main()
{
  char str1[41], str2[41];
  int index, len;
  clrscr();
  printf("                  01234567890123456789012345678901234567890\n");
  printf("                            1         2         3         4\n");
  printf("Enter a string -> ");
  gets(str1);
  printf("\nEnter string to be inserted -> ");
  gets(str2);
  len = strlen(str1);
  do {
     printf("\nEnter location : ");
     scanf("%d", &index);
     printf("\n");
  } while (inde" >= len);
  in_insert(str1, str2, index);
  printf("\nThe string is now '%s'", str1);
}
```

The **in_overwrite** function overwrites a string with another at a specified character location. The function is declared as:

```
void in_overwrite(char* str, char* substr, unsigned int index)
```

The second string used to overwrite the first may cause it to expand in size. This is due to the relative string lengths and/or the overwrite location. If the specified character index is located beyond the string delimiter, the second string is simply appended to the first one. To demonstrate how **in_overwrite** functions, consider the following code:

```
/* program to demonstrate overwriting string characters
   using in_overwrite() in library "strops2.h" */
#include <stdio.h>
#include <string.h>
#include <strops2.h>
#include "conio.h"
main()
```

```
{
  char str1[41], str2[41];
  int index, len;
  clrscr();
  printf("                    0123456789012345678901234567890123456789O\n");
  printf("                              1         2         3         4\n");
  printf("Enter a string -> ");
  gets(str1);
  printf("\nEnter overwriting string -> ");
  gets(str2);
  len = strlen(str1);
  do {
     printf("\nEnter location : ");
     scanf("%d", &index);
     printf("\n");
  } while (index >= len);
  in_overwrite(str1, str2, index);
  printf("\nThe string is now '%s'", str1);
}
```

The **in_delete** function removes part or all of the characters in a string. The function is declared as:

```
int in_delete(char* str, unsigned int index, unsigned int count)
```

If the character index lies beyond the string delimiter, no characters are deleted. If the value of the count parameter is greater than the available number of characters to be deleted, the slack is ignored. An example for using **in_delete** is:

```
/* program to demonstrate deleting string characters
   using in_delete() in library "strops2.h" */
#include <stdio.h>
#include <string.h>
#include <strops2.h>
#include "conio.h"
main()
{
  char str1[41];
  int count, index, len;
  clrscr();
  printf("                    01234567890123456789012345678901234567890\n");
  printf("                              1         2         3         4\n");
  printf("Enter a string -> ");
  gets(str1);
```

```
  printf("\nEnter the number of characters to delete : ");
  scanf("%d", &count);
  len = strlen(str1);
  do {
     printf("\nEnter location : ");
     scanf("%d", &index);
     printf("\n");
  } while (index >= len);
  in_delete(str1, index, count);
  printf("\nThe string is now '%s'", str1);
}
```

The **in_replace_str** function is engaged in translating substrings into a larger string. The function is declared as:

```
int in_replace_str(char* str,
                   char* find,
                   char* replace,
                   unsigned int start_index,
                   unsigned int freq)
```

The **start_index** parameter specifies the character index where the translation begins (and is also equal to the number of characters to be bypassed, minus one). The **freq** parameter defines the maximum number of translations allowed. These two parameters give you control to fine-tune the text translation process. The following short program demonstrates the use of the **in_replace_str** function:

```
   /* program to demonstrate translating string characters
   using in_replace_str() in library "strops2.h" */
#include <stdio.h>
#include <string.h>
#include <strops2.h>
#include "conio.h"
main()
{
  char str1[41], find[41], replace[41];
  int start = 1, count = 1;
  clrscr();
  printf("Enter a string -> ");
  gets(str1);
  printf("\nEnter the string to find -> ");
  gets(find);
  printf("\nEnter the string to replace -> ");
  gets(replace);
```

```
  in_replace_str(str1, find, replace, start, count);
  printf("\nThe string is now '%s'", str1);
}
```

The **int_pos_mid** is a function that extracts a function by specifying the first and last character index. The function is declared as:

```
int in_pos_mid(char* str, unsigned int first, unsigned int last)
```

When the first parameter points to a character beyond the null string terminator, the string parameter is returned unchanged. When the last parameter points to a character beyond the null string terminator, the string is returned after removing its former leading characters. Values for the first and last parameters that are within the string's length should remove portions of the left and right sides of the string. The following program illustrates how this function works:

```
/* program to demonstrate extracting string characters
   using in_pos_mid() in library "strops2.h" */
#include <stdio.h>
#include <string.h>
#include <strops2.h>
#include "conio.h"
main()
{
  char str1[41];
  int first, last;
  clrscr();
  printf("                    01234567890123456789012345678901234567890\n");
  printf("                              1         2         3         4\n");
  printf("Enter a string -> ");
  gets(str1);
  do {
     printf("\nEnter first character to extract : ");
     scanf("%d", &first);
     printf("\nEnter last character to extract : ");
     scanf("%d", &last);
  } while (first >= last);
  in_pos_mid(str1, first, last);
  printf("\nThe string is now '%s'", str1);
}
```

The **in_count_mid** function is a sister function to in_pos_mid. The difference is that the last parameter provides a count for the number of extracted characters. The function is declared as:

```
int in_count_mid(char* str, unsigned int index, unsigned int count)
```

When the first parameter points to a character beyond the null string terminator, the string parameter is returned unchanged. When the count parameter is greater than the actual number of available characters, the string is returned after removing its former leading characters. Values for the first and count parameters that are within the string's length should remove portions of the left and right sides of the string. The following program illustrates how this function operates:

```
/* program to demonstrate extracting string characters
   using in_count_mid() in library "strops2.h" */
#include <stdio.h>
#include <string.h>
#include <strops2.h>
#include "conio.h"
main()
{
  char str1[41];
  int first, count;
  clrscr();
  printf("                    0123456789012345678901234567890123456789\n");
  printf("                              1         2         3         4\n");
  printf("Enter a string -> ");
  gets(str1);
  do {
     printf("\nEnter first character to extract : ");
     scanf("%d", &first);
     printf("\nEnter the number of characters to exctract : ");
     scanf("%d", &count);
  } while (first < 0 || count <= 0);
  in_count_mid(str1, first, count);
  printf("\nThe string is now '%s'", str1);
}
```

The **strops2.c** library contains the following three string-padding functions:

```
void pad_left(char* str, char pad_char, int num_chars)
void pad_right(char* str, char pad_char, int num_chars)
void pad_ends(char* str, char pad_char, int each_end)
```

These functions pad a specified number of copies of a character to either or both ends of a string.

The counterpart of the string-padding functions are the following string-trimming functions:

```
void trim_left(char* str, char ch)
void trim_right(char* str, char ch)
void trim_ends(char* str, char ch)
```

These functions are characterized by the fact that you can specify the character to be trimmed. You are not limited to removing only the space. An example for using the padding and trimming functions is the following short program.

```
#include <stdio.h>
#include "strops2.h"
main()
{
  char str[81] = "0123456789";
  char c = '-';
  void pad_ends(char*, char, int);
  void trim_ends(char*, char);

  pad_ends(str, c, 3);
  puts(str); /* displays "—0123456789—" */
  trim_ends(str, c);
  puts(str); /* displays "0123456789" */
}
```

AN APPLICATION: A BASIC TEXT FILE TRANSLATOR

Listing 6.5 contains the source code for "translan.c", an application that performs basic text file translation. Although the application performs straightforward translation, it is driven by a script file. The script file provides the application with the exact text manipulation instructions. A script file is a text file that contains a series of commands that can be one of the following:

1. **Case-sensitive text deletion** This uses the syntax "D |<text>|" where the bar symbols enclose the pattern of the text to be deleted.
2. **Case-insensitive text deletion** This utilizes the syntax "K |<text>|" where the bar symbols enclose the pattern of the text to be deleted.
3. **Case-sensitive text translation** This employs the syntax "R |<old text>|<new text>|" to replace <old text> with <new text>.

Listing 6.6 contains the source code for the script file **pas2c.src** used in the preliminary translation of Turbo Pascal programs to Turbo C. The **translan.c** is written such that the **pas2c.src** file is the default file. You can add or remove specific script instructions from **pas2c.src**. If you are translating between other languages, you need to write your own script file. The power of the **translan.c** utility is its programmability. You can add new script commands to the **translan.c** file to carry out more advanced text translation involving text patterns.

In order to demonstrate the **translan.c** program, the Turbo Pascal version of the sieve benchmark, shown in Listing 6.7, is used as the input file. The output file is shown in Listing 6.8 and contains a source code file with Pascal and C syntax! The hand-edited working file is shown in Listing 6.9. This should give you an idea of the amount of work performed to convert the listing from the intermediate state to the final form.

Listing 6.1 Source code for header file "stropsl.h"

```
void pt_insert(char*, char*);
void pt_overwrite(char*, char*);
void pt_delete(char*, unsigned int);
int pt_replace_str(char*, char*, char*, unsigned int);
void repeat_str(char*, char*, int);
```

Listing 6.2 Source code for library file "stropsl.c"

```
#include <string.h>
void pt_insert(char* ptr, char* substr)
/* insert substring */
{
   unsigned int m = strlen(substr);
   memmove((ptr+m),ptr,strlen(ptr)+1); /* move character out */
   memmove(ptr,substr,m);              /* copy substring */
}
void pt_overwrite(char* ptr, char* substr)
{
   unsigned int m = strlen(substr)-1;
   unsigned int n = strlen(ptr);
   unsigned int shift;
   shift = (n < m) ? m : (m+1);
   memmove(ptr,substr,shift);
}
void pt_delete(char* ptr,  unsigned int count)
{
   unsigned int n = strlen(ptr);
   if (count >= n)
      *ptr = '\0'; /* simply truncate string pointer */
   else /* move characters to overwrite deleted substring */
      memmove(ptr,(ptr+count),n-count+1);
}
int pt_replace_str(char* ptr,
                   char* find,
                   char* replace,
                   unsigned int freq)
{
    unsigned int findlen = strlen(find);
    unsigned int repl_strlen = strlen(replace);
    unsigned int sstrlen = strlen(ptr);
    char* match_ptr;
    /*————Argument-checking————*/
    if ((findlen * sstrlen) == 0)
       return -1;
    match_ptr = strstr(ptr, find);
    while ((match_ptr != 0) && (freq > 0)) {
        freq—;
```

```
        /* remove string found */
        pt_delete(match_ptr, findlen);
        /* replace it with new string */
        if (repl_strlen > 0)
            pt_insert(match_ptr, replace);
        /* find next matching strings */
        match_ptr = strstr(ptr, find);
    }
    return 0;
}
void repeat_str(char* str, char* pattern, int num)
{
    while (num-- > 0)
        strcat(str, pattern);
}
```

Listing 6.3 Source code for header file "strops2.h"

```
int pos_str(char*, char*, unsigned int);
int pos_str2(char*, char*, unsigned int);
int pos_char(char*, char, int);
void in_insert(char*, char*, unsigned int);
void in_overwrite(char*, char*, unsigned int);
int in_delete(char*, unsigned int, unsigned int);
int in_replace_str(char*, char*, char*, unsigned int, unsigned int);
int in_pos_mid(char*, unsigned int, unsigned int);
int in_count_mid(char*, unsigned int, unsigned int);
void pad_left(char*, char, int);
void pad_right(char*, char, int);
void trim_left(char*, char);
void trim_right(char*, char);
void trim_ends(char*, char);
```

Listing 6.4 Source code for string library "strops2.c"

```
#include <string.h>
int pos_str(char* str, char* substr, unsigned int start_index)
{
    int i, j, k, last;
    unsigned int sstrlen = strlen(str);
    unsigned int substrlen = strlen(substr);
    unsigned char nomatch;
    if ((substrlen == 0) || (start_index >= sstrlen))
        return -1;
    k = -1;
    if (sstrlen > substrlen) {
        i = start_index - 1;
        last = sstrlen - substrlen;
        nomatch = 1;
```

```
        while ((i <= last) && (nomatch == 1)) {
            i++;
            if (substr[0] == str[i]) {
                k = i;
                j = 1;
                i++;
                nomatch = 0;
                while ((j < substrlen) && (nomatch == 0) )
                    if (substr[j] == str[i]) {
                        i++;
                        j++;
                    }
                    else
                     nomatch = 1;
               /* restore index before complete matching was attempted */
                if (nomatch == 1) {
                    i = k + 1;
                    k = -1;
                }
            } /* if (substr[0] == str[i]) */
        } /* while ((i <= last) && (nomatch)) */
    } /* if (sstrlen > substrlen) */
    return k;
}
int pos_str2(char* str, char* substr, unsigned int start_index)
{
  char* ptr;
  ptr = strstr((str+start_index), substr);
  if (ptr != 0)
     return (ptr - str);
  else
     return -1;
}
int pos_char(char* str, char ch, int start_index)
{
   int k;
   unsigned int n = strlen(str);
   for (k = start_index; ((*(str+k) != ch) && (k < n)); k++);
   if (k == n)
      k = -1;
   return k;
}
void in_insert(char* str, char* substr, unsigned int index)
/* insert or append substring */
{
   unsigned int m = strlen(substr);
   unsigned int n = strlen(str);
   if (index < n) { /* insert substring */
      { int i;
```

```
      memmove((str+index+m),(str+index),n+1-index);
      /* *(str+n+m) = '\0';
    for (i = n+1-index; i >= 0; i-)
       *(str+index+m+i) = *(str+index+i); */
      }
      memmove((str+index),substr,m);
   }
   else /* append substring */
      memmove((str+n),substr,m+1);
}
void in_overwrite(char* str, char* substr, unsigned int index)
{
   unsigned int m = strlen(substr);
   unsigned int n = strlen(str);
   unsigned int first, shift;
   if (index < n) { /* overwrite substring */
      first = index; /* substring index in inside string   */
      shift = m;     /* assume substring does not go beyond
                        end-of-string                      */
      if ((index+m) > n)
         shift++; /* add one more char count for \0 */
   }
   else { /* append substring */
      first = n;
      shift = m + 1;
   }
   memmove((str+first),substr,shift);
}
int in_delete(char* str, unsigned int index, unsigned int count)
{
   unsigned int n = strlen(str);
   if (index < 0 ) index = 0;
   if (index < n) {
      if ((index+count-1) >= n) /* truncate string */
         str[index] = '\0';
      else /* move characters to overwrite deleted substring */
         memmove((str+index),(str+index+count),n-index-count+1);
      return 0; /* no-error code */
   }
   else
      return -1; /* error code */
}
int in_replace_str(char* str,
                   char* find,
                   char* replace,
                   unsigned int start_index,
                   unsigned int freq)
{
```

```
    unsigned int findlen = strlen(find);
    unsigned int repl_strlen = strlen(replace);
    unsigned int sstrlen = strlen(str);
    int match_pos;
    /*----------Argument-checking----------*/
    if ( ((findlen * sstrlen) == 0) || (start_index >= sstrlen) )
       return -1;
    match_pos = pos_str(str, find, 0);
    while (match_pos > -1 && freq > 0) {
        freq--;
        /* remove string found */
        in_delete(str, (unsigned int) match_pos, findlen);
        /* replace it with new string */
        if (repl_strlen > 0)
       in_insert(str, replace, (unsigned int) match_pos);
        /* find next matching strings */
        match_pos = pos_str(str, find, 0);
    }
   return 0;
}
int in_pos_mid(char* str, unsigned int first, unsigned int last)
{
   unsigned int len = strlen(str);
   unsigned count;
    if (len == 0 || last < first) /* bad arguments */
       return -1;
    if (first > len) first = len;
    if (last > len)  last = len;
    /* second comparison of first and last values */
    if (first > last)
      return -1;
    count = last - first + 1;
    if (first > 0) {
        in_delete(str, 0, first);
        last -= first; /* adjust value of last */
        /* update len with new string length */
        len -= first;
    }
    if (last < len)
      in_delete(str, (last+1), (len-last));
    return 0;
}
int in_count_mid(char* str, unsigned int index, unsigned int count)
{
   unsigned int len = strlen(str);
    if (len == 0)
      return -1;
    if (index > len)
```

```
        index = len;
    if ((index + count) > len)
            count = len - index + 1;
    if (index > 0) {
        in_delete(str, 0, index);
        /* update len with new string length */
        len -= index;
    }
    if (count < len)
      in_delete(str, count, (len-count+1));
    return 0;
}
void pad_left(char* str, char pad_char, int num_chars)
{
   char pad_str[41];
   memset(pad_str, pad_char, num_chars);
   pad_str[num_chars] = '\0';
   in_insert(str, pad_str, 0);
}
void pad_right(char* str, char pad_char, int num_chars)
{
   char pad_str[41];
   memset(pad_str, pad_char, num_chars);
   pad_str[num_chars] = '\0';
   in_insert(str, pad_str, strlen(str)+1);
}
void trim_left(char* str, char ch)
{
   int i, count = 0;
   for (i = 0; ( (*(str+i) != '\0') && (*(str+i) == ch) ); i++)
      count++;
   in_delete(str, 0, count);
}
void trim_right(char* str, char ch)
{
   int i, count = 0;
   unsigned int len = strlen(str);
   for (i = len-1; ( (i >= 0) && (*(str+i) == ch) ); i--)
      count++;
   str[len-count] = '\0';
}
void trim_ends(char* str, char ch)
{
   trim_left(str, ch);
   trim_right(str, ch);
}
```

Listing 6.5 Source code for the application "tanslan.c"

```
/*
  C file that manipulates text in a set of files.
  Two files are involved: the file containing the names of
  the processed files, and the script file containing the
  operations to be performed on each file.
  If the output filename is omitted, the manipulated text is
  sent back to the input file.
  The script file contains the following patterns:
  D |<text>|   <== case sensitive deletion of <text>
  K |<text>|   <== case insensitive deletion of <text>
  R |<old text>|<new text>| replace <old text> with <new text>
*/
#include <stdio.h>
#include "conio.h"
#include "string.h"
#include "strops2.h"
#define TITLE "MULTI-FILE TEXT MANIPULATION"
#define VERSION "Version 1.0"
#define DEFAULT_SCRIPT_FILE "PAS2C.SRC"
#define MAX_SCRIPT_LINES 45
typedef char STRING[81];
typedef unsigned int word;
typedef unsigned char byte;
enum booleans { FALSE, TRUE };
typedef enum booleans boolean;
struct script_cmd {
         char op_char;
         STRING dtext;
     };
main()
{
   FILE *infile_var, *outfile_var, *script_var;
   STRING infile, outfile, script;
   STRING line, genstr;
   struct script_cmd script_lines[MAX_SCRIPT_LINES];
   word num_script, i;
   char go_on, quit_ch;
   boolean ok, use_same_script, have_read_script;
   go_on = 'Y';
   strcpy(script, DEFAULT_SCRIPT_FILE);
   have_read_script = FALSE;
   do {
    clrscr();
    center(TITLE,1);
```

```
center(VERSION,2);
printf("\n\n\n");;
do {
    printf("Enter source filename -> ");
    gets(infile); printf("\n");
    infile_var = fopen(infile, "rt");
    if (infile_var == NULL)  {
        printf("Cannot open file %s\n\n",infile);
        printf("Exit ? (Y/N) ");
        quit_ch = getche();
        if ((quit_ch == 'Y') || (quit_ch == 'y'))
           exit(0);
        printf("\n");
    }
} while (infile_var == NULL);
do {
    printf("Enter destination filename -> ");
    gets(outfile); printf("\n");
    outfile_var = fopen(outfile, "wt");
    if (outfile_var == NULL) {
        printf("Cannot open file %s\n\n",outfile);
        printf("Exit ? (Y/N) ");
        quit_ch = getche();
        if ((quit_ch == 'Y') || (quit_ch == 'y'))
           exit(0);
        printf("\n");
    }
} while (outfile_var == NULL);
do {
    printf("The default script filename is %s\n",script);
    printf("Enter script filename ");
    printf("press [Enter] for default) -> ");
    gets(genstr); printf("\n");
    if (strlen(genstr) != 0)  {
        strcpy(script,genstr);
        use_same_script = FALSE;
    }
    else
        use_same_script = TRUE;
    script_var = fopen(script, "rt");
    if (script_var == NULL)  {
        printf("Cannot open file %s\n\n",script);
        printf("Exit ? (Y/N) ");
        quit_ch = getche();
        if ((quit_ch == 'Y') || (quit_ch == 'y'))
           exit(0);
        printf("\n");
    }
```

```
    } while (script_var == NULL);
    if (have_read_script == FALSE ||
        use_same_script == FALSE)  {
        printf("Reading and processing the script file ...");
        num_script = 0; /* initialize script line counter*/
        while ((! feof(script_var)) &&
              (num_script < (MAX_SCRIPT_LINES-1)))  {
            fgets(genstr,80,script_var);
            get_script(genstr, &script_lines[num_script], &ok);
            if (ok == TRUE) num_script++;
        }
        have_read_script = TRUE;
        printf("\n");
    }
    fclose(script_var);
    if (num_script > 0)  {
      while (!feof(infile_var))  {
        fgets(line,80,infile_var);
        if (strlen(line) > 0)  {
          for (i = 0; i < num_script; i++)
            switch (script_lines[i].op_char) {
              case 'D':
                  delstr(line, script_lines[i].dtext);
                  break;
              case 'K':
                  kilstr(line, script_lines[i].dtext);
                  break;
              case 'R':
                  translate(line, script_lines[i].dtext);
                  break;
            }
        }
        printf("%s",line);
        fprintf(outfile_var,"%s",line);
      }
      fclose(infile_var);
      fclose(outfile_var);
    }
    printf("\n");
    printf("Want to process more files? (Y/N) ");
    go_on = getche();
   } while (!(go_on != 'Y' || go_on == 'y'));
}
int center(char* strng, byte line_num)
/* center string on specified line */
{
    gotoxy(40 - strlen(strng) / 2,line_num);
    printf("%s",strng);
```

```
}
int get_script(char* strng,
               struct script_cmd *script_line,
               boolean *good_line)
/* parse string into script commands */
{
   char ch;
   byte index1, index2, index3;
   STRING str0;
    ch = *strng;
    if (ch >= 'a' && ch <= 'z') ch += 'A' - 'a';
    *good_line = FALSE;
    if (ch == 'D' || ch == 'K' || ch == 'R')  {
        script_line->op_char = ch;
        index1 = pos_char(strng, '|', 0);
        if (index1 > -1)  {
            index2 = pos_char(strng, '|', index1 + 1);
            if (index2 > -1)  {
                strcpy(script_line->dtext,strng);
                in_pos_mid(script_line->dtext, index1+1,index2-1);
                *good_line = TRUE;
                if (ch == 'R')  {
                  index3 = pos_char(strng, '|', index2+1);
                  if (index3 > -1) {
                     strcpy(str0,strng);
                     strcat(script_line->dtext,"|");
                     in_pos_mid(str0,index2+1,index3-1);
                     strcat(script_line->dtext, str0);
                  }
                  else
                      *good_line = FALSE;
                }
            }
        }
    }
}
int delstr(char* strng, char* substr)
/* delete substring from string.  case sensitive. */
{
   int i;
   unsigned int len = strlen(substr);
   i = pos_str(strng, substr, 0);
   while (i > -1)  {
        in_delete(strng, i, len);
        i = pos_str(strng, substr, 0);
    }
}
int kilstr(char* strng, char* substr)
/* delete substring from string.  case insensitive. */
```

```
{
    int i;
    unsigned int len = strlen(substr);
    STRING strcopy;
    strcpy(strcopy, strng);
    /* convert both string copy and substring to uppercase */
    strupr(strcopy);
    strupr(substr);
    i = pos_str(strcopy, substr, 0);
    while (i > -1) {
        in_delete(strng, i, len);   /* delete from argument */
        in_delete(strcopy, i, len); /* delete from copy */
        i = pos_str(strcopy, substr, 0);
    }
}
int translate(char* strng, char* pattern)
/* replace a substring with another */
{
    unsigned int findlen, replen;
    int i;
    STRING find, replace;
    i = pos_char(pattern,'|',0);
    strcpy(find,pattern);
    in_delete(find,i,strlen(pattern)-i);
    strcpy(replace,pattern);
    in_delete(replace,0,i+1);
    findlen = strlen(find);
    replen = strlen(replace);
    i = pos_str(strng, find, 0);
    while (i > -1)  {
        in_delete(strng, i, findlen);
        in_insert(strng, replace, i);
        i = pos_str(strng, find, i+replen+1);
    }
}
```

Listing 6.6 Contents of file "pas2c.src"

```
R |Turbo Pascal|C|
R |(*|/*|
R |{|/*|
R |*)|*/|
R |}|*/|
R |BEGIN|{|
R |END|}|
R |FUNCTION|void|
R |PROCEDURE|void|
D |THEN|
D |DO|
```

```
R |REPEAT|do|
R |clrscr|clrscr()|
R |clreol|clreol()|
R |ClrScr|clrscr()|
R |FOR|for|
R |SQR(|^^(|
R | = | == |
R |:=|=|
R |WRITELN(|printf("\n |
R |WRITE(|printf(|
R |READLN(|scanf("%|
R |READ(|scanf("%|
R |'|"|
R |WRITELN|printf("\n");|
R |UNTIL|while not|
R |<>|!=|
R |NOT|!|
R |AND|&&|
R |WORD|word|
R | OR | || |
R |IF|if|
R |ELSE|else|
R |CASE|switch|
R |WHILE|while|
R |TO|; <=|
R |Length(|strlen(|
R |};|}|
```

Listing 6.7 Sample Turbo Pascal program used as an input for the "translan.c" program

```
PROGRAM SIEVE_TEST;
CONST size = 7000;
      MAX_ITER = 100;
VAR i, prime, k, count, iter : INTEGER;
    flags : ARRAY [0..size] OF BOOLEAN;
BEGIN
    WRITELN('START ',MAX_ITER,' iterATIONS');
    FOR iter := 1 TO MAX_ITER DO BEGIN
        count := 0;
        FOR i := 0 TO size DO flags[i] := TRUE;
        FOR i := 0 TO size DO
            IF flags[i] THEN BEGIN
                prime := k + k + 3;
                k := k + prime;
                WHILE k <= size DO BEGIN
                    flags[i] := FALSE;
                    k := k + prime
                END;
```

```
                count := count + 1
            END;
    END;
    WRITELN(^G,count,' primeS');
END.
```

Listing 6.8 Sample listing emitted by the TRANSLAN.C program

```
PROGRAM SIEVE_TEST;
CONST size == 7000;
      MAX_ITER == 100;
VAR i, prime, k, count, iter : INTEGER;
    flags : ARRAY [0..size] OF BOOLEAN;
{
    printf("\n "START ",MAX_ITER," iterATIONS");
    for iter = 1 ; <= MAX_ITER  {
        count = 0;
        for i = 0 ; <= size  flags[i] = TRUE;
        for i = 0 ; <= size
            if flags[i]  {
                prime = k + k + 3;
                k = k + prime;
                while k <= size  {
                    flags[i] = FALSE;
                    k = k + prime
                };
                count = count + 1
            };
    };
    printf("\n ^G,count," primeS");
}.
*/.
```

Listing 6.9 Manually-edited C program based on the listing emitted by the "translan.c" program

```
/* Sieve test program */
#include <stdio.h>
#define size 7001
#define MAX_ITER 100
#define TRUE 1
#define FALSE 0
main()
{
    int i, prime, k, count, iter;
    unsigned char flags[size];
    printf("START %d iterATIONS\n",MAX_ITER);
    for (iter = 0 ; iter < MAX_ITER; iter++)  {
        count = 0;
```

```
      for (i = 0; k < size; k++)
     flags[i] = TRUE;
      for (i = 0; k < size; k++) {
          if (flags[i] == 1)  {
              prime = k + k + 3;
              k = k + prime;
              while (k <= size)  {
                  flags[i] = FALSE;
                  k += prime;
              }
              count++;
          }
   }
   }
   printf("\n\007%d primeS\n",count);
}
```

CHAPTER

7

Advanced Pointer and Memory Allocation Techniques

Advanced techniques for manipulating pointers and handling memory allocation problems are discussed in this chapter. The concepts are explained in a practical setting by developing a dynamic string package. Along the way, advanced memory allocation techniques, the ins and outs of typecasting, and tricky pointer manipulation are also discussed. Although the code developed here is specifically for dynamic strings, many of the techniques can be applied to other memory allocation and pointer-handling problems as well.

If you came from the BASIC world before learning C, the one thing that probably puzzled you most was how C handled strings. You might have been a little shocked at how low level they were. Many long hours were probably spent painfully learning that before copying into a string, you must first make sure that enough space is allocated for it. In a complex program, this can be difficult to do. It would not be so bad, except the kind of errors resulting from inadequate or faulty memory allocation can be hard to spot and debug.

In this chapter you will find ways to alleviate some of these problems, and in fact, you will see a way to go above and beyond the kind of strings that BASIC provides. Developed here is a method for implementing strings not only of characters, but strings *of any type*. In addition, these generic strings can be programmed to automatically grow, if needed.

First let us review just how standard C strings work. The strings of C are just arrays of characters. The end of the string is indicated by a *null* character (having a value of 0x00). This kind of null termination has three important consequences. In order to find the length of a string, you must scan that string looking for the null character. For a supposedly efficient language like C, this is decidedly inefficient. The second consequence is that you cannot use strings to store any kind of binary data (e.g., part codes and quantities), because 0x00 (the *null* character) is a valid byte for types like integers and floats. The standard string functions provided with C would misinterpret such bytes as the end of the string. The third, and probably most important consequence, is that there is no way to tell how much space is available in the string when copying from one string to another. This makes writing general string functions very difficult.

Even with all these problems, C has one trump card. Since it is in many ways a low-level language, it is very powerful, so it is easy to build up strings that work very differently from the standard ones. We will start by examining how other languages handle strings. A classic example is the strings used in Turbo Pascal™ 3.0, which have the following equivalent C structure:

```
struct turbo_pascal_string {
   unsigned char currlen;
   unsigned char data[MAXSIZE];
};
```

In Turbo Pascal, the current length of the string is maintained by the compiler and run-time system, and is stored with the string. This makes finding the string length much more efficient than scanning for a *null* byte. However, two deficiencies exist: Because the length is stored in one byte, the strings cannot be over 255 characters long. Also, the dimensioned (i.e., maximum) size of the string must be determined at compile time. So while this representation solves some problems, it still has its limits.

Some BASICs use the equivalent of the following structure for their strings:

```
struct basic_string {
   unsigned int dimlen;
   unsigned int currlen;
   unsigned char data[CURRDIMSIZE];
};
```

This type of string can store up to 64K of data, and the storage for the string characters is allocated dynamically. The amount allocated can vary. The dimlen field indicates the number of bytes currently allocated, and the currlen field indicates the currently used length of the string. This turns out to be one of the best ways to represent strings, since they can be virtually any length (well, at least to 64K), and you are not limited as to the kind of data stored in the string.

DYNAMIC STRINGS

In implementing this type of string in C, you would probably use the following structure instead, and you would make a new type in the process:

```
typedef struct dynamic_str_struct {
   unsigned int dimlen;
   unsigned int currlen;
   unsigned char *data;
} dynamic_str;
```

Instead of storing the string data immediately after currlen, a pointer to the data is stored. This allows you to conveniently allocate and point to space for the string data, independent of the string structure itself.

To use such a string, you must first declare a variable of type **dynamic_str**, and then allocate space for the data. The number of bytes allocated is then stored in **dimlen**. The current length of the string is also set to 0. This value is then updated every time data is added or deleted from the string. As an example:

```
#include <alloc.h>
#include <string.h>
dynamic_str mystr;
char msg[] = "hello";
main() {
   mystr.data = malloc(25);
   mystr.dimlen = 25;
   mystr.currlen = 0;
   memcpy(mystr.data, msg, sizeof(msg));
   mystr.currlen += sizeof(msg);
}
```

Suppose there was not enough room to store the data? What would be nice is a way for the string to grow dynamically. The Turbo C function **realloc()** allows you to do just that. This function permits you to change the dimensions of an allocated block to make it bigger or smaller. If the new dimension is at least as large as the old one, the stored data is kept intact. Resizing to a smaller dimension causes the data to be truncated, with a resulting loss of information.

When enlarging a block, **realloc()** tries to obtain the additional bytes from those bytes directly following the existing data on the heap. In this case, no memory needs to be moved. If this is not possible, then the first free block on the heap of sufficient size is used. The existing data is then copied to the new location, and the old block is placed back on the heap.

This possible copying has two consequences. The first is that it represents the tradeoff in using this approach over a linked list, for example. In a linked list scheme, no memory needs to be copied; instead, pointers can just be manipulated. We will have more to say about this later.

The second consequence is that since data might be moved, the pointer variable pointing to the data may change its value, and you can no longer rely on it being the same after the **realloc()** call. For example, using the pointer **q** after the following code sequence would not be safe:

```
#include <alloc.h>
main() {
   char *p, *q;
   p = malloc(200);  /* allocate 200 bytes */
   q = p;            /* set pointers equal */
   p = realloc(300); /* enlarge the allocated space */
   /* q may now point to freed memory. Don't use !! */
}
```

This gets especially tricky if you use a dynamic string in a function. You are never quite sure when it is safe to point to it, as you may not know if the function uses **realloc()** or not. The way around this is to wrap another structure around the dynamic string pointer and always reference the string from that structure. This is exactly what you can do with the dynamic string structure given earlier. You might then have code like the following:

```
#include <alloc.h>
void myfunc(dynamic_str *s);
main() {
  dynamic_str mystr;
  mystr.data = malloc(200);
  myfunc(&mystr);
  if (mystr.data[1] == 'Y') /* then do something useful. */ ;
```

```
  /* ... */
}
void myfunc(dynamic_str *s)
{
  s->data = realloc(s->data,600);
}
```

Even though the data pointer might get changed by the **realloc()** call in **myfunc()**, the use of **mystr.data[i]** in the main program would still be perfectly safe.

GENERIC STRINGS

With the dynamic string type (just defined) and the appropriate functions, we can create strings that work much like those in most BASIC's. But you can also go one step further. One of the strengths of C is its typecasting, which is the ability to force one data type to be used like another. Typecasting is especially useful with pointers. An example is:

```
char *p;
int *i;
/* ... */
i = (int *) p;
```

The character data to which **p** points can be treated like integer data after the typecast. The last section showed a dynamic string structure that pointed to character strings. There is no reason you could not store other types of data using the same method. For instance, you could have strings of integers, floats, "widgets", or any structure we wish. You just have to make the compiler "think" that the data is of the appropriate type. This can be done by using pointer casting, storing the size of each element in the string, and scaling **dimlen** and **currlen** appropriately. You then arrive at the following general string structure:

```
typedef struct vstr_struct {
   unsigned int dimlen;     /* initial size of allocated space    */
   unsigned int currlen;    /* current length of string           */
   int esize;               /* size of string element             */
   int inc;                 /* no. of elements to add on resizing */
   void *data;              /* pointer to string data             */
} vstr;
```

The new structure is of type **vstr**, which stands for *variable-length string*. Because this structure can be used for any type of string, the data pointer is now typed as void.

We have added two fields to this structure, **esize** and **inc**. The **esize** field stores the number of bytes taken up by each element of the string. The **inc** field is used whenever you want to enlarge the string. It tells you how many additional elements to allocate whenever more space is requested. Since data may need to be copied during a **realloc()** call, you might as well add as many elements as possible to make the copy worthwhile. The **inc** field can be adjusted to optimize performance for your particular application. Wasted space results from making it too big, but more frequent copying (from having more calls to **realloc()**) results if it is too small.

Suppose you wished to make a string of integers. The following code sequence shows how to dimension a **vstr** for 25 integers and set the increment size to 10 integers:

```
#include <alloc.h>
void init_vstr(vstr s) {
   s.dimlen  = 25;
   s.currlen = 0;
   s.esize   = sizeof(int);
   s.inc     = 10;
   s.data    = calloc(25,sizeof(int));
}
```

Note the use of **sizeof()** to determine the number of bytes per element. Even though integers are two bytes on most PCs, you cannot be sure of that for other machines. The safest way is to let the compiler decide. Using the **sizeof()** function for this purpose is highly recommended.

POINTER CASTING

Now that you have dimensioned your integer string, how do you store and access data in it? The proper way is to use pointer casting, as is shown in the following example. It stores the 10 integers 0–9 in your integer string, and then walks through the string, printing them out:

```
/*  Simple dynamic string example  (vstrex1.c)   */
#include <stdio.h>
#include <alloc.h>
typedef struct vstr_struct {
   unsigned int dimlen;     /* initial size of allocated space    */
   unsigned int currlen;    /* current length of string           */
   int esize;               /* size of string element             */
   int inc;                 /* no. of elements to add on resizing */
   void *data;              /* pointer to string data             */
} vstr;
main() {
 vstr s;
 int i, *ip;
 s.dimlen  = 25;
 s.currlen = 0;
 s.esize   = sizeof(int);
 s.inc     = 10;
 s.data    = calloc(25,sizeof(int));
 for (i=0; i < 10; i++)
     ((int *)(s.data))[i] = i;  /* store data */
 s.currlen = 10; /* good thing to do, even if we don't use it here */
 for (i=0, ip = (int *)(s.data); i < 10; i++, ip++)
     printf("%d\n",*ip);
}
```

The string has been purposely accessed by two different methods. In the first case, **s.data** was cast directly to be of type integer pointer. You can then address the array pointed to by **s.data** as though it were an integer array. Recall how C does pointer arithmetic: whenever you add a number to a pointer variable, C determines the size of the type to which the pointer variable points. It then uses that as a scale factor in computing the actual number to add to the address stored in the pointer. If you have the code fragment **p = p+n**, where **p** is a pointer and **n** is an integer, the arithmetic actually taking place looks something like:

```
p = p + sizeof(*p) * n
```

The second thing to recall is that in C, the following statements are equivalent:

```
(1) x = *(p + n);
(2) x = p[n];
```

In the integer string example, the s.data pointer was first cast to an integer pointer to set the appropriate scale factor. Then you can use subscripting to access integers in the string.

The second loop in the example shows another method for accessing string data. In this case, an auxiliary integer pointer is declared, and then it is set it equal to **s.data** via typecasting. Then, as you are scanning the array, this pointer is incremented, causing the effective address stored in the pointer to be incremented by 2, the size of an integer. This second method is often more convenient than the first, because once you set the auxiliary pointer, you do not have to keep typecasting every time you access the array. However, this method can be dangerous if you use **realloc()** to change the size of the string, because the actual pointer to the data might change. If you were to execute code like the following, it would most likely crash your system:

```
vstr s;
int *p;
/* ... initialize s here ... */
p = (int *)s.data;    /* then set p to point to string data */
/* ... */
s.data = realloc(500);
*p = 57;    /* DON'T DO: p might be a dangling pointer here */
```

The best method for accessing general strings is by using macros. For the integer string, you might have a macro like:

```
#define int_array ((int *)(s.data))
```

You can then access a string element with **int_array[i]**, which gets expanded to ((int *)(s.data))[i]. One problem is that this macro assumes your vstr is named **s**. You could make a more general macro, as follows:

```
#define int_array(x) ((int *)(x.data))
```

and then write macros like **int_array(s)[i]**. None of these methods are entirely satisfactory, so it is best to just pick a convention and stick to it.

THE VSTR PACKAGE

Now that all of the basic concepts have been introduced, you are ready for the VSTR package. The code is given in Listings 7.1 and 7.2, and includes the following functions:

Function	Use
vstr_inited()	Checks for proper initialization
dimvstr()	Dimensions a vstr
clrvstr()	Either dimensions a vstr if it has not already been done, or sets the current length to 0
redimvstr()	Resizes a vstr
delvstr()	Frees up memory allocated for a vstr
copyvstr()	Copies one vstr into another
vstrdel()	Deletes elements from a vstr
vstrins()	Inserts elements into a vstr

All of these functions return a 1 if successful or a 0 if there was some kind of error (such as not enough memory, or an invalid set of parameters). Each function will be explained in turn.

Our **vstr** structure is a slight modification of the one we have been using, and looks like this:

```
typedef struct vstr_struct {
  char marker[5];          /* special initialization marker      */
  unsigned int dimlen;     /* initial size of allocated space    */
  unsigned int currlen;    /* current length of string           */
  int esize;               /* size of string element             */
  int inc;                 /* no. of elements to add on resizing */
  void *data;              /* pointer to string data             */
} vstr;
```

A five-byte initialization marker has been added. This marker is set to the special code "(@)%" when a **vstr** is first dimensioned. Whenever a **vstr** is passed to one of the functions above, a check is made to see whether the marker bytes have this code. If not, the **vstr** was not properly initialized. An error message is printed and the program aborts. This safety check is mostly for debugging purposes while you get used to using the vstr package, after which it can be removed. You may choose to just leave it in, as it does not cost that much overhead.

DIMENSIONING VSTR'S

The **dimvstr()** function is used to allocate memory for the **vstr**, and to set the **esize** and **inc** parameters. Suppose you wished to have a string of (x,y) points, like those used by the Turbo C polygon draw and fill routines. You could create a point data type and then allocate a string of points as follows:

```
typedef struct point_struct {
   int x,y;
} point;
vstr pstr;
dimvstr(&pstr, 50, sizeof(point), 5);
```

This would allocate room for 50 points, with a redimensioning increment of 5 points. Note again the recommended use of **sizeof()** to determine the element size of your vstr.

An alternative way to initialize a **vstr** is by the use of the **clrvstr()** function. This function has the same parameters as **dimvstr()**, and works as follows: suppose you have a **vstr v**. If **v.data** is null when **clrvstr()** is called, then the parameters are used to call **dimvstr()** to allocate memory for the string. If it is not NULL, it is assumed that the string has already been allocated, and **v.currlen** is merely set to 0, which means "empty string". The **clrvstr()** function is useful any time you wish to reuse a **vstr** inside a loop. When reusing a **vstr**, all you really need to do is simply set its current length to 0. It is not necessary to deallocate and then reallocate space for it, unless you have an old, large string you wish to free up for other uses. You must allocate memory the first time it is used, however. The following code fragment shows a convenient way to do this:

```
typedef struct point_struct {
   int x,y;
} point;
vstr pstr;
int i;
```

```
pstr.data = NULL;    /* get things started by doing this */
/* ... */
for (i=0; i<10; i++) {
   /* allocate or reset the string */
   clrvstr(&pstr,50,sizeof(point),5);
   /* ... some code that builds and uses pstr ... */
}
/* ... */
delvstr(&pstr);     /* free up memory for good */
```

After declaring a **vstr**, set its data pointer to NULL. You can then use **clrvstr()** any time after that to reset or allocate the string. Although you do not have to do it this way, this technique is useful as your program gets larger and it becomes more difficult to keep track of allocated memory. Following this convention can save you many hours of debugging. Unfortunately, you still have to remember to set the data pointer to NULL at the beginning of the program. You can do this by initializing the whole **vstr** structure at compile time.

```
vstr pstr = {
  {0,0,0,0,0},      /* Set marker to zero  */
  0,                /* Set dimlen to zero  */
  0,                /* Set currlen to zero */
  0,                /* Set esize to zero   */
  0,                /* Set inc to zero     */
  NULL              /* Most importantly, set data pointer to NULL */
};
```

The macro NULLVSTR defined in the **vstr** header file (Listing 7.1) does just this. An example of using it is:

```
#include <stdlib.h>
#include "vstr.h"
vstr pstr = NULLVSTR;
```

Remember that NULL (which is referenced by NULLVSTR) is a macro that is defined in **stdlib.h** (as well as in **stddef.h**, **stdio.h**, **mem.h**, and **alloc.h**). You must include one of these header files when using the NULLVSTR macro.

The function **redimvstr()** is used whenever you wish to change the size of memory allocated for a string. It is mainly for internal use by the other **vstr** functions, although you can use it directly as well. The **redimvstr()** function calls the Turbo C **realloc()** function to do the resizing. If you should make the string smaller, it also adjusts the currlen field to reflect any truncation that may take place. To use this routine you simply pass to it the address of the already allocated **vstr** and the new desired dimension, as in the following example:

```
#include <stdlib.h>
#include "vstr.h"
main() "
  vstr float_str = NULLVSTR;
  clrvstr(&float_str,20,sizeof(float),5); /* room for 20 floats */
  /* ... */
  redimvstr(&float_str,500);     /* now there's room for 500 */

  /* ... */
}
```

INSERTING AND DELETING WITH DYNAMIC STRINGS

Two functions missing from the standard C library for null-terminated strings are operations for inserting and deleting. The vstr package provides such functions for dynamic strings.

The **vstrins()** allows you to insert an array of elements at any position of a **vstr**. Before the insertion, it checks to see whether there is enough room allocated for the new length of the string. If there is not, it automatically calls **redimvstr()** for more. Because the array of elements to add is passed as a void pointer, you can insert any kind of data into the string. However, you must also pass the number of elements n, so it assumes that the array contains **n*esize** bytes of data. If **redimvstr()** cannot allocate more memory (e.g., when **inc = 0**), the data is inserted but the string may have to be truncated.

The position for inserting begins counting at 0, where 0 is the start of the string. If you give it a position equal to or greater than the current length of the string, then the data is effectively concatenated onto the end. The following example shows some data being inserted at the beginning, the middle, and the end of a **vstr**:

```
/*
   Example of inserting into a vstr  (vstrex2.c)
   Must link with: vstr.obj
*/
#include <stdio.h>
#include "vstr.h"
void main() {
 vstr v = NULLVSTR;
 clrvstr(&v,10,sizeof(char),4);  /* allocate 10 bytes */
 if (!vstrins(&v,0,"hello",5));  /* insert at the beginning */
 if (!vstrins(&v,3,"p me ",5));  /* insert in the middle */
 if (!vstrins(&v,v.currlen,"ad my truck",11)); /* add onto the end */
 if (!vstrins(&v,v.currlen,"",1));  /* add a null byte to end */
 printf("The vstr data is '%s'.\n",v.data);
 printf("The current length is %d bytes.\n", v.currlen);"
}
```

The program prints out the following when executed:

```
The vstr data is 'help me load my truck'.
The current length is 22 bytes.
```

There are several things to note. One is that the string is not terminated automatically with a null byte. In fact, that was one of the main reasons for developing dynamic strings. However, if the vstr holds character data that you would like to print out, you must add a null byte at the end so that **printf()** will work properly. You could not simply pass a 0 for the data; **vstrins()** is expecting an address instead. A convenient way of passing the address of a null byte is to simply pass a null string. The compiler will allocate memory for the null byte and then pass its address to **vstrins()**.

The second thing to note is that even though you originally allocated only 10 bytes for your string, the final result contains more than this. You did not have to explicitly resize the vstr; **vstrins()** did that for you.

Figure 7.1 shows the resizing process. The resizing algorithm for **vstrins()** uses max(**numbytesneeded,inc)** for the number of bytes to add to the **vstr**. Here,

numbytesneeded is the number of additional bytes needed in the string to accommodate the insertion, and **inc** is the **inc** field of the vstr structure. In the previous example above, **inc** was set to 4 bytes. When the string **ad my truck** was inserted, the string space was already full, so **vstrins()** knew that it would have to add some bytes. Since the number of bytes to add (11) was bigger than **inc** (4), exactly 11 bytes were added to the dimension of the string. At this point, the string is again full with 21 bytes of data. When the null byte is then concatenated to the end, **vstrins()** must again redimension the string, but this time, **inc** bytes are added, since 4 is greater than 1. The final string contains room for 25 bytes. The current length of the string, however, is 22 bytes, as the output shows.

Deleting elements from a vstr is essentially the reverse process, except the vstr is not resized, and no memory is returned to the heap. The currlen field does reflect the change, though. The following example does the opposite of the insert example:

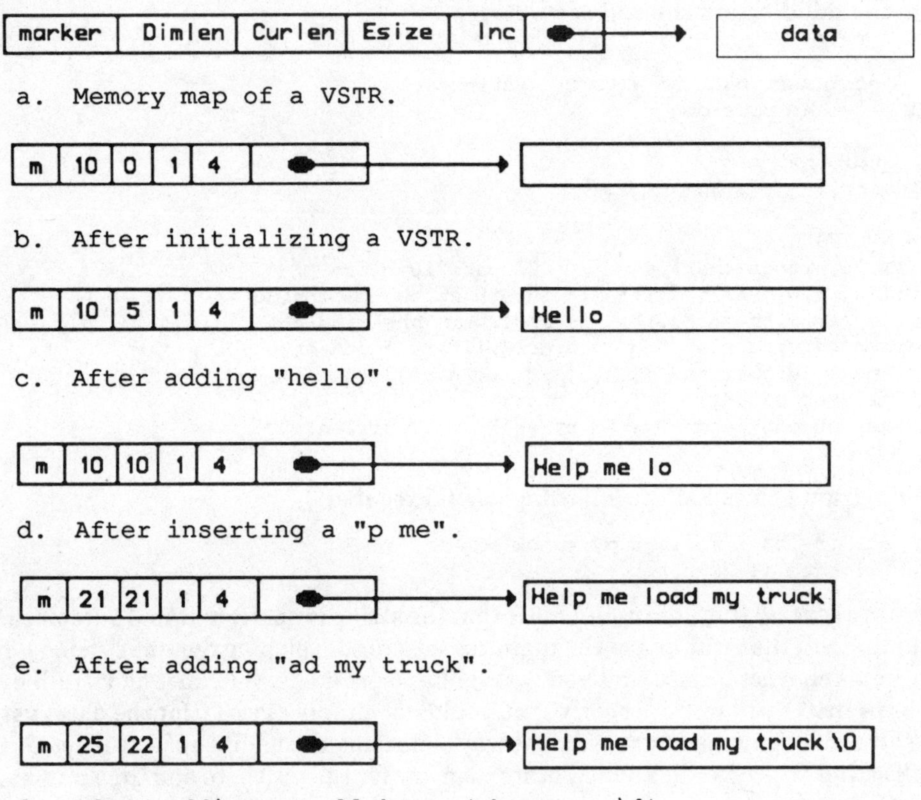

Figure 7.1 Resizing a VSTR

```
/*
   Example of deleting data in a vstr  (vstrex3.c)
   Must link with: vstr.obj
*/
#include <stdio.h>
#include "vstr.h"
void main() {
 vstr v = NULLVSTR;
 clrvstr(&v,30,sizeof(char),4);  /* allocate 30 bytes */
 /* load up the vstr */
 vstrins(&v,0,"help me load my truck",21);
 vstrins(&v,v.currlen,"",1);  /* add null byte */
 vstrdel(&v,3,5);    /* delete "p me " */
 vstrdel(&v,5,11);  /* delete "ad my truck" */
 printf("The vstr data is '%s'.\n",v.data);
 printf("The current length is %d bytes.\n", v.currlen);
}
```

This program would print out the following when executed:

```
The vstr data is 'hello'.
The current length is 6 bytes.
```

DYNAMIC STRINGS VERSUS LINKED LISTS

Before using any data structure, you should always consider the alternatives and tradeoffs involved. The generic dynamic strings presented are not usually discussed in most textbooks on data structures, but nevertheless they are quite viable for many applications. These applications are ones which are traditionally associated with linked lists.

One such application is storing a list of points, as might be used to represent objects in a CAD package. A simple example of this is shown later on, but here, let us concentrate on the difference between using linked lists and dynamic strings.

For both methods, you would probably create a **point** structure, which might, for example, hold the (x,y) coordinate of the point:

```
typedef struct point_struct {
   int x,y;
} point;
```

Using linked lists, you could represent a list of points by creating a point_list type, which is a structure holding the (x,y) coordinates and a link to the next point:

```
typedef struct point_link_struct {
   point data;
   point_link_struct *next;
} point_list;
```

Let us examine the cost of such a representation. As far as memory is concerned, each element has additional overhead to store a pointer to the next point in the list. In Turbo C, this overhead is two bytes for the tiny, small, and medium memory models, and four bytes for the other memory models.

There is also another type of overhead to consider: the time to access each point in the list. Basically, a linked list is a sequential data type. You must sequentially scan down the list, chasing the "next" pointers in order to access any given point in the list. How does this compare with using dynamic strings?

If you were to use the generic string package, the only overhead is the size of the vstr structure, from 15 to 17 bytes (if we keep the marker bytes, 10 to 12 bytes if we do not), depending on the memory model. This is a fixed cost, regardless of the length of the string. You can store a list of points very efficiently this way. Access to any point is also very efficient, since it involves just a simple subscript operation (basically a multiplication plus an addition). Another plus is that you can conveniently use some of the built-in array functions provided by Turbo C, such as **qsort()**, **bsearch()**, and so on.

The tradeoff with the string approach is in insertion and deletion, which require memory to be shuffled. For linked lists, just some pointer manipulation is needed, which is far less costly. Also, if **realloc()** is called to expand the string, then there may be some copying. But just how costly is moving memory? On the IBM PC, there are special operations that can move blocks of memory in a single instruction. This is fast enough not to be noticeable in most situations. The only problem, (and the only restriction with the generic strings), is that each block of memory can be up to only 64K bytes in size. For many applications, this is plenty of room. Note that nothing stops you from having more memory effectively associated with the string. You could, for instance, have an array of pointers, each pointing to a string.

AN EXAMPLE: REPRESENTING POLYGONS WITH DYNAMIC STRINGS

We will now show a complete example of using strings for things other than characters. In this example, a series of points in graphics mode are collected into a **vstr** using the mouse. We then call the Turbo C **fillpoly()** routine to draw a closed polygon on the screen. Thefollowing program uses the mouse package developed earlier, along with the vstr package and the Turbo C graphics package:

```
/*
   Example of storing polygons via vstr's  (vstrex4.c)
   Must link with: mouse.obj, vstr.obj, graphics.lib
*/
#include <graphics.h>
#include <stdio.h>
#include "mouse.h"
#include "vstr.h"
/* Convenient macro to access point data */
#define POINT ((point *)(v.data))
typedef struct {
  int x,y;
} point;
void main()
{
```

```
int gd=DETECT, gm=0;
unsigned int k;
vstr v = NULLVSTR;
point p;
initgraph(&gd,&gm,"");
init_mouse(MOUSE_NEEDED, gd, gm);
clrvstr(&v,30,sizeof(point),5);
do {
   while(!(k = mouse_trigger(0)));
   if (k == LEFT_MOUSE_REL) {
      p.x = mouse_grph_x;
      p.y = mouse_grph_y;
  vstrcat(&v,&p);
  /* if we have more than one point, draw a line */
  if (v.currlen > 1) {
         mouse_off(1);
     line(POINT[v.currlen-1].x,POINT[v.currlen-1].y,
      POINT[v.currlen-2].x,POINT[v.currlen-2].y);
     mouse_on(1);
  }
  else { /* draw starting pixel */
     mouse_off(1);
     putpixel(p.x, p.y, WHITE);
     mouse_on(1);
  }
   }
} while (k != RIGHT_MOUSE_REL);
vstrcat(&v,v.data);   /* make a closed polygon boundary */
setfillstyle(8,4);    /* cross hatch fill, red color    */
mouse_off(1);
fillpoly(v.currlen, (int far *)(v.data));
mouse_on(1);
while(!(k = mouse_trigger(0)));
mouse_reset();
closegraph();
/* print out the points in text mode */
for (k=0; k < v.currlen; k++) {
    printf("%d %d\n", POINT[k].x, POINT[k].y);
}
}
```

The program works by waiting for a series of left mouse button releases. Lines are drawn as the mouse button is released. The end points of the lines are stored in **vstr v**, which is set up to hold a collection of points. This process is continued until a right mouse button release, at which time the polygon represented by the lines is filled.

The Turbo C **fillpoly()** routine requires that the polygon points represent a closed boundary. You can do that by copying the first point onto the end of the point string. The **fillpoly()** routine is then called with the fill style set to cross hatching, and the fill color set to red. After another button release (either left or right), the screen is set back to text mode and the point coordinates are printed out.

Note the use of the macro **vstrcat()**. This macro is available in **vstr.h** and is defined as follows:

```
#define vstrcat(v,e)  vstrins(v, (v)->currlen,e,1)
```

The **vstrcat()** function allows you to add exactly one element onto the end of a string. This is very convenient for situations just like the previous example.

This example shows quite clearly a situation in which using strings is far superior to linked lists. In this case, the data structure perfectly matches that required by **fillpoly()**. Yet, you still are able to allocate the number of points dynamically and allow an arbitrary number of points per polygon.

Note the typecasting that was needed. You had to typecast the string data pointer as an integer pointer, since this is what **fillpoly()** is expecting. Also, the order of (x,y) in the point structure is very critical, as it is the order required by **fillpoly()**. You are taking advantage of knowing the exact memory representation used by **fillpoly()** for the points array.

It does not take much imagination to see that this simple example could be extended to become an actual CAD package, with which you could draw and store objects based on line segments. In later chapters you will see how to write a series of such strings to a file, allowing the building of a database of line figures.

Listing 7.1 Source code for file "vstr.h"

```
/* Variable length string toolkit header file (vstr.h) */
/* Convenient macro to concatenate one element to end of string */
#define vstrcat(v,e)  vstrins(v, (v)->currlen,e,1)
/* Macro to initialze a vstr at compile time */
#define NULLVSTR {{0,0,0,0,0},0,0,0,0,NULL}
/*
 *  Generic "virtual" (ie. variable length, dynamic) string package
 */
typedef struct vstr_struct {
  char marker[5];           /* special initialization marker */
  unsigned int dimlen;      /* initial size of allocated space */
  unsigned int currlen;     /* current length of string (in elements) */
  int esize;                /* size of string element */
  int inc;                  /* no. of elements to add on resizing */
  void *data;               /* pointer to string data */
} vstr;
extern int vstr_inited(vstr *v);
extern int dimvstr(vstr *v, unsigned int dimlen, int esize, int inc);
extern int redimvstr(vstr *v, unsigned int newdimlen);
extern int clrvstr(vstr *v, unsigned int dimlen, int esize, int inc);
extern int delvstr(vstr *v);
extern int copyvstr(vstr *t, vstr *s);
extern int vstrdel(vstr *v, int p, int n);
extern int vstrins(vstr *v, int p, void *s, int n);
```

Listing 7.2 Source code for file "vstr.c"

```
/***************************************************************
 *  Variable length string toolkit  (vstr.c)
 ***************************************************************/
#include <stddef.h>
#include <stdio.h>
#include <alloc.h>
#include <conio.h>
#include <string.h>
#include <process.h>
#include "vstr.h"
#define MAX(a,b)  ((a) > (b) ? (a) : (b))
#define MIN(a,b)  ((a) < (b) ? (a) : (b))
static char vinitflag[] = "(@)%";   /* special internal marker code */
int vstr_inited(vstr *v)
/* Checks for proper initialization, if not, it aborts the program */
{
   if (strcmp(v->marker,vinitflag))  {
      printf("Serious error: vstr not init'ed\nPress return ...");
      getch();
      exit(1);
   }
   return 1;
}
int dimvstr(vstr *v, unsigned int dimlen, int esize, int inc)
/*
   Dimension a virtual string to be initially dimlen elements long,
   with each element being esize bytes wide, and adding up to
   inc bytes during a redimension.  If inc = 0, it means the string
   will not be allowed to grow beyond its allocated space.
   Returns 1 on success, 0 if any errors occur.
*/
{
   if ((v->data = calloc(dimlen, esize)) != NULL) {
      v->dimlen = dimlen;
      v->currlen = 0;
      v->inc = inc;
      v->esize = esize;
      strcpy(v->marker, vinitflag);  /* set special marker flag */
      return 1;
   }
   else return 0;  /* calloc failed */
}
int redimvstr(vstr *v, unsigned int newdimlen)
/*
   Redimensions a vstr to the new dimension length newdimlen.
   If v->inc = 0, or a can't get more memory, a 0 is returned,
   else, a 1 is returned.  If the new length is shorter than
```

```
   the old current length of the string, the string is truncated,
   and data is lost.
*/
{
   if (vstr_inited(v)) {
      if ((v->inc) &&  /* check this flag first */
         (v->data = realloc(v->data, newdimlen*v->esize)) != NULL) {
         v->dimlen = newdimlen;
         /* possibly truncate data */
         v->currlen = MIN(v->currlen, newdimlen);
         return 1;  /* success */
      }
   }
   return 0;  /* failed */
}
int clrvstr(vstr *v, unsigned int dimlen, int esize, int inc)
/*
   If v->data is NULL, the string is dimensioned using the given parms
   by calling dimvstr.  If v->data is not NULL, the current length
   of the already allocated data is set to zero.
   An 0 is returned if any errors occur, else a 1 is returned.
*/
{
   if (v->data == NULL) {
      return dimvstr(v, dimlen, esize, inc);
   }
   else {
     if (vstr_inited(v)) {
        v->currlen = 0;
        return 1;
     }
     return 0;
   }
}
int delvstr(vstr *v)
/* De-allocates the data portion of a vstr.
   Sets current length to zero.
   If v->data already = NULL,  nothing happens.
   An error code is returned if the array has never been
   dimensioned and v->data != NULL.
   Does not free up any dynamic memory pointed to by the data,
   so that better have been done before calling this.
*/
{
   if (v->data != NULL) {
     if (vstr_inited(v)) {
        free(v->data);
        v->data = NULL;
        v->currlen = 0;
        return 1;
```

```
      }
      else return 0;
   }
   return 1;
}
int copyvstr(vstr *t, vstr *s)
/*
   Copies source virtual string s into target virtual string t.
   If t->data comes in NULL, then memory for t will be allocated
   and t will take on the same sizing parms as s, else the old
   data in t is replaced, and t will be enlarged if necessary.
   Errors return 0, else 1 is returned.
*/
{
   if (vstr_inited(s)) {
      if (clrvstr(t, s->dimlen, s->esize, s->inc)) {
         memmove(t->data, s->data, s->currlen*s->esize);
         t->currlen = s->currlen;
         return 1; /* successful */
      }
   }
   return 0;  /* default is error */
}
int vstrdel(vstr *v, int p, int n)
/*
   Deletes UP TO n elements from virtual string v at pos'n p.  If p
   is out of range nothing happens.  If n <= 0, nothing happens.
   An error code of 0 is returned if the string has never been
   dimensioned, else a 1 is returned.
*/
{
    int k;
    char *t;
    if (vstr_inited(v)) {
       if ((p>=0) && (n>0) && (p < v->currlen)) { /* in range ? */
          if ( (k = p+n) >= v->currlen ) {
             v->currlen = p;    /* chop off end */
          }
          else {
            t = (char *)v->data;
            memmove(t+p*v->esize, t+k*v->esize, (v->currlen-k)*v->esize);
            v->currlen -= n;
          }
          return 1;  /* successful */
       }
    }
    return 0;  /* error */
}
int vstrins(vstr *v, int p, void *s, int n)
/*
```

```
    Inserts the data pointed to by s into vstr v.  It is assumed
    that the data has the same element size as v.  Up to n elements
    are inserted, starting at position p, (counted by zero).
    If p >= v->currlen, then the data is concatenated on the end.
    If we need to allocate more memory, then MAX(n,v->inc) elements
    are added.  However, if v->inc is zero, then the data will be
    inserted, but data will be truncated off the end of the string.
    Returns 0 if there's an error, else a 1 is returned.
*/
{
    char *t;
    int addsize;
    /* check for initialization and p in range */
    if (vstr_inited(v) && p >= 0) {
       addsize = v->currlen + n - v->dimlen;
       if (addsize > 0) {
          /* we need more room */
          if (v->inc != 0) {  /* are we allowed to add any? */
              addsize = MAX(addsize, v->inc);
              if (!redimvstr(v, v->dimlen+addsize)) return 0;
          }
          else {  /* string not enlarged, so data will be truncated */
             if (p < v->currlen) {
                t = (char *)v->data; /* point to start of data */
                if (n > (v->currlen-p)) {
                   n = v->currlen - p; /* we'll be replacing */
                }
                else {  /* make room for inserted data */
                  memmove(t+(p+n)*v->esize, t+p*v->esize, v->currlen-p-n);
                }
                memmove(t+p*v->esize, s, n*v->esize);  /* copy in source */
                return 1;  /* success */
             }
             return 0;  /* can't concatenate on end, no room */
          }
       }
       t = (char *)v->data;   /* point to start of data */
       if (p >= v->currlen) { /* just concatenate */
          p = v->currlen;
       }
       else {  /* make room for inserted data */
         memmove(t+(p+n)*v->esize, t+p*v->esize, (v->currlen-p)*v->esize);
       }
       memmove(t+p*v->esize, s, n*v->esize);  /* copy in source */
       v->currlen += n;
       return 1;
    }
    else return 0;
}
```

CHAPTER

8

Generic Programming in Turbo C

Turbo C supports generic programming and provides a number of generic routines to perform sorting and searching. This chapter briefly looks at the these routines, discusses the methods to write generic functions, and presents a library of additional generic sort and search routines.

Generic programming is one of the techniques fostered by modern software engineering. The basic idea is to develop routines that are able to work with as many different types as possible. Certain algorithms can be applied to all data types, but others are still more limited to a certain class. For example, sorting and searching algorithms can be applied to numeric and nonnumeric types, such as integers, reals, characters, and strings. By contrast, routines that return statistics like the minimum, maximum, and mean value are obviously limited to the numeric data types. In either case, when generic routines are developed for some or all data types, you need not rewrite routine versions that are customized to the recipient data types. The benefits from generics are enormous and truly time-saving.

GENERIC ROUTINES

The generic sorting and searching functions in Turbo C are prototyped in **stdlib.h**:

1. **qsort** sorts an array using the QuickSort algorithm. The **qsort** function is prototyped as:

```
void qsort(void *base, size_t nelem, size_t width,
           int (*fcmp)(const void*, const void*));
```

The **base** parameter is the pointer to the array's base address (i.e., 0th element). The **nelem** and **width** parameters provide the **qsort** routine with the number of elements to be sorted and the size of each element, respectively. The **fcmp** is a pointer to a function that compares any two array elements. The general form for the **fcmp** function is:

```
int fmcp(const void *element1, const void *element2)
```

The result of the comparison function falls into one of these three categories:

Result of fcmp	Significance
`< 0`	`element1 <  element2`
`= 0`	`element1 == element2`
`> 0`	`element1 >  element2`

2. **bsearch** performs a binary search for an element in a perfectly ordered array. The **bsearch** function is prototyped as:

```
void *bsearch(void *key, void *base,
              size_t nelem, size_t width,
              int (*fcmp)(const void*, const void*));
```

   The **key** parameter is a pointer to the sought element. The **base** parameter is the pointer to the array's base address (i.e., 0'th element). The **nelem** and **width** parameters provide the search routine with the number of elements to be scanned and the size of each element, respectively. The **fcmp** is a pointer to a function that compares any two array elements. The **bsearch** function returns a pointer to the location of the matching element if one is found; otherwise, a NULL pointer is returned.

3. **lsearch** performs a linear search for an element in an array. The **bsearch** function is declared as:

```
void *lsearch(void *key, void *base,
              size_t nelem, size_t width,
              int (*fcmp)(const void*, const void*));
```

   The **key** parameter is a pointer to the sought element. The **base** parameter is the pointer to the array's base address (i.e., 0th element). The array need not be sorted for this search routine to properly work. The **nelem** and **width** parameters provide the search routine with the number of elements to be examined and the size of each element, respectively. The **fcmp** is a pointer to a function that compares any two array elements. The **lsearch** function returns a pointer to the location of the matching element, if one is found. If no match is found, the key element is appended to the array.

4. **lfind** performs a linear search for an element in an array. The **bsearch** function is declared as:

```
void *lfind(void *key, void *base,
            size_t nelem, size_t width,
            int (*fcmp)(const void*, const void*));
```

   The **key** parameter is a pointer to the sought element. The **base** parameter is the pointer to the array's base address. The array need not be sorted for this search routine to properly work. The **nelem** and **width** parameters provide the search routine with the number of elements to be scanned and the size of each element, respectively. The **fcmp** is a pointer to a function that compares any two array elements. The **lfind** function returns a pointer to the location of the matching element if one is found; otherwise, a NULL pointer is returned.

The following simple program demonstrates the use of **qsort** and **bsearch** with an array of integers. The program displays the array of integers in ascending order and then indicates the index of the array that contains the integer 34. The function **intcmp** is included to perform comparison on int type elements. The source code is as follows:

```
#include <stdio.h>
#include <stdlib.h>
main()
{
   int num[] = { 12, 34, 5, 67, 232, 22, 133 };
   int i, n = sizeof(num) / sizeof(int);
   int j = 67;
   int intcmp(const void*, const void*);
   qsort(num, n, sizeof(int), intcmp);
   for (i = 0; i < n; i++)
      printf("%d  %3d\n", i, num[i]);
   i = (int*) bsearch(&j, num, n, sizeof(int), intcmp) - (int*) num;
   printf("\nFound %d in array index number %d\n", j, i);
}
int intcmp(const void *i, const void *j)
{
    return (*((int*)i) - *((int*)j));
}
```

The next program sorts and searches an array of strings. The **qsort** routine is employed to put the array in order. The **lfind** is utilized to perform a linear search for the string **Paul**. The program displays the array index containing the sought string and then displays the ordered string. The **string.h** header is used since the strcmp function is invoked in comparing strings:

```
#include <stdio.h>
#include <stdlib.h>
#include "string.h"
main()
{
   char str[10][11] = { "Robert", "Bobbi", "Keith", "James", "David",
                "Kim", "Thomas", "Paul", "Peter", "John" };
   char name[11] = "Kim";
   int i, n = 10;
   unsigned found;
   qsort(str, n, 11, strcmp); /* sort array */
   /* search for name */
   found = ((unsigned) lfind(name, str, (size_t*) n, 11, strcmp) -
        (unsigned) str) / sizeof(name);
   printf("found %s in index %u\n\n", name, found);
```

```
   for (i = 0; i < n; i++)
      printf("%d  %s\n", i, str[i]);
}
```

The next program applies the generic sort and search routines to structures. The program defines the structure **mail_rec**. A structured array of five members is initialized, sorted, and subjected to a binary search. The structured array is sorted based on its string-typed field. The program displays the array index of the matching data and then displays the array in ascending order:

```
#include <stdio.h>
#include <stdlib.h>
#include "string.h"
struct mail_rec {
      char name[31];
      unsigned int age;
      double wt;
      };
typedef struct mail_rec mail;
int struct0_cmp(const void* e1, const void* e2)
{
   return strcmp( ((mail*)e1)->name, ((mail*)e2)->name);
}
main()
{
   mail person[5] = { { "Namir", 34, 180.0 },
                      { "Bobbi", 31, 165.0 },
                      { "Keith", 29, 155.0 },
                      { "James", 35, 190.0 },
                      { "David", 41, 190.0 } };
   mail who = { "Keith", 29, 155.0 };
   unsigned i, n = 5;
   unsigned found;
   qsort(person, n, sizeof(mail), struct0_cmp);
   found = ( (unsigned) bsearch(&who, person, n, sizeof(mail),
                                struct0_cmp) -
         (unsigned) person) / sizeof(mail);
   printf("Found %s in index %d\n\n", who.name, found);
   for (i = 0; i < n; i++)
      printf("%d  %s is %2d years old and weighs %lg bounds \n",
            i, person[i].name, person[i].age, person[i].wt);
}
```

BUILDING GENERIC PROGRAMS

This section examines the basic components of building your own generic sorting and searching functions. As it turns, out the building blocks for such software components are fairly simple.

The first and most important aspect is manipulating the void-typed pointers that are used to pass arrays of data and single data items. Since they are declared void, the compiler cannot perform any needed pointer arithmetic. The solution lies in typecasting these void pointers into unsigned char pointers and using the later throughout the generic routine. This allows the use of a data type that occupies a single byte. Using the typecast pointers, the compiler is able to successfully perform pointer arithmetic. Pointer arithmetic in generic routines is just a bit more elaborate than in nongeneric ones. To access the i'th element, given the size of each element), the general form is:

```
address of i'th element = ptr + i * element_size
```

The second component of generic routines handles assigning and copying array elements. It requires using the **memmove** function to copy one or more elements.

The third component is the use of local scalar or array variables. This is performed by first declaring unsigned char pointers and then using them with **malloc** or **calloc** (or even **realloc**) in dynamic memory allocation. It is highly recommended that the free function be utilized to deallocate the dynamic memory before the generic routine exits.

The fourth component is using the comparison function to carry out decision making that involves generic data. This is rather simple and appears in the general form of:

```
(*fcmp)((ptr + i * elmsize),(ptr + j * elmsize))
```

where **ptr** is the typecast pointer, elmsize is the element size in bytes, and i and **j** are indices of the compared generic array elements.

The following is the source code for a generic shell sort routine. This routine is slower than the qsort, but it requires far less stack space since no recursion takes place:

```
void gen_shell_sort(void *base, int nelem, int elmsize,
                    int (*fcmp)(const void*, const void*))
{
    int i, j, jump = nelem;
    unsigned char done;
    unsigned char *tempo, *ptr = (unsigned char *) base;
    tempo = (unsigned char *) malloc(elmsize);
    while (jump > 1) {
        jump /= 2;
        do {
            done = 1;
            for (j = 0; j < (nelem - jump); j++) {
                i = j + jump;
                if ((*fcmp)((ptr+i*elmsize),(ptr+j*elmsize)) < 0) {
                    /* swap i'th and j'th elements */
```

```
                done = 0;
                memmove(tempo, (ptr+i*elmsize), elmsize);
                memmove((ptr+i*elmsize), (ptr+j*elmsize), elmsize);
                memmove((ptr+j*elmsize), tempo, elmsize);
            }
        }
    } while (!done);
  }
  free(tempo); /* restore dynamic memory */
}
```

SUPPLEMENTARY GENERIC SORT/SEARCH LIBRARY

Listings 8.1 and 8.2 contains the source code for **gensort.h** and **gensort.c**, a library of supplementary sort and search routines. The library contains three sets of functions:

1. **Functions that compare two elements** These functions include ones for the int, unsigned int, long, unsigned long, and double types. These functions are rather trivial, but are required in generic programming. They can serve as a nucleus for additional type-comparing functions that you may want to insert.
2. **Generic sort routines** These include the following:

   a. **gen_shell_sort** sorts an array using the Shell-Metzner algorithm. The function is declared as:

   ```
   void gen_shell_sort(void *base, int nelem, int elmsize,
                       int (*fcmp)(const void*, const void*));
   ```

   The base parameter is the pointer to the array's base address (i.e., 0th element). The nelem and elmsize parameters provide the sort routine with the number of elements to be sorted and the size of each element, respectively. The **fcmp** is a pointer to a function that compares any two array elements. The parameter list of this sort routine is identical to that of **qsort**.

   b. **gen_insert_sor** inserts a new element in an array and maintains the sorted order. The function is declared as:

   ```
   int gen_insert_sort(void *base, void* key,
                       int *nelem, int elmsize,
                       int (*fcmp)(const void*, const void*))
   ```

   The base parameter is the pointer to the array's base address. The key parameter points to the inserted element. The nelem and elmsize parameters provide the sort routine with the number of elements to be sorted and the size of each element, respectively. The **fcmp** is a pointer to a function that compares any two array elements.

   c. **gen_merge_sort** merges one sorted array with another. The function is declared as:

   ```
   int gen_merge_sort(void *base1,  void *base2,
                      int *nelem1, int nelem2,
   ```

```
                int elmsize,
                int (*fcmp)(const void*, const void*))
```

The basel parameter is the pointer to the first array's base address. The base2 parameter is the pointer to the second array's base address (i.e., 0th element). The neleml, nelem2, and elmsize parameters provide the sort routine with the number of elements to be sorted and the size of each element, respectively. The **fcmp** is a pointer to a function that compares any two array elements. The first array returns with the elements of the second array placed in their proper locations.

d. **gen_reverse_array** reverses the order of the elements of an array. The function is declared as:

```
5int gen_reverse_array(void *base, int nelem, int elmsize)
```

The base parameter is the pointer to the first array's base address (i.e., 0'th element). The nelem and elmsize parameters provide the sort routine with the number of elements to be reversed and the size of each element, respectively.

3. **Generic search routines** This includes the following:

a. **bidir_find** performs bidirectional linear search in an array. This function is somewhat similar to Turbo C's **lfind** linear search function. The basic difference lies in the type of algorithm employed. The **bidir_find** resorts to the statistical probability of finding an element in an array, assuming that all elements have the same likelihood to be sought. Statistical analysis shows that averaging the indices of such searches points to the median member and the region around it. Thus, the median element of the array is the first element to be examined. The next search steps employs two indices to alternate the search below and above the median element. With each unsuccessful iteration, the search indices move further away from the median and closer towards the array's upper and lower limits.

The function is declared as:

```
int bidir_find(void *key, void *base,
               int nelem, int elmsize,
               int (*fcmp)(const void*, const void*))
```

The key parameter points to the inserted element. The base parameter is the pointer to the array's base address (i.e., 0th element). The nelem and elmsize parameters provide the sort routine with the number of elements to be examined and the size of each element, respectively. The **fcmp** is a pointer to a function that compares any two array elements. The function **bidir_find** returns the index of the matching array element or -1 if no match is found.

b. **bidir_search** performs bidirectional linear search in an array. This function uses the same algorithm as **bidir_find**. The difference is that if the element is not found in the array, it is added as the new last array member.

The function is declared as:

```
int bidir_search(void *key, void *base,
                 int *nelem, int elmsize,
                 int (*fcmp)(const void*, const void*))
```

The key parameter points to the inserted element. The base parameter is the pointer to the array's base address (i.e., 0th element). The nelem and elmsize parameters provide the sort routine with the number of elements to be examined and the size of each element, respectively. The **fcmp** is a pointer to a function that compares any two array elements. The function **bidir_search** returns the index of the matching array element, or the index of the newly added array member if there is no match.

c. **set_index_table** initializes the index search table based on the data of a sorted array. The function is defined as:

```
int set_index_table(void *table, int *index, void *base,
                    int tbl_size, int nelem, int elmsize)
```

The table parameter is the pointer to the index table. The index parameter is the pointer to the array of indices used by the table. The base parameter is the pointer to the array's base address (i.e., 0th element). The tbl_size is the assigned table size. The nelem and elmsize parameters provide the sort routine with the number of elements to be examined and the size of each element, respectively. If there are too few array elements, this function returns 0; otherwise, it returns 1.

d. **search_index_table** searches for a given datum in a sorted array by using an index search table to accelerate the search. The entries of the index table serve to narrow the array index range to be examined. Within that given range, the binary search algorithm is applied to accelerate the search even further.

The function is declared as:

```
int search_index_table(void *key, void *table,
                       int *index, void *base,
                       int tbl_size, int nelem,
                       int elmsize,
                       int (*fcmp)(const void*, const void*))
```

The key parameter points to the sought element. The table parameter is the pointer to the index table. The index parameter is the pointer to the array of indices used by the table. The base parameter is the pointer to the array's base address (i.e., 0th element). The **tbl_size** is the assigned table size. The nelem and elmsize parameters provide the sort routine with the number of elements to be examined and the size of each element, respectively. An unsuccessful search returns -1; otherwise, the array index of the matching element is returned.

Examples follow for using the different routines in the **gensort.c** library, using a series of short, self-contained programs. The programs employ arrays of various types that are internally initialized.

The following program sorts an array of integers using the generic shell sort routine. The array is examined using the **bidir_find** function to locate the array member storing the integer 22. The index of the matching array element and the list of the sorted array are displayed:

```
#include <stdio.h>
#include <stdlib.h>
#include "string.h"
```

```
#include "gensort.h"
main()
{
   int num[] = { 12, 34, 5, 67, 232, 22, 133 };
   unsigned i, n = sizeof(num) / sizeof(int);
   int found, j = 22;
   /* sort array */
   gen_shell_sort(num, n, sizeof(int), intcmp);
   /* search for array element storing the value in 'j' */
   found = bidir_find(&j, num, n, sizeof(int), intcmp);
   printf("Found %d in array element %d\n\n", j, found);
   puts("The sorted array of integer is :");
   for (i = 0; i < n; i++)
      printf("%u  %3d\n", i, num[i]);
}
```

The next program sorts an array of strings also using the generic shell sort routine. The array is examined using the **bidir_find** function to locate the array member storing the string **James**. The index of the matching array element and the list of the sorted array are displayed:

```
#include <stdio.h>
#include <stdlib.h>
#include "string.h"
#include "gensort.h"
main()
{
   char str[5][11] = { "Namir", "Bobbi", "Keith", "James", "David" };
   unsigned i, n = 5;
   int found;
   char name[11] = "James";
   /* sort array */
   gen_shell_sort(str, n, 11, strcmp);
   /* search for array element storing the string "James" */
   found = bidir_find(name, str, n, 11, strcmp);
   printf("Found %s in array element %d\n\n", name, found);
   puts("The sorted array of names is:");
   for (i = 0; i < n; i++)
      printf("%u  %s\n", i, str[i]);
}
```

The following program gradually builds an ordered array of strings by inserting one string per call to routine gen_insert_sort. The array is examined using the **bidir_search** function to locate the array member storing the string **Keith**. The index of the matching array element and the list of the sorted array are displayed:

```
#include <stdio.h>
#include <stdlib.h>
#include "string.h"
#include "gensort.h"
main()
{
   char str[5][11];
   char name[11] = "Keith";
   unsigned i, n = 0;
   int found;
   /* insert names */
   gen_insert_sort(str, "Namir", &n, 11, strcmp);
   gen_insert_sort(str, "Bobbi", &n, 11, strcmp);
   gen_insert_sort(str, "Keith", &n, 11, strcmp);
   gen_insert_sort(str, "James", &n, 11, strcmp);
   gen_insert_sort(str, "David", &n, 11, strcmp);
   /* search for array element storing the string "Keith" */
   found = bidir_search(name, str, &n, 11, strcmp);
   printf("Found %s in array element %d\n\n", name, found);
   puts("The sorted array of names is:");
   for (i = 0; i < n; i++)
      printf("%u  %s\n", i, str[i]);
}
```

The next program adds a new level of complexity to the generic sorting. A structure-type array is put in order using the generic shell sort routine, and then displayed. The structure is defined as:

```
struct mail_rec {
      char name[31];
      unsigned int age;
      double wt;
      };
```

The name field is used for sorting the array. A special element-comparison function, **struct0_cmp**, is written and engaged in the argument list of the generic sort routine:

```
#include <stdio.h>
#include <stdlib.h>
#include "string.h"
#include "gensort.h"
struct mail_rec {
      char name[31];
      unsigned int age;
```

```
      double wt;
      };
typedef struct mail_rec mail;
int struct0_cmp(void *e1, void *e2)
{
   return strcmp(((mail*)e1)->name, ((mail*)e2)->name);
}
main()
{
   mail person[5] = { { "Namir", 34, 180.0 },
                      { "Bobbi", 31, 165.0 },
                      { "Keith", 29, 155.0 },
                      { "James", 35, 190.0 },
                      { "David", 41, 190.0 } };
   unsigned i, n = 5;
   gen_shell_sort(person, n, sizeof(mail), struct0_cmp);
   for (i = 0; i < n; i++)
      printf("%s is %2d years old and weighs %lg bounds \n",
            person[i].name, person[i].age, person[i].wt);
}
```

The following program initializes two structured arrays. Each array is sorted separately, using qsort, and then the arrays are merge-sorted. The order of the new large array is then reversed and its contents displayed. The program demonstrates the call to functions **gen_merge_sort** and **gen_reverse_array**.

```
#include <stdio.h>
#include <stdlib.h>
#include "string.h"
#include "gensort.h"
struct mail_rec {
      char name[31];
      unsigned int age;
      double wt;
      };
typedef struct mail_rec mail;
int struct0_cmp(void *e1, void *e2)
{
   return strcmp( ((mail*)e1)->name, ((mail*)e2)->name);
}
main()
{
   mail person1[10] = { { "Namir0", 34, 180.0 },
                        { "Bobbi0", 31, 165.0 },
```

```
                         { "Keith0", 29, 155.0 },
                         { "James0", 35, 190.0 },
                         { "David0", 41, 190.0 } };
    mail person2[5] = { { "Namir1", 34, 180.0 },
                         { "Bobbi1", 31, 165.0 },
                         { "Keith1", 29, 155.0 },
                         { "James1", 35, 190.0 },
                         { "David1", 41, 190.0 } };
    unsigned i, n = 5, m = 5;
    /* sort first array */
    qsort(person1, n, sizeof(mail), struct0_cmp);
    /* sort second array */
    qsort(person2, m, sizeof(mail), struct0_cmp);
    /* merge sort both arrays */
    gen_merge_sort(person1, person2, &n, m, sizeof(mail), struct0_cmp);
    /* reverse the order of the array */
    gen_reverse_array(person1, n, sizeof(mail));
    /* display structured array in descending order */
    for (i = 0; i < n; i++)
       printf("%s is %2d years old and weighs %lg bounds \n",
            person1[i].name, person1[i].age, person1[i].wt);
}
```

The final example illustrates the use of the generic index search table routine. An array of ten strings is first sorted using qsort. The ordered array is then employed to build a modest index table with three entries. The index table is involved in searching for the array member storing the string **Paul**. The program displays the index of the element storing the sought string and then displays the array of sorted strings:

```
#include <stdio.h>
#include <stdlib.h>
#include "string.h"
#include "gensort.h"
#define TABLE_SIZE 3
#define ARRAY_SIZE 10
#define STRING 11
main()
{
   char str[ARRAY_SIZE][STRING]
          = { "Namir", "Bobbi", "Keith", "James", "David",
              "Kim", "Thomas", "Paul", "Peter", "John" };
   char name[STRING] = "Keith";
   char table[TABLE_SIZE][STRING];
   unsigned index[TABLE_SIZE];
```

```
  unsigned i, n = ARRAY_SIZE, tbl_size = TABLE_SIZE;
  int found;
  qsort(str, n, STRING, strcmp); /* sort the array of string */
  /* setup the index search table */
  set_index_table(table, index, str, tbl_size,  n, STRING);
  /* use the index search table */
  found = search_index_table(name, table, index, str,
                    tbl_size, n, 11, strcmp);
  printf("found %s in index %d\n\n", name, found);
  for (i = 0; i < n; i++)
     printf("%u  %s\n", i, str[i]);
}
```

Listing 8.1 Source code for the generic sort/search header file "gensort.h"

```
int intcmp(int*, int*);
long longcmp(long*, long*);
int uintcmp(unsigned int*, unsigned int*);
long ulongcmp(unsigned long*, unsigned long*);
int doublecmp(double*, double*);
void gen_shell_sort(void*, unsigned, unsigned,
                    int (*fcmp)(const void*, const void*));
void gen_insert_sort(void*, void*, unsigned*, unsigned,
                     int (*fcmp)(const void*, const void*));
int gen_reverse_array(void*, unsigned, unsigned);
int gen_merge_sort(void*,  void*, unsigned*, unsigned, unsigned,
                    int (*fcmp)(const void*, const void*));
int bidir_find(void*, void*, unsigned, unsigned,
               int (*fcmp)(const void*, const void*));
int bidir_search(void*, void*, unsigned*, unsigned,
                 int (*fcmp)(const void*, const void*));
int set_index_table(void*, unsigned*, void*,
                    unsigned, unsigned, unsigned);
int search_index_table(void*, void*, unsigned*,
                       void*, unsigned, unsigned, unsigned,
                       int (*fcmp)(const void*, const void*));
```

Listing 8.2 Source code for the supplementary generic sort/search library "gensort.c"

```
#include <stdlib.h>
#include <string.h>
int intcmp(int *i, int *j)
{
    return (*i - *j);
}
```

```
long longcmp(long *i, long *j)
{
    return (*i - *j);
}
int uintcmp(unsigned int *i, unsigned int *j)
{
    return (int)(*i - *j);
}
long ulongcmp(unsigned long *i, unsigned long *j)
{
    return (long)(*i - *j);
}
int doublecmp(double *x, double *y)
{
    if (*x < *y)
       return -1;
    else if (*x > *y)
       return 1;
    else
       return 0;
}
void gen_shell_sort(void *base, unsigned nelem,
                    unsigned elmsize,
                    int (*fcmp)(const void*, const void*))
{
    unsigned i, j, jump = nelem;
    unsigned char done;
    unsigned char *tempo, *ptr = (unsigned char *) base;
    tempo = (unsigned char *) malloc(elmsize);
    while (jump > 1) {
        jump /= 2;
        do {
            done = 1;
            for (j = 0; j < (nelem - jump); j++) {
                i = j + jump;
                if ((*fcmp)((ptr+i*elmsize),(ptr+j*elmsize)) < 0) {
                    done = 0;
                    memmove(tempo, (ptr+i*elmsize), elmsize);
                    memmove((ptr+i*elmsize), (ptr+j*elmsize), elmsize);
                    memmove((ptr+j*elmsize), tempo, elmsize);
                }
            }
        } while (!done);
    }
    free(tempo); /* restore dynamic memory */
}
void gen_insert_sort(void *base, void* key,
                     unsigned *nelem, unsigned elmsize,
```

```
                    int (*fcmp)(const void*, const void*))
{
    unsigned i, found ;
    unsigned char *ptr = (unsigned char *) base;
    unsigned char *kee = (unsigned char *) key;
    if (*nelem > 0) {
        for (i = 0, found = 0; (i < *nelem && !found); i++)
            if ((*fcmp)((ptr+i*elmsize),kee) > 0) {
                memmove((ptr+(i+1)*elmsize),
                        (ptr+i*elmsize),
                        (*nelem - i) * elmsize);
                memmove((ptr+i*elmsize), kee, elmsize);
                found = 1;
            }
        (*nelem)++;
        if (!found)
            memmove((ptr + *nelem * elmsize), kee, elmsize);
    }
    else {
        memmove(ptr, kee, elmsize);
        (*nelem)++;
    }
}
int gen_reverse_array(void *base, unsigned nelem, unsigned elmsize)
{
    unsigned median = nelem / 2, i, j;
    unsigned char *tempo, *ptr = (unsigned char *) base;
    if (nelem < 3)
        return 0;
    tempo = (unsigned char *) malloc(elmsize);
    for (i = 0, j = nelem-1; i < median; i++, j--) {
        memmove(tempo, (ptr+i*elmsize), elmsize);
        memmove((ptr+i*elmsize), (ptr+j*elmsize), elmsize);
        memmove((ptr+j*elmsize), tempo, elmsize);
    }
    free(tempo);
    return 1;
}
int gen_merge_sort(void *base1, void *base2,
                   unsigned *nelem1, unsigned nelem2,
                   unsigned elmsize,
                   int (*fcmp)(const void*, const void*))
{
    unsigned i, j, k;
    unsigned char *ptr0 = (unsigned char *) base1;
    unsigned char *ptr1 = (unsigned char *) base1;
    unsigned char *ptr2 = (unsigned char *) base2;
    if (*nelem1 < 1 || nelem2 < 1)
```

```
        return 0;
     ptr0 = (unsigned char *) calloc(*nelem1, elmsize);
     /* copy main array into temporary array */
     memmove(ptr0, ptr1, *nelem1 * elmsize);
     for (i = 0, j = 0, k = 0; (i < *nelem1 && j < nelem2); k++) {
        if ( (*fcmp)((ptr0+i*elmsize),(ptr2+j*elmsize)) < 0 )  {
       memmove((ptr1+k*elmsize),(ptr0+i*elmsize),elmsize);
       i++;
        }
        else {
       memmove((ptr1+k*elmsize),(ptr2+j*elmsize),elmsize);
       j++;
        }
     }
     if (i < *nelem1) /* copy the rest of array1 */
        memmove((ptr1+k*elmsize),
            (ptr0+i*elmsize),
            (*nelem1-i)*elmsize);
     else /* copy the rest of array2 */
        memmove((ptr1+k*elmsize),
            (ptr2+j*elmsize),
            (nelem2-j)*elmsize);
     *nelem1 += nelem2;
     free(ptr0);
     return 1;
}
int bidir_find(void *key, void *base,
               unsigned nelem, unsigned elmsize,
               int (*fcmp)(const void*, const void*))
/* function that performs linear bidirectional search starting with
   the median element and searching towards the ends */
{
     int i, j;
     unsigned char *ptr = (unsigned char *) base;
     unsigned char *kee = (unsigned char *) key;
     if (nelem < 2)
        return -1;
     for(i = nelem / 2 - 1, j = i + 1;
     (i > -1 || j < nelem);
     i--, j++) {
      if (i > -1) {
             if ( (*fcmp)((ptr+i*elmsize),kee) == 0)
            return i;
      }
           if (j < nelem) {
          if ( (*fcmp)((ptr+j*elmsize),kee) == 0)
            return  j;
      }
```

```
    }
    return -11;
}
int bidir_search(void *key, void *base,
                 unsigned *nelem, unsigned elmsize,
                 int (*fcmp)(const void*, const void*))
/* function that performs linear bidirectional search starting with
   the median element and searching towards the ends.
   If the element is not found it is added to the end of the array.
*/
{
    unsigned i, j;
    unsigned char *ptr = (unsigned char *) base;
    unsigned char *kee = (unsigned char *) key;
    if (*nelem > 1) {
       for(i = *nelem / 2 - 1, j = i + 1;
       (i > -1 || j < *nelem);
       i--, j++) {
        if (i > -1) {
              if ( (*fcmp)((ptr+i*elmsize),kee) == 0)
                return i;
        }
            if (j < *nelem) {
           if ( (*fcmp)((ptr+j*elmsize),kee) == 0)
                return  j;
        }
       }
    }
    /* add new element */
    memmove((ptr + *nelem * elmsize), kee, elmsize);
    (*nelem)++;
    return (*nelem - 1);
}
int set_index_table(void *table, unsigned *index, void *base,
                    unsigned tbl_size, unsigned nelem, unsigned elmsize)
{
    unsigned i, j, offset = nelem / tbl_size;
    unsigned char *ptr = (unsigned char *) base;
    unsigned char *tbl = (unsigned char *) table;
    if (offset < 1)
       return 0;
    for (i = 0, j = 0; j < tbl_size; j++, i += offset) {
       memmove((tbl+j*elmsize),(ptr+i*elmsize),elmsize);
       *(index+j) = i;
    }
    return 1;
}
int search_index_table(void *key,
```

```
                        void *table,
                        unsigned *index,
                        void *base,
                        unsigned tbl_size,
                        unsigned nelem,
                        unsigned elmsize,
                        int (*fcmp)(const void*, const void*))
{
    unsigned i, first, last, found = 0;
    unsigned median;
    unsigned char *ptr = (unsigned char *) base;
    unsigned char *tbl = (unsigned char *) table;
    unsigned char *kee = (unsigned char *) key;
    for (i = 1; (i < tbl_size && found == 0); i++) {
      if ( (*fcmp)(kee, (tbl+i*elmsize)) <= 0 ) {
     found = 1;
     first = *(index+i-1);
     if (i < (tbl_size - 1))
        last = *(index+i);
     else
        last = nelem - 1;
      }
    }
   if (found == 0) {
      first = *(index+tbl_size-1);
      last = nelem - 1;
   }
   found = 0; /* reset found flag */
   while ( (first+1) < last && found == 0 ) {
      /* calculate median index */
      median = (first + last) / 2;
      if ( (*fcmp)(kee, (ptr+median*elmsize)) < 0 )
         last = median;
      else if ( (*fcmp)(kee, (ptr+median*elmsize)) > 0 )
         first = median;
      else
         found = 1;
   }
   if (found == 0) {
     if ( (*fcmp)(kee, (ptr+last*elmsize)) == 0)
       return last;
     else if ( (*fcmp)(kee, (ptr+first*elmsize)) == 0)
        return first;
     else
      return -1;
   }
   return median;
}
```

CHAPTER

9

Directory Utilities

This chapter looks at building functions that extend frequently used DOS commands. The code is written as functions that can easily be incorporated into your custom applications. The four utilities presented are:

1. **Extended-directory listing generator function and application** This extends the MS-DOS DIR command (and also emulates the OS/2 DIR command) by allowing up to ten wildcard programs to be specified.
2. **File copier function and application that supports multiple wildcards** This extends the DOS COPY command by supporting multiple wildcards, and optional verbose and safe copy modes. The safe copy mode examines the destination directory for the presence of each copied file. If a file is present in the current and target directories, the user is prompted to authorize copying that file.
3. **An application that implements a multifile lister** The application employs the extended-directory listing function to invoke a child program that actually handles the source code listing.
4. **Smart directory jump function application** This function scans the directory tree and enables your programs to zoom in on a directory by simply invoking its name, without requiring the full pathname!

EXTENDED DIRECTORY FUNCTION AND APPLICATION

The above utilities are built on calls to function **fn_edir**, found in Listings 9.1 and 9.2. This function employs two basic Turbo C functions involved in filename query—namely, findfirst and findnext. The headings of the findfirst and findnext functions are declared as:

```
struct ffblk* fn_edir(char wildcard[][MAX_WILDCARD_LEN],
                      int num_wildcard,
                      struct ffblk *files,
                      int *num_files)
int findfirst(const char *pathname, struct ffblk *ffblk, int attrib)
int findnext(struct ffblk *ffblk)
```

The pathname parameter defines the exact directory path and includes either unambiguous filenames or wildcards. The attrib parameter defines the type of directory entries to be selected. The attribute can be an archive, a read-only, a system, a hidden, a directory name, or the disk volume name. The structure ffblk is defined as:

```
struct ffblk {
          char ff_reserved[21];   /* reserved area      */
          int ff_ftime;           /* file time stamp   */
          int ff_fdate;           /* file date stamp   */
          long ff_fsize;          /* file size         */
          char ff_name[13];       /* complete filename */
      }
```

A call to **findfirst** should specify the pathname and attribute. The function returns a nonzero integer, if at least one file is found to match the requested attribute for the specified pathname. The data for the located file entry is returned through the file block pointer parameter, *ffblk. A nonzero result returned by findfirst also means that there may be more matching file entries. Normally, a WHILE loop is used to contain calls to function **findnext**. Like **findfirst**, the **findnext** function returns a nonzero integer if it succeeded in locating more matching files specified by a call to **findfirst**. The **findnext** is repeatedly called until it returns 0, indicating that the end of the list of matching files has been reached.

The function **fn_edir** builds the list of matching files using a dynamic array that maintains the filenames in sorted order. Since there is no way for predicting (or even approximating) the actual array size ahead of time, dynamic allocation and reallocation are used. The array of filenames is dynamically allocated to some arbitrary size specified by the macro DYN_ARRAY_SIZE. When the array is full, it is dynamically reallocated by INC_ARRAY_SIZE elements using the **realloc** function. This approach has been made very easy with the **realloc** function. Without it, a programmer has two other choices. The first is to develop his or her own version of **realloc**. The second alternative is to use ordered singlylinked lists.

Maintaining an ordered array reduces the time involved with searching for duplicate names. This is an important aspect of function **fn_edir**. Suppose the wildcards like "*.*" and "*.C" are specified. This tends to fetch a number of duplicate filenames from the same directory. To prevent this redundancy, the **fn_edir** function traps duplicate filenames. This also resolves the potential problem of duplicate filenames with the other utilities presented in this chapter that invoke function **fn_edir**.

The **fn_edir** function returns a pointer to the ffblk structure. The result should be reassigned to the pointer-typed parameter, files, to update the address of the dynamic array. It is important that the applications or functions which directly invoke **fn_edir** deallocate the dynamic array once its data is no longer needed.

Listing 9.3 contains the source code for **edir.c**, an application that lists the filenames and file sizes. When the compiled program is run with no arguments, the application behaves as though you had typed the argument ***.*** and displays the entire list of files in the current directory. The application is able to display filenames from different directories and/or drives. However, this is not recommended, since discerning the exact file location becomes very confusing. When multiple wildcards are specified along with their pathnames, the latter should all be identical. Figure 9.1 shows a sample session with the compiled "edir.c" program. The output is generated by specifying the ***.C** and ***.BAT** wildcards by typing the following from the DOS command level:

```
> EDIR *.C *.BAT
```

Filename	Size	Time	Date
BASTATO.C	882	02:36:13	01-27-1987
BGIDEMO.C	42530	01:05:00	12-10-1987
BJBASTAT.C	882	20:34:15	03-09-1988
BJBGIDEM.C	42530	20:34:16	03-09-1988
CHILDLIS.C	3137	20:38:22	03-10-1988
CHILDMN1.C	1456	17:10:15	03-10-1988
CHILDMN2.C	1917	17:07:00	03-10-1988
CHILDMN3.C	1949	17:14:02	03-10-1988
CHILDPRN.C	1647	15:26:24	03-10-1988
CHILDWS2.C	1969	16:00:06	03-10-1988
CPASDEMO.C	1682	01:05:00	12-10-1987
DIROPS.C	7797	22:03:02	03-17-1988
FILECOMP.C	11073	01:00:00	05-13-1987
GENSORT.C	7009	22:26:00	03-15-1988
GETOPT.C	4228	01:05:00	12-10-1987
LIST.C	2948	11:28:21	03-16-1988
MAIN.C	1102	01:05:00	12-10-1987
MATHERR.C	3850	01:05:00	12-10-1987
OPEN.C	478	14:27:11	01-19-1988
STROPS1.C	1675	11:41:12	03-16-1988
STROPS2.C	6349	17:45:08	03-08-1988

```
press any key to continue
```

Filename	Size	Time	Date
T.C	8891	16:01:05	03-07-1988
TRANSLAN.C	7848	15:40:06	03-10-1988

```
23 files matching in 163829 bytes
26 files matching in 168124 bytes
```

Figure 9.1 Sample output of a session with application **edir.c**. The command line arguments supplied is ***.C *.BAT**.

EXTENDED FILE COPYING FUNCTION AND APPLICATION

The second file/directory management function is copyto and is shown in Listings 9.4 and 9.5. The heading of the function declaration is:

```
int fn_copyto(char* destination,
              char wildcard[][MAX_WILDCARD_LEN],
              int num_wildcard,
              int verbose,
              int safe_mode)
```

The destination parameter is the pathname of the target directory. The wildcard parameter passes an array of strings that contain the wildcards. The num_wildcard parameter specifies the number of wildcards. The verbose parameter is utilized to indicate whether or not the function should display the names of the files as they are being copied. A nonzero verbose parameter value turns on the verbose mode, and a zero value turns it off. The safe_mode parameter is employed in making sure that the destination directory does not blindly overwrite existing files during the file copy process. A nonzero safe_mode parameter value turns on the safe copy mode. If a copied file already exists in the destination directory, the enduser is prompted for an authorization.

The **copyto** function calls on the **fn_edir** function to access the array of filenames. The function assumes that the filenames are all located in the current directory. The low-level file I/O functions **open**, **write**, **read**, and **close** are used to perform fast buffered I/O. The buffer size is currently set at about 4K. In addition, the function employs the predefined Turbo C flags O_CREATE, O_RDONLY, O_WRONLY, and O_BINARY to control the modes of the opened files. Using these flags, the function is able to detect the presence of the same file in both the current and the destination directories. The **copyto** function returns a value of 0 if no file matches any of the specified wildcards; otherwise, a value of 1 is returned.

Listing 9.6 contains an application program that drives the **copyto** function. The program scans the command-line arguments, and prompts you to use the verbose and safe copy modes. If no arguments are supplied, the program displays an on-line help message and exits. For example, the compiled application is invoked from DOS to copy .C and .EXE files to the root directory of a RAM disk as follows:

```
>COPYTO E:\ *.C *.EXE
```

MULTIPLE-FILE LISTING UTILITY

Listing 9.7 contains **lister.c**, a short C program that combines the power of the **fn_edir** function with the versatility of the system calls. The program itself may be regarded as a type of shell that reads the command-line arguments to obtain the file wildcards. If none are found, the program uses the ***.*** wildcard. A call to **fn_edir** returns a pointer to the dynamic array that contains the filenames (assumed to be in the current directory) to be viewed. A FOR loop is employed to build a DOS command that invokes the **list.c** program (shown in Listing 9.8) and supply it with a single unambiguous filename. Once the **list.c** exits, you return to the **lister.c** program, which prompts to see if you wish to stop viewing the remaining files. For example, the compiled application is invoked from DOS to view .C and .BAT files to the root directory of a RAM disk as follows:

```
>LISTER *.C *.BAT
```

The **list.c** program is a separate, stand-alone program that is invoked using the system function. You can substitute the program name with another one that is able to read the filename supplied as a command-line argument. The **list.c** program writes directly to the screen using a far pointer. The far pointer is used since the physical address of the video most likely lies outside the program's data segment. You may use the PgUp, PgDn, Home, End, and up and down cursor keys to navigate throughout the text. Pressing the Q key results in exiting the **list.c** program. The **list.c** program reads up to 700 lines of text file and ignores the extra lines.

DIRECTORY JUMPS

This next utility is a particularly handy one for moving around in directories. The directory tree structure, useful in grouping files together, can become quite bothersome when trying to move from one directory to another, since you must walk up and down the tree in doing so. The jump directory program, shown in Listing 9.7, provides a shortcut to this process. It also shows more examples of using the Turbo C functions **findfirst()**, **findnext()** and **chdir()**.

The jump program allows you to jump to a different subdirectory merely by specifying its name. You give just the subdirectory name, not its full pathname. The name can be a partial one, and the program will prompt you to resolve any ambiguities. You can then jump directly to that subdirectory, regardless of where you are in the tree. If the name is unique, no prompting is done, and you go immediately to the subdirectory.

The program works as follows: a "flattened" form of the complete directory tree on the current drive is created. The "flattened" tree is put into a special file in your root directory. The file stores information on the names of each subdirectory and it's level in the tree. This file is then consulted whenever you use the jump command to quickly generate the full path name of the subdirectory. This name is then used as an input to the Turbo C function **chdir()**, which allows you to change directories.

The jump program is called two different ways:

```
>jump -s
```

to create a directory map, or

```
>jump <partial_dir_name>
```

to move to another directory.

The jump program, then, has two modes: one mode is to create the special directory file, the other to provide the jump function. The main routines in the jump program are **savedir()** and **jumpdir()**, which handle these two modes, respectively.

The **savedir()** routine recursively walks the directory routine, starting from the root. The Turbo C functions **findfirst()** and **findnext()** are used to return the name and attribute of each file in the directory. Those that are directories rather than just normal files are weeded out. Each one of these directories is then visited, and the process recurses. In essence, the directory tree is walked in a depth-first fashion.

In order to distinguish between directories and normal files, the program checks an attribute flag found in the structure **struct ffblk**, which is returned by both **findfirst()** and **findnext()**. This structure is:

```
struct ffblk {
   char ff_reserved[21];
   char ff_attrib;
   int ff_ftime;
   int ff_fdate;
   int ff_fsize;
   char ff_name[13];
}
```

The flag ff_attrib gives the DOS file attribute, which can take on the following codes, defined in the **dos.h** header:

FA_RDONLY	Read only file
FA_HIDDEN	Hidden file
FA_SYSTEM	System file
FA_LABEL	Volume Label
FA_DIREC	Directory
FA_ARCH	Archive

The one you're looking for is FA_DIREC. Note that you must check specifically for the directories "." and "..". These special directories are names for the current directory and parent directory, respectively. In order to prevent an infinite loop, you must be sure not to visit them over and over.

When a directory is found, its name and level are added to the special file \save.dir, which is created in your root directory. The name stored is not the full path name, but rather just the name of the subdirectory. The level is an integer indicating how deep in the directory structure you are, where 0 means the subdirectory is accessed from the root directory. An example of the contents of \save.dir as follows:

```
0 DOS        1 QUICKY     0 TC         2 V2
0 MSC        2 TST        1 WORK       3 KEYS
1 LIB        2 CQ         1 TSR        0 CG
1 RMRL       0 MOUSE      1 GUIDE      0 TALK
```

In this example, the subdirectories DOS, MSC, MOUSE, TC, CG, and TALK all reside under the root directory.

The following list shows the full pathnames for all of the directories:

Directory	Pathname
0 DOS	\dos
0 MSC	\msc
1 LIB	\msc\lib
1 RMRL	\msc\rmrl
1 QUICKY	\msc\quicky
2 TST	\msc\quicky\tst

Directory	Pathname
2 CQ	\msc\quicky\cq
0 MOUSE	\mouse
0 TC	\tc
1 WORK	\tc\work
1 TSR	\tc\work\tsr
1 GUIDE	\tc\guide
2 V2	\tc\guide\v2
3 KEYS	\tc\guide\v2\keys
0 CG	\cg
0 TALK	\talk
1 CG	\talk\cg

Once \save.dir is built, the program can then be used to jump to different directories. The function **jumpdir()** does all of the work. Basically, \save.dir is loaded into memory as an array of level-name pairs. Then, given a subdirectory name, the program scans this array sequentially, looking for a partial match. Along the way, the full pathname of the candidate directory is constructed, using the level information stored in the array.

When a match is found, the program looks to see if it is unique. If it is, the **chdir()** function is called to do the jump, and is given the full pathname. If the name is not unique, then the user is prompted with the candidate pathnames. The choice is made by pressing **y** or **Y**. Any other key causes a prompt with the next matching pathname.

For instance, with the sample directory given earlier, the following jumps could be used:

```
>jump tst           jumps to \msc\quicky\tst
>jump gu            jumps to \tc\guide
>jump ke            jumps to \tc\guide\v2\keys
>jump cg            not unique, so it will prompt for \cg, and then \talk\cg
>jump \tc\guide     NOT allowed, can't give pathnames!!
```

One problem with the jump program is that every time a directory is added or deleted, you must run **jump -s** in order to rebuild \save.dir. This is somewhat of a nuisance, which could be alleviated by making the program memory resident and monitoring all make directory and delete directory commands to DOS. This would require some fancy footwork and is probably not warranted. The simplistic approach used here is quite adequate.

The \save.dir file was designed to be small, so that reading this file when the jump command is executed is as quick as possible. Of course, if you're using a floppy disk, it could get pretty slow, so it works best for hard disks.

Another limitation is the pathnames cannot be used, even partial ones. One challenge would be to change the code to allow, for instance, ">jump work\ts" which, given the example above, would jump to \tc\work\tsr.

Listing 9.1 Contents of the header file "fn_edir.h"

```
#define MAX_WILDCARD_LEN 31
#define DYN_ARRAY_SIZE 50
#define INC_ARRAY_SIZE 25
struct ffblk* fn_edir(char[][], int, struct ffblk*, int*);
```

Listing 9.2 Source code for function "fn_edir.c"

```
#include "stdlib.h"
#include "dos.h"
#include "dir.h"
#include "string.h"
#include "fn_edir.h"
struct ffblk* fn_edir(char wildcard[][MAX_WILDCARD_LEN],
                      int num_wildcard,
                      struct ffblk *files,
                      int *num_files)
{
   int n = DYN_ARRAY_SIZE;
   unsigned int blk_size = sizeof(struct ffblk);
   int i, j, k, nomatch, not_unique, found;
   struct ffblk *ptr;
   /* allocate new block for file structures */
   files = (struct ffblk *) calloc(n,blk_size);
   ptr = (struct ffblk*) calloc(n,blk_size);
   *num_files = 0; /* initialize matching file count */
   /* loop to look for the specified wildcards */
   for (i = 0; i < num_wildcard; i++) {
      /* search for the first matching entry */
      nomatch = findfirst((wildcard+i),ptr,0);
      /* while a match is found */
      while (!nomatch) {
         not_unique = 0; /* assume filename is unique */
         /* search in the available array of filenames */
         if (*num_files > 0)
            for (j = 0; (j < *num_files) && (!not_unique); j++)
               if (!strcmp(ptr->ff_name, (files+j)->ff_name))
                  not_unique = 1; /* found a match */
         /* if filename is unique process it */
         if (!not_unique) {
            (*num_files)++; /* increment file count */
            /* need more dynamic memory? */
            if (*num_files > n) {
               n += INC_ARRAY_SIZE;
               files = (struct ffblk *) realloc(files, n * blk_size);
            }
            /* insert in order */
```

```
        if (*num_files > 1) {
           found = 0;
           k = *num_files - 1;
           /* search for proper insersion lcoation */
           for (j = 0; (j < k) && (!found); j++) {
         if (strcmp(ptr->ff_name,(files+j)->ff_name) < 0) {
              found = 1;
              /* move rest of array updaward */
              memmove((files+j+1),(files+j),(k-j)*blk_size);
              /* insert new element */
              *(files+j) = *ptr;
                    }
                }
           if (!found)  /* insert as last array element */
         *(files + k) = *ptr;
              }
        else  /* assign first entry */
                *files = *ptr;
         }
         /* search for the next matching entry */
         nomatch = findnext(ptr);
      }
   }
   return files; /* return pointer to dynamic array */
}
```

Listing 9.3 Source code for utility program "edir.c"

```
#include <stdio.h>
#include "conio.h"
#include "stdlib.h"
#include "dos.h"
#include "dir.h"
#include "errno.h"
#include "string.h"
#include "fcntl.h"
#include "sys\stat.h"
#include "fn_edir.h"
main(int argc, char* argv[])
{
  char wildcard[10][MAX_WILDCARD_LEN];
  int num_wildcard, num_files, i, count;
  struct ffblk *files = NULL;
  long sum = 0;
  clrscr();
  directvideo = 1;
  if (argc < 2) {
     num_wildcard = 1;
     strcpy(wildcard[0],"*.*");
```

```
  }
  else {
   num_wildcard = argc - 1;
   for (i = 0; i < num_wildcard; i++)
      strcpy(wildcard[i],argv[i+1]);
  }
  files  = fn_edir(wildcard, num_wildcard, files, &num_files);
  if (num_files > 0) {
     puts("  Filename         Size");
     puts("————   ————");
     for (i = 0, count = 0; i < num_files; i++, count++) {
   if (count > 20) {
       printf("\npress any key to continue");
       getch();
       clrscr();
       puts("  Filename         Size");
           puts("————   ————");
       count = 0;
   }
         printf("%-13s  %10ld\n",
                  (files+i)->ff_name,
                  (files+i)->ff_fsize);
   sum += (files+i)->ff_fsize;
     }
   }
   printf("\n%d files matching in %ld bytes\n", num_files, sum);
   free(files);
}
```

Listing 9.4 Contents of the header file "fn_copy.h"

```
int fn_copyto(char*, char [][], int, int, int);
```

Listing 9.5 Source code for function "fn_copy.c"

```
#include "stdlib.h"
#include "dos.h"
#include "dir.h"
#include "string.h"
#include "fcntl.h"
#include "fn_edir.h"
int fn_copyto(char* destination,
              char wildcard[][MAX_WILDCARD_LEN],
              int num_wildcard,
              int verbose,
              int safe_mode)
{
   struct ffblk *files;
   int num_files, num_bytes, i;
```

```
char ch, path[65];
char buffer[4096];
int infile, outfile;
unsigned int const BUF_SIZE = 4096;
int line_num;
files = fn_edir(wildcard, num_wildcard, files, &num_files);
if (num_files > 0) {
   for (i = 0; i < num_files; i++)   {
      strcpy(path, destination);
  strcat(path, (files+i)->ff_name);
  infile  = open((files+i)->ff_name, O_RDONLY | O_BINARY);
      outfile = open(path, O_WRONLY | O_BINARY);
      if ((safe_mode) && (outfile > 0)) {
     line_num = wherey(); /* store cursor row number */
     do {
        gotoxy(1,line_num);
        clreol();
        printf("overwrite %s in destination ? Y/N -> ",
           (files+i)->ff_name);
        ch = getche(); printf("\n");
        if (ch >= 'a' && ch <= 'z') ch += 'A' - 'a';
     } while (ch != 'Y' && ch != 'N');
     if (ch == 'N') {
           close(infile);
        close(outfile);
        continue;
     }
  }
      close(outfile);
      /* reopen file handle to allow new file creation */
      outfile = open(path, O_CREAT | O_WRONLY | O_BINARY);
  /* are both files are opened ok */
  if ((infile > 0) && (outfile > 0)) {
     if (verbose)
        printf("%s -> %s\n",
           (files+i)->ff_name,path);
     while ( (num_bytes = read(infile, buffer, BUF_SIZE)) > 0)
        write(outfile, buffer, num_bytes);
          close(infile);
     close(outfile);
  }
      else {
     if (infile  > 0) close(infile);
     if (outfile > 0) close(outfile);
  }
   }
   free(files);
   return 1;
}
```

```
   else
      return 0;
}
int backup(char* destination,
          char wildcard[][MAX_WILDCARD_LEN],
          int num_wildcard,
      int verbose)
{
   struct ffblk *files, *ptr;
   int num_files, num_bytes, i, nomatch;
   char ch, path[65];
   char buffer[4096];
   int infile, outfile;
   unsigned int const BUF_SIZE = 4096;
   int t1, t2, d1, d2;
   long int s1, s2;
   long sum_size;
   files = fn_edir(wildcard, num_wildcard, files, &num_files);
   if (num_files > 0) {
      for (i = 0; i < num_files; i++)  {
         strcpy(path, destination);
    strcat(path, (files+i)->ff_name);
         nomatch = findfirst(path, ptr, 0);
         if (!nomatch) {
        /* get source file size, time and date stamps */
        s1 = (files+i)->ff_fsize;
        t1 = (files+i)->ff_ftime;
            d1 = (files+i)->ff_fdate;
            /* get destination file size, time and date stamps */
        s2 = ptr->ff_fsize;
        t2 = ptr->ff_ftime;
            d2 = ptr->ff_fdate;
            /* do files match in size, time and date */
            if ( (s1 != s2) || (t1 != t2) || (d1 != d2) )
          continue;
     }
     infile  = open((files+i)->ff_name, O_RDONLY | O_BINARY);
         outfile = open(path, O_CREAT | O_WRONLY | O_BINARY);
     /* are both files are opened ok */
     if ((infile > 0) && (outfile > 0)) {
        if (verbose)
           printf("%s -> %s\n",
               (files+i)->ff_name,path);
        while ( (num_bytes = read(infile, buffer, BUF_SIZE)) > 0)
           write(outfile, buffer, num_bytes);
             close(infile);
        close(outfile);
     }
```

```
            else {
              if (infile  > 0) close(infile);
              if (outfile > 0) close(outfile);
         }
          }
          free(files);
          return 1;
     }
     else
          return 0;
}
```

Listing 9.6 Source code for program "copyto.c"

```
#include <stdio.h>
#include "stdlib.h"
#include "dir.h"
#include "errno.h"
#include "conio.h"
#include <io.h>
#include "string.h"
#include "fcntl.h"
#include "sys\stat.h"
#include "fn_edir.h"
#include "fn_copy.h"
main(int argc, char* argv[])
{
   char wildcard[10][MAX_WILDCARD_LEN];
   unsigned int num_wildcard, num_files, i;
   char ch, destination[65];
   int verbose, safe_mode;
   clrscr();
   directvideo = 1;
   if (argc < 2) {
       puts("proper usage is: copyto <destination> <wildcard 1>...\n\n");
       exit(0);
    }
    else {
      strcpy(destination, argv[1]);
      num_wildcard = argc - 2;
      for (i = 0; i < num_wildcard; i++)
       strcpy(wildcard[i],argv[i+2]);
   }
   printf("\n\nUse verbose mode ? (Y/N) ");
   ch = getche(); printf("\n\n");
   verbose = (ch == 'y' || ch == 'Y') ? 1 : 0;
   printf("Use safe copy mode ? (Y/N) ");
   ch = getche(); printf("\n\n");
```

```
  safe_mode = (ch == 'y' || ch == 'Y') ? 1 : 0;
  fn_copyto(destination, wildcard, num_wildcard, verbose, safe_mode);
}
```

Listing 9.7 Source code for program "lister.c"

```
#include <stdio.h>
#include "stdlib.h"
#include "dir.h"
#include "errno.h"
#include "conio.h"
#include "string.h"
#include "fcntl.h"
#include "sys\stat.h"
#include "fn_edir.h"
main(int argc, char* argv[])
{
  char wildcard[10][MAX_WILDCARD_LEN];
  unsigned int num_wildcard, num_files, i, count;
  struct ffblk *files = NULL;
  char ch;
  char dos_cmd[81];
  clrscr();
  directvideo = 1;
  if (argc < 2) {
     num_wildcard = 1;
     strcpy(wildcard[0],"*.*");
  }
  else {
   num_wildcard = argc - 1;
   for (i = 0; i < num_wildcard; i++)
      strcpy(wildcard[i],argv[i+1]);
  }
  files  = fn_edir(wildcard, num_wildcard, files, &num_files);
  if (num_files > 0) {
     for (i = 0 ; i < num_files; i++) {
         strcpy(dos_cmd,"LIST ");
         strcat(dos_cmd, (files+i)->ff_name);
         system(dos_cmd);
         printf("press the [X] key to exit or any other key to continue");
         ch = getch();
         if (ch == 'X' || ch == 'x') exit(0);
     }
   }
   free(files);
}
```

Listing 9.8 Source code for program "list.c"

```
/* C program that lists small programs.  The cursor
  and screen control keys are used to navigate in the listing.
  The listings are protected from any modification.          */
#include <stdio.h>
#include "conio.h"
enum booleans { FALSE, TRUE };
typedef enum booleans boolean;
#define MAX_LINES 750
#define LINES_PER_SCREEN 23
main(int argc, char* argv[])
{
    char filename[65];
    FILE *filevar;
    char line[MAX_LINES][81];
    int i, j, k, n, m, count, offset;
    char ch;
    int far *screen = (int far*) 0xB8000000L; /* for color */
 /* int far *screen = (int far*) 0xB0000000L; for mono */
    clrscr();
    gotoxy(33,1);
    puts("PROGRAM LISTER");
    gotoxy(33,2);
    puts("______________\n\n\n");
    do {
       if (argc < 2) {
         printf("Enter filename -> ");
         gets(filename); putch('\n');
       }
       else
         strcpy(filename,argv[1]);
       /* set argc to 1 so that subsequent filenames are queried */
       argc = 1;
       if ( (filevar = fopen(filename,"rt")) == NULL)
        printf("\nCannot open file %s\n\n",filename);
    } while (filevar == NULL);
    printf("\nReading ");
    n = 0;
    m = 0;
    while (n < MAX_LINES && !feof(filevar))  {
        if ((n % 50) == 0) putch('.');
        fgets(line[n], 80, filevar);
        n++;
    }
    fclose(filevar);
    n--;
    do {
```

```
      clrscr();
    k = 80;
    puts(filename);
      for (count = 1; count < LINES_PER_SCREEN; count++) {
          j = m + count;
        offset = 0;
        for (i = 0; (line[j][i] != '\0' && line[j][i] != 0x0A); i++) {
              if (line[j][i] == 0x09)
             offset += 7;
           else
              *(screen + i + k + offset) = line[j][i] | 0x700;
        }
        k += 80;
    }
    gotoxy(1,25);
        printf("use cursor/page control keys, [Q] to quit");
        ch = getch();
        if (ch == 0) {
            ch = getch(); /* get second byte */
        switch (ch) {
                case  71 :
                    m = 0; /* Home */
                    break;
                case 79 :
                    m = n - LINES_PER_SCREEN; /*End*/
                    break;
                case 73 :  /* PageUp */
                         if (m > 1)  m -= LINES_PER_SCREEN;
                         if (m < 0)  m = 0;
                         break;
                case 81 :  /* PageDown */
                         if (m < n)  m += LINES_PER_SCREEN;
                         if (m >= (n - LINES_PER_SCREEN))
                              m = n - LINES_PER_SCREEN;
                         break;
                case 72 :  /* Arrow Up */
                         if (m > 0)  m--;
                    break;
                case 80 :  /* Arrow Down */
                         if (m < n)  m++;
                         if (m >= (n - LINES_PER_SCREEN))
                              m = n - LINES_PER_SCREEN;
                         break;
        } /* switch */
        ch = ' ';
      }
    } while (ch != 'Q' && ch != 'q');
    clrscr();
}
```

Listing 9.9 The source code for the jump directory program "jump.c".

```
/*******************************************************************
 *
 *                        Jump Directory Program
 *
 *  Calling sequence: >j partial_dir_name  % jumps to directory
 *
 *                        or
 *
 *                     >j -s                % save directory tree
 *
 *  This program uses a fast lookup file created by the "-s" option to
 *  find a match on a directory name, and then jumps there.  Since the
 *  match may be a partial one, it prompts the user if the match is not
 *  unique and verifies that it is the one wanted.  If no match is
 *  found, or the user says no to each prompt, then no jump takes place.
 *
 *  This program reads/creates the file \save.dir in your root directory.
 *
 *
 *******************************************************************/
#include <stdio.h>
#include <string.h>
#include <dos.h>
#include <dir.h>
/* change this constant if you have more directories than this */
#define MAXNUMDIRS 256
void savedir(void);
int  scandir(int level, char *path, FILE *f, struct ffblk ffblk);
void jumpdir(char *dirname);
int  srch_tree(int level, char *path, char *dir);
int  verify(char *dir, char *newpath);
struct dirstruct {
  int level;
  char dir[MAXFILE];  /* MAXFILE = maximum size of file name + null */
} table[MAXNUMDIRS];
FILE *f;
int numdirs, index;
char path[MAXPATH];   /* MAXPATH = maximum size of path name + null */
main(int argc, char *argv[]) {
 int i,n;
 if (argc > 1) {
    if (!strcmp(argv[1],"-s")) {
       savedir();      /* -s option: he wants to save directory tree */
    }
    else {
       jumpdir(argv[1]);  /* else jump to a directory */
```

```
      }
   }
   else {
      printf("Usage: j partial_dir_name   or   j -s\n");
   }
}
void savedir(void)
/*
 * This routine scans the current drive and collects the path names
 * of all directories.  The names are stored in a special file
 * called "save.dir" in your root directory.  This file can then
 * be used to quickly find the directory to jump to.
 */
{
   struct ffblk ffblk;
   FILE *f;
   printf("Creating directory table \save.dir\n");
   f = fopen("\\save.dir","wt");  /* open save.dir in root directory */
   strcpy(path, "\\*.*");         /* start with root path */
   scandir(0, path, f, ffblk);
   fclose(f);
}
int scandir(int level, char *path, FILE *f, struct ffblk ffblk)
/*
 * This is a recursive routine that walks the directories in a
 * depth-first fashion and accumulates the full path name of
 * each subdirectory, then computes its depth in the directory tree.
 * The subdirectory name and its level are then written to file f.
 *
 * NOTE: since char *path is modified, it should NOT come in as a
 *       string literal.
 */
{
   int done, oldlen;
   oldlen = strlen(path);    /* keep track of "base" path length */
   done = findfirst(path,&ffblk,FA_DIREC);  /* grab first directory */
   while(!done) {
     path[oldlen] = 0;  /* reset to base path name */
     /* check to see if we found a directory, and that it is not the
        special directories "." (current directory) or ".." (parent
        directory).  These last two checks prevent infinite recursion.
      */
     if ((ffblk.ff_attrib == FA_DIREC) && stricmp(ffblk.ff_name,".")
          && stricmp(ffblk.ff_name,"..")) {
        printf("%d ",level);                          /* feedback to user */
        fprintf(f,"%d %s\n",level,ffblk.ff_name);  /* and store */
        path[strlen(path)-3] = 0;       /* remove "*.*" search pattern */
        strcat(path,ffblk.ff_name);     /* add new directory name */
        strcat(path,"\\*.*");           /* and search pattern */
```

```
        scandir(level+1, path, f, ffblk);
     }
     if (findnext(&ffblk) == -1) done = 1;  /* no more files */
   }
   return;
}
void jumpdir(char *dirname)
/* Opens the directory tree table \save.dir and then searches for
 * the directory node char *dirname.  This name can be a partial one.
 */
{
 int i,n;
 if ((f = fopen("\\save.dir","rt")) == NULL) {
    printf("Directory table file \\save.dir not found\n");
    exit(0);
 }
 numdirs = -1;
 while(!feof(f)) {  /* read in the number of directories */
  if (numdirs == MAXNUMDIRS - 1) {
     printf("WARNING: out of room in directory table, ");
     printf("only first %d read\n", MAXNUMDIRS);
     break;
  }
  numdirs++;
  fscanf(f,"%d %s\n",&(table[numdirs].level), table[numdirs].dir);
 }
 fclose(f);
 index = 0;           /* initialize directory table index */
 strcpy(path,"\\");  /* start with root directory       */
 if (!srch_tree(0,path,dirname)) printf("sub-directory not found\n");
}
int srch_tree(int level, char *path, char *dir)
/*
 * Searches our directory tree for a match, and changes directories
 * and returns a 1 if we do find one, else 0 is returned.
 *
 * "path" is the full path name of the directory we are currently
 * trying. "dir" is the partial or full name of the directory
 * we would like to jump to.
 *
 * NOTE: This is a recursive routine, and uses index and numdirs as
 *       global variables.  They must be initialized before this
 *       routine is called the first time.
 *       Also, since char *path is modified, NEVER pass it as a
 *       string literal.
 */
{
  int oldlen;
  oldlen = strlen(path);            /* keep track of base path */
```

```
  while(index < numdirs) {
    path[oldlen] = 0;              /* reset to base path name */
    strcat(path,table[index].dir); /* tack on our target dir  */
    /* check for match, if found, verify it is the desired one */
    if (!strnicmp(dir,table[index].dir,strlen(dir))) {
       if (verify(dir,path)) {
          chdir(path);    /* yep, so jump there */
          return 1;       /* signal we've done so */
       }
    }
    index++;
    if (index < numdirs) {
       if (table[index].level != table[index-1].level) {
          if (table[index].level > table[index-1].level) {
             strcat(path,"\\");  /* get ready to go down the tree */
             if (srch_tree(level+1,path,dir)) return 1;
             /* might be several levels deep, so keep popping */
             if (level > table[index].level) return 0;
          }
          else {       /* new level < old level */
            return 0; /* so go back up to parent */
          }
       }
    }
  }
  return 0;
}
int verify(char *dir, char *newpath)
/*
 *  Sees if the directory name is unique.  If it's not,
 *  the user is prompted with the full path name to verify
 *  it's the one he wants.  If it is unique, no prompting
 *  is done.
 *  Returns 1 if it's the right directory, else 0.
 */
{
    int i,cnt,c;
    for (i=0, cnt=0; i <= numdirs; i++) /* count number of matches */
        if (!strnicmp(dir,table[i].dir,strlen(dir))) cnt++;
     if (cnt > 1) {
       printf("\n%s ?",newpath);
       c = getche();
       if (c == 'y' || c == 'Y') return 1;
       return 0;
     }
    return 1;
}
```

CHAPTER

10

Advanced File I/O

This chapter picks up where Chapter 5 left off and discusses more advanced file applications. This is done by developing yet another application-oriented package built on top of the FILE I/O package.

The record-oriented file I/O discussed earlier only works for fixed-length records. There are many applications that need varying amounts of data in each record. Some examples are CAD databases, where figures might be drawn and stored using a list of points or as variable-sized bit mapped images. Another example is an on-line reference program, where each reference has a varying amount of text. The new hypertext applications that are becoming increasingly popular also require some way of storing varying amounts of data. Although you could use fixed-length records for these applications, using variable-length records can result in significantly smaller files.

This chapter introduces a Variable-length Record (VLR) package. Along with showing many of the file I/O functions in practical use, you will see the Pop-up Window and Dynamic String packages in action as well. The chapter ends with a very simple "slide-show" program, which stores and retrieves graphic objects and uses variable-length records. In a later chapter, you will see a hypertext application that also uses these variable-length records.

VARIABLE-LENGTH RECORD FILES

Handling files with variable-length records is more complicated than with fixed-length records. There are basically three issues involved.

- How do you locate records in the file?
- How do you insert and delete records?
- How do you alleviate fragmentation of records in the file?

We will discuss each of these issues, in addition to discussing how our VLR package handles them:

LOCATING VLRS IN A FILE

Locating records in a fixed-length record file is easy. The byte offset of a record can be found by multiplying the size of a record by the record number. For VLRs, some form of index must be used.

In general, the index for a VLR file contains a key identifying each record and the starting address of that record in the file. There could be more than one set of indices, either to group the records into categories or to provide multiple keys into the database. These indices could be stored separately from the data file itself, as is often done in btree databases, or stored within the data file. Each approach has its tradeoffs.

Keeping the index separate from the data file itself allows you to organize and reorganize the keys independently of the data file. It also makes it easy to add multiple sets of indices by merely creating another index file. However, this means you must keep track of more files for any given database and, more importantly, have multiple files opened at once. In general, it is a good idea to minimize the number of files opened, since there are a limited number of file handles available from DOS. With the separate index approach, you can quickly use up all the file handles if you need to have multiple databases open simultaneously.

By storing the index with the data itself, you can get around these problems, but other problems are created in the process. Since the number of records in the file is variable, the size of the index is, too. You could just set a limit on the number of records available in the file. Then the index could be fixed length, and you could reserve space in the file (probably at the beginning) for the index. However, it is better not to impose such arbitrary limits, so what *do* you do?

One way to handle this situation is to store the index as a VLR itself. The index is then read into memory to be used. This may impose a limitation that the index must fit in memory, so the maximum number of records you can handle is fixed. However, in many applications, this limitation is not really a problem.

Although indexing is not strictly a part of the VLR package, we will show the internal indexing approach in our examples.

INSERTING AND DELETING VLRS

Inserting or deleting records is a problem for both fixed-length and variable-length files. Many fixed-length record databases keep a list of free or unused records. When a record is deleted, it is placed on the "free" list. When a new record is to be added, one from the free list is used. The same idea is used for variable-length records.

The VLR files store each variable-length record as blocks of data hooked together in a linked list. (We will thus use the terms *list* and *record* interchangeably throughout this discussion.) The blocks themselves are of variable length and can be up to 256 bytes long.

There is a special record, called the *free space list,* which contains all blocks that were once used but have been deleted. When more space is needed, blocks from the free space list are used first. Should the free space list become empty, then bytes are added to the end of the file. When a list is deleted, all of its blocks are added to the free space list.

RECORD FRAGMENTATION

When a variable-length record is reused, the new data may be larger or smaller than the original data. Making the record grow in size is relatively easy. New blocks are simply acquired from the free space list. But what if the new data is smaller, and in particular, substantially smaller? Rather than cause waste, you would like to return as much space as possible to the free space list. However, you must be careful not to cause undue fragmentation in the file, (i.e., create a large number of short blocks). A fragmented file leads to much wasted space, as an inordinate number of pointers are stored, relative to the data itself. Such files also have slower access.

This fragmentation problem is present in every memory management system, whether that memory is in RAM or is stored on disk. Even the DOS file system has this problem. For our VLR files, the fragmentation problem is handled in the following manner.

The VLR algorithms try to use full 256 byte blocks whenever possible. When a new list is added, as many full 256 byte blocks as possible are used. Rather than waste a whole 256-byte block, any remaining bytes are stored in a short block. We could just make this last block exactly as large as needed; instead, the last block is padded with extra bytes. This gives the record a little room to grow without having to allocate new blocks. The size of the padding is application-dependent. By using the appropriate size, you can help minimize fragmentation.

Whenever a record is updated, its old list is reused. If the size of the new data is smaller, then you need to return bytes from the remaining blocks to the free space list. To keep fragmentation to a minimum, once a block is created, it is never split up. That is, you do not reuse a block partially and then return the rest of it to the free space list. Only the completely unused blocks remaining are returned. Although this may waste some space, it avoids having blocks that have only a few bytes in them. Also, if the record is updated and made larger, then the empty space in the last block is readily available for the expansion, and you may not have to create any new blocks at all.

Padding the last block has one unfortunate consequence: you cannot tell where the actual data ends merely by scanning to the end of the last block. Thus, the length of the data must be recorded in some other manner. If you were storing ASCII text, you could simply signal the end with a NULL byte. Even with binary data, you might have a special marker-byte sequence to signal the end. A more general way is to just store the length of the record at the beginning. This is the approach used in the VLR package: the first block of a VLR record contains the number of actual bytes of data.

THE VLR FILE FORMAT

Figure 10.1 shows the format for VLR files as used in the VLR package.

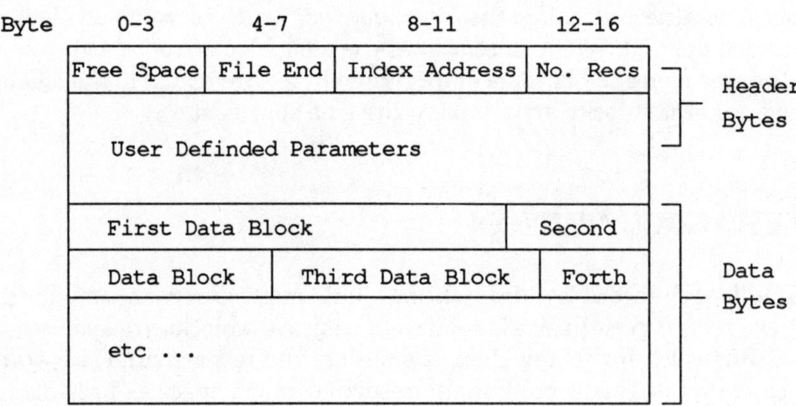

Figure 10.1 VLR file format

THE VLR FILE HEADER

The first part of the file contains a block of header bytes. There are four parameters in the header. The **free space** parameter points to the start of the free space list. The **file end** parameter points to the last byte in the file. When these two parameters are equal, it is a signal that there is no more free space in the file; that is, the file is full, and if more bytes need to be added, then the file must grow in size.

The **index address** parameter points to the start of the index for the file. This parameter is optional, and is provided in case you wish to store the index along with the data in the same file. The **free space** and **file end** parameters are meant for internal use only, but the **index address** parameter is not a part of the VLR package itself, and it is handled completely by the user.

The last parameter is the number of records currently stored in the file and is provided mainly for convenience. It is maintained entirely by the VLR package.

Following the four parameters is a region of reserved space. The size of this space is specified when a new VLR file is created. It is provided as an area to keep additional parameters that you may wish to store in the file, and it is totally under user control. For instance, you may want to have multiple indices stored with the file. This space could be used to store the starting addresses of those indices.

THE VLR RECORD FORMAT

Following the header bytes are the start of the variable-length records themselves. Each record is stored as a singly linked list of data blocks. Each data block can be from 6 bytes to 256 bytes long. The blocks have the format shown in Figure 10.2.

Byte	0	1	2-5	6-7*	8-255	
	L	S	Next Location	N	Data	

* For the first block, this is the number of actual bytes of data in the list. For all other blocks, these bytes are data.

Figure 10.2 Format of variable-length record data blocks

The first byte contains the length L, which represents the number of bytes in the block, not including the length byte itself. For instance, if L = 15, it means that the block is 16 bytes long. L can range from 5 to 255. If L = 5, that means there is no data in the block; the block just contains a link to the next block. Empty blocks represent wasted space and do not normally occur in a VLR file if the routines are used properly.

The second byte is called the **sync byte**, and always has the code 0xfd. This byte serves as an integrity check. When scanning a list, this byte is checked to make sure it has the code of 0xfd. If it does not, it means that the file has somehow been garbled.

Following the sync byte is a 4-byte integer which is the address of the next block in the list. For example, if it had the value of 0x0100, then the next block would start 256 bytes (0x100) from the beginning of the file. If the next location is 0x0000, it means that you have reached the end of the list.

Following the next location field is the data itself. If this block is the first one in the list, then the first two bytes store the actual number of bytes of data for the whole list.

THE VLR PACKAGE

Now that we have discussed the issues involved with variable-length records and have seen the format of VLR files, the VLR package can be introduced. The code is given in Listings 10.1 and 10.2. The package contains the following external routines:

Routine	Use
openvlr	Open/create a VLR file.
readhdr	Read the file header bytes.
writehdr	Write the file header bytes.
getvlr	Read in a VLR record.
addvlr	Add a VLR record.
delvlr	Delete a VLR record.
reuse_vlr	Reuse or update a VLR record.

These functions make extensive use of the Error Reporting and File I/O packages given earlier. The VLR package also works hand-in-hand with the VSTR package. The dynamic strings handled by the VSTR package are useful for storing varying amounts of data in RAM, and VLR records are useful for storing that same type of data in a file.

OPENING AND CREATING VLR FILES

The **openvlr()** function is used to open or create a VLR file. Its prototype is:

```
int openvlr(char *fname, char *access_type, long rs);
```

The first parameter is the filename and the second is the access mode, given as a string just as it is for any standard I/O file. The third parameter indicates the byte location where the data records are to start.

The file handle is returned. Like all of the standard file I/O functions, a return value of -1 is used to indicate errors. Note that the file handle returned is not the DOS file handle, but rather the pseudohandle used by the File I/O package.

A typical call to create a VLR file might be as follows:

```
/*
   Opening VLR files example  (vlrex1.c)
   Must link with: popup.obj, mouse.obj, sayerr.obj,
        fileio.obj, vstr.obj, vlr.obj
*/
#include <stdio.h>  /* must include for std I/O routines     */
#include "popup.h"  /* all of these must be included as well */
#include "fileio.h"
#include "vstr.h"
#include "vlr.h"
void main() {
  int fh;
  init_win();       /* always, always, always do */
  init_files();
  if ((fh = openvlr("mydata.vlr","w+b", 32L)) != -1) {
     mprintf("mydata.vlr file created successfully\r\n");
     closefile(fh);
  }
  else {
     mprintf("mydata.vlr file not created successfully\r\n");
  }
}
```

Here, "w+b" is used for the access mode to indicate that you wish the file created and to use binary mode. It is important never to use an append mode and to always use binary access; otherwise, the VLR routines may not work properly.

In this example, we have told **openvlr()** to start the data records at byte location 32. This basically tells the VLR package the size of the header section of the file. You can use any value greater than 16, as you see fit. The four parameters FS (free space address), FE (file end address), IA (index address), and NR (number of records) are stored in the first 16 bytes. The area between these and the start of the data records is uninitialized, so if you were to inspect the file via a hex dump, you would just see harmless garbage there. It is up to the user to initialize this area as he or she sees fit.

When a VLR file is first created, the FS, FE, IA, and NR parameters are initialized. The FS and FE parameters are both set to the start of the data records. By setting them to be equal, it indicates that there is currently no free space. The IA parameter is set to 0, (it is updated by the user whenever appropriate), and the NR parameter is also set to 0. The VLR file is now ready for use.

ACCESSING THE HEADER SECTION

The routines **readhdr()** and **writehdr()** are used to access the four parameters FS, FE, IA, and NR in the header section. They have the following prototypes:

```
int  readhdr(int fh, long *fs, long *fe, long *ia, long *nr);
int writehdr(int fh, long fs,  long fe,  long ia,  long nr);
```

The FS and FE parameters are for internal use only and should not be tampered with. In fact, the only reason to use **readhdr()** and **writehdr()** in an application is to access the index address and number of records in the file. Any other user-defined parameters in the header must be accessed directly with your own routines.

Since the four parameters are critical to file integrity, whenever **writehdr()** is called, the file buffer is flushed.

ADDING AND RETRIEVING RECORDS

The routines **addvlr()** and **getvlr()** are used to add a new record to the file and to retrieve the data of an existing record. The data to be added or retrieved is passed via a dynamic string. For **addvlr()**, the new location of the record is returned. For **getvlr()**, you must pass it this location. The prototypes for these two functions are:

```
int addvlr(int fh, vstr *s, long *locn);
int getvlr(int fh, vstr *s, long locn);
```

The following program shows an example of storing and retrieving a record. The assumption is made that the records will start at byte 32.

```
/*
   Example of accessing a vlr file  (vlrex2.c)
   Must link with: popup.obj, mouse.obj, sayerr.obj,
          fileio.obj, vstr.obj, vlr.obj
*/
```

```
#include <stdio.h>
#include "popup.h"
#include "fileio.h"
#include "vstr.h"
#include "vlr.h"
void main() {
  int fh;
  vstr mydata = NULLVSTR;
  long locn;
  long fs, fe, ia, nr;     /* four parms in header section */
  init_win();     /* always, always, always do */
  init_files();
  /* Start a character string, add a null
     terminated message to it */
  clrvstr(&mydata, 20, sizeof(char), 5);
  vstrins(&mydata, 0, "hello world\0", 12); /* notice null byte */
  /* Open file.  If successful, write, and then read the data */
  /* Also, retrieve number of records in the file */
  if ((fh = openvlr("mydata.vlr","w+b", 32L)) != -1) {
mprintf("mydata.vlr created successfully\r\n");
     addvlr(fh, &mydata, &locn);  /* add record      */
     getvlr(fh, &mydata, locn);    /* read it back in */
     mprintf("First record at locn %ld contains: '%s'\r\n",
          locn, mydata.data);
     readhdr(fh, &fs, &fe, &ia, &nr);
     mprintf("Free space at %ld\r\n", fs);
     mprintf("File ends at %ld\r\n", fe);
     mprintf("Number of records is %ld\r\n", nr);
     closefile(fh);
  }
  else {
mprintf("mydata.vlr not created successfully\r\n");
  }
}
```

The function **addvlr()** takes the data in the dynamic string and, if there is free space, reuses the free space list to store the data. If there is no free space, the data is appended to the file. In either event, the starting address of the record is returned. When reading an existing record using **getvlr()**, the starting address must be specified. Typically, the address is kept in some index table associated with the file. In this simple example, we have merely kept it in a local variable.

TYPING VLRS

When a dynamic string is written to a VLR file, the current length of the string is multiplied by the element size to determine the actual number of bytes in the string. This number is stored along with the data. When a variable-length record is read, the associated string is first reset (by setting the current length to 0), and the data is read in. The stored length of the data is then divided by the element size to determine the length of the string.

What this means is that the "type" of the stored data is determined by the "type" of dynamic string passed. The typing information used is simply the size of one element in the string. Thus it is important to use the same "type" of string for reading and writing a variable-length record. In particular, if the element size is not a multiple of the number of bytes written, then an improper length will be returned and data could be lost. If you wish to access the data in raw binary form, then use a string with an element size of a character.

UPDATING VLRS

Records of a VLR file are updated by using the **reuse_vlr()** function and can be deleted using the function **delvlr()**. Their prototypes are:

```
int reuse_vlr(int fh, long locn, vstr *w, int offset, int use_fs);
int delvlr(int fh, long locn);
```

Deleting a record is straightforward. The blocks of the record are added to the front of the free space list, and the record count is decremented.

The **reuse_vlr()** function is the longest of the routines, and the most complicated. It first takes the dynamic string stored in **w** and scans the old variable-length record at location **locn**, filling up its blocks. If there are any remaining blocks that are completely unused, they are returned to the free space list. The remaining bytes of the last partial block are simply left as they are.

If the old record is not big enough, then the free space list is used. This is accomplished by calling **reuse_vlr()** recursively, with the free space list being "reused." When recursing, the parameter offset points to the remaining bytes of the string to be written. The parameter **use_fs** signals the routine to reuse the free space.

Should the free space list get exhausted, then the internal routine **extend_file()** is called to append bytes to the file. This routine fills as many 256-byte blocks as are needed and pads the last block with extra bytes. The padsize external variable can be set to any size desired. It defaults to 10 bytes.

The following example shows a VLR file being created and a record being added, updated, and finally deleted.

```
/*
   More examples of vlr file I/O  (vlrex3.c)
   Must link with: popup.obj, mouse.obj, sayerr.obj,
         fileio.obj, vstr.obj, vlr.obj
*/
    #include <stdio.h>
```

```
#include "popup.h"
#include "fileio.h"
#include "vstr.h"
#include "vlr.h"
void main() {
  int fh;
  vstr mydata = NULLVSTR;
  long locn;
  long fs, fe, ia, nr; /* four parms in header section */
  init_win();          /* always, always, always do */
  init_files();
  /* start a character string, add a
     null terminated message to it */
  clrvstr(&mydata, 20, sizeof(char), 5);
  vstrins(&mydata, 0, "hello world\0", 12); /* notice null byte */
  /* open file.  If successful, write, and then read the data */
  /* Also, retrieve number of records in the file */
  if ((fh = openvlr("mydata.vlr","w+b", 32L)) != -1) {
   mprintf("mydata.vlr created successfully\r\n");
     addvlr(fh, &mydata, &locn);  /* add record      */
     getvlr(fh, &mydata, locn);   /* read it back in */
     mprintf("First record at locn %ld contains: '%s'\r\n",
          locn, mydata.data);
     readhdr(fh, &fs, &fe, &ia, &nr);
     mprintf("Free space at %ld\r\n", fs);
     mprintf("File ends at %ld\r\n", fe);
     mprintf("Number of records is %ld\r\n", nr);
     /* update record, then read it back in */
     vstrins(&mydata,6,"cruel ",6);
     mprintf("adding %s\r\n", mydata.data);
     reuse_vlr(fh, locn, &mydata, 0, 0);
     getvlr(fh, &mydata, locn);
     mprintf("Record now contains: '%s'\r\n", mydata.data);
     readhdr(fh, &fs, &fe, &ia, &nr);
     mprintf("Free space at %ld\r\n", fs);
     mprintf("File ends at %ld\r\n", fe);
     mprintf("Number of records is %ld\r\n", nr);
     /* delete the record */
     delvlr(fh, locn);
     mprintf("Record now deleted\r\n");
     readhdr(fh, &fs, &fe, &ia, &nr);
     mprintf("Free space at %ld\r\n", fs);
```

```
    mprintf("File ends at %ld\r\n", fe);
    mprintf("Number of records is %ld\r\n", nr);
    closefile(fh);
  }
  else {
    mprintf("mydata.vlr not created successfully\r\n");
  }
}
```

When executed, this program will print out:

```
New vlr file created successfully
First record at locn 32 contains: 'hello world'
Free space at 62
File ends at 62
Number of records is 1
adding hello cruel world
Record now contains: 'hello cruel world'
Free space at 62
File ends at 62
Number of records is 1
Record now deleted
Free space at 32
File ends at 62
Number of records is 0
```

Note how the last two parameters **offset** and **use_fs** are handled. For an external call to **reuse_vlr()**, these two parameters should always be 0. Only the internal recursive call should set these parameters to nonzero values.

BUILDING AN INTERNAL VLR INDEX

We will now show you how to build an index for a set of variable-length records and then how to store this index as a record itself. In this example, the index will not store any keys, just the addresses of the records. The easiest way to do this is to build the index as a dynamic string of long integers. All of the records are added to the VLR file, and their starting addresses are recorded in the integer string. This string is then written to the file, and the index address itself is added to the header block.

```
/*
   Example of an internal vlr file index  (vlrex4.c)
   Must link with: popup.obj, mouse.obj, sayerr.obj,
         fileio.obj, vstr.obj, vlr.obj
    */
    #include <stdio.h>
    #include "popup.h"
```

```
#include "fileio.h"
#include "vstr.h"
#include "vlr.h"
void main() {
  int fh;
  vstr rec1data = NULLVSTR;
  vstr rec2data = NULLVSTR;
  vstr rec3data = NULLVSTR;
  vstr buffer   = NULLVSTR;
  vstr index    = NULLVSTR;
  long locn;
  long fs, fe, ia, nr;    /* four parms in header section */
  init_win();     /* always, always, always do */
  init_files();
  /* make the null terminated character strings */
  clrvstr(&rec1data, 20, sizeof(char), 5);
  vstrins(&rec1data, 0, "This is record one\0",19);
  clrvstr(&rec2data, 20, sizeof(char), 5);
  vstrins(&rec2data, 0, "This is record two\0",19);
  clrvstr(&rec3data, 20, sizeof(char), 5);
  vstrins(&rec3data, 0, "This is the third record\0",25);
  clrvstr(&buffer, 20, sizeof(char), 5);  /* temp buffer */
  /* and then the index itself */
  clrvstr(&index, 10, sizeof(long), 5);
  /* open file.  If successful, add the records, and record the
     addresses in the index table.
  */
  if ((fh = openvlr("mydata.vlr","w+b", 32L)) != -1) {
     mprintf("New vlr file created successfully\r\n");
     addvlr(fh, &rec1data, &locn);
     vstrcat(&index, &locn);
     addvlr(fh, &rec2data, &locn);
     vstrcat(&index, &locn);
     addvlr(fh, &rec3data, &locn);
     vstrcat(&index, &locn);
     /* Add the index itself to the file, then update the
        header bytes to point to index
     */
     addvlr(fh, &index, &locn);
     readhdr(fh, &fs, &fe, &ia, &nr);
     writehdr(fh, fs, fe, locn, nr);
     /* Now, read in the index, and then each record */
```

```
      readhdr(fh, &fs, &fe, &ia, &nr);  /* get index address */
      getvlr(fh, &index, ia);
      locn = ((long *)(index.data))[0];
      getvlr(fh, &buffer, locn);
      mprintf("First record at locn %ld contains: '%s'\r\n",
              locn, buffer.data);
      locn = ((long *)(index.data))[1];
      getvlr(fh, &buffer, locn);
      mprintf("Second record at locn %ld contains: '%s'\r\n",
              locn, buffer.data);
      locn = ((long *)(index.data))[2];
      getvlr(fh, &buffer, locn);
      mprintf("Third record at locn %ld contains: '%s'\r\n",
              locn, buffer.data);
      mprintf("Free space at %ld\r\n", fs);
      mprintf("File ends at %ld\r\n", fe);
      mprintf("Number of records is %ld\r\n", nr);
      closefile(fh);
   }
   else {
      mprintf("File not created successfully\r\n");
   }
}
```

When executed, this program prints out:

```
New vlr file created successfully
First record at locn 32 contains: 'This is record one'
Second record at locn 69 contains: 'This is record two'
Third record at locn 106 contains: 'This is the third record'
Free space at 179
File ends at 179
Number of records is 4
```

Note how the index record is counted in the record count.

EXAMPLE: A SIMPLE SLIDE-SHOW PROGRAM

This section gives an extended example of using VLR files. Presented are two programs, one to create a series of "slides" of graphical objects and one to show these slides. The slide-creation program is given in Listing 10.3, and the slide-show program in Listing 10.4. Upon examining them, you will see that the two programs are very similar, using basically the same code.

The slide-creation program allows you create graphical polygon objects within a frame. You can then store these objects and create other ones, generating a series of frames. The program uses the mouse (our apologies if you do not have one) to do the drawing and to select commands. Figure 10.3 shows a sample screen. The objects are drawn within the rectangular region (with clipping turned on) by building up a series of line segments. A line segment is drawn whenever the left mouse button is clicked inside the frame.

Commands are selected by pointing at the desired entry and clicking the left mouse button. The commands are:

Command	Use
`Store`	`Stores the current slide`
`Fill`	`Makes a closed polygon by connecting the first point with the last, and then filling the polygon with red crosshatches`
`Clear`	`Clears the slide, and resets the object's point list`
`Quit`	`Closes the slide file and quits the program`

To draw an object, simply move the mouse to a desired position and click the left mouse button. A line will be drawn from the previous point to the new point. Continue this process until you wish to close off the polygon. Then select the FILL command. You can draw more than one polygon on a slide. When finished, select the STORE command to save the slide. If you make a mistake when making a slide, select CLEAR to clear the screen and reset the polygon lists. When all finished, select QUIT to close the file and exit the program. Your series of slides are now all saved in one VLR file.

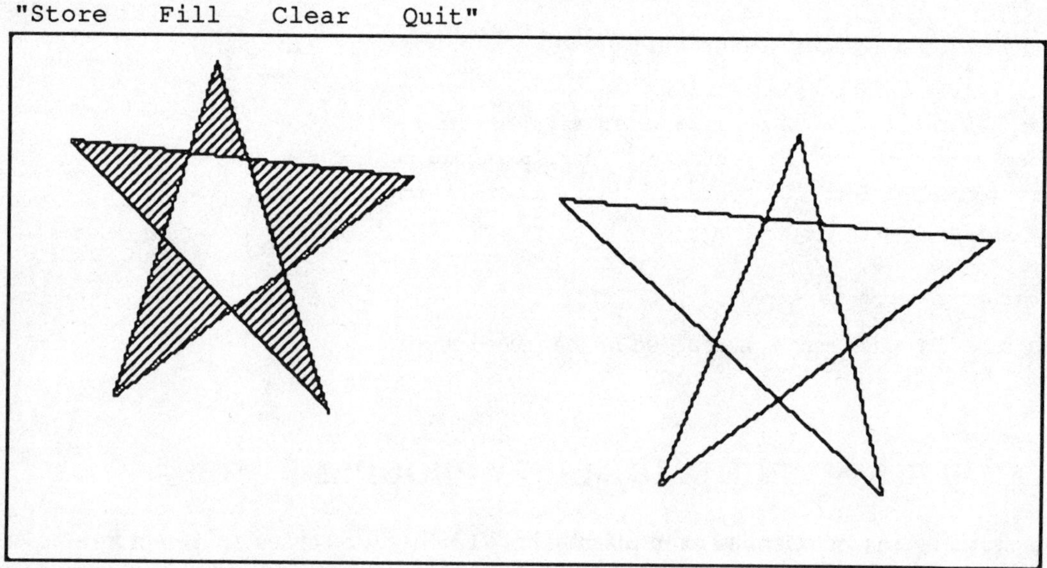

Figure 10.3 Using the polygon slide show creation program

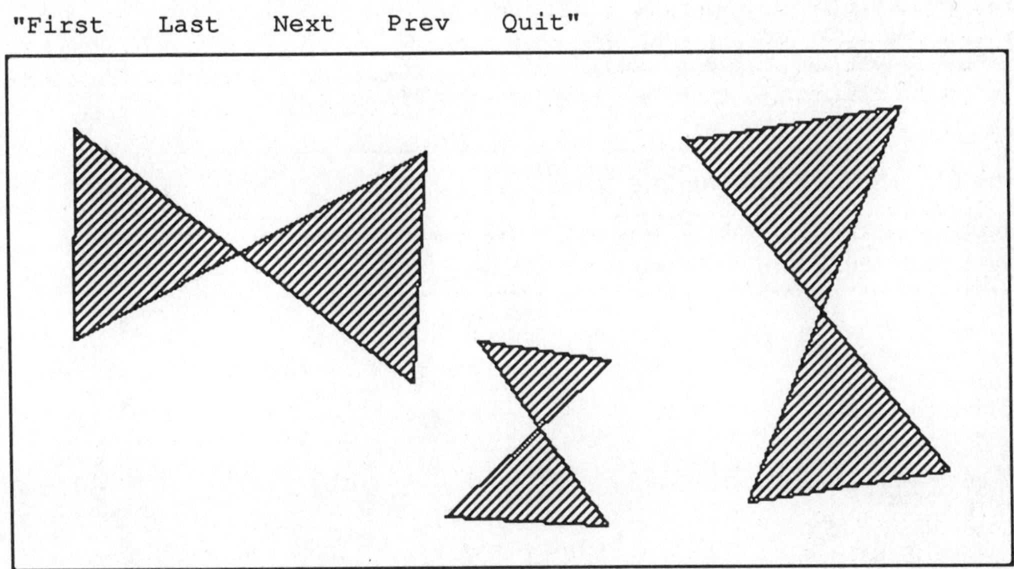

Figure 10.4 Using the polygon slide show browser program

To view the slides, execute the program given in Listing 10.4. A sample screen is given in Figure 10.4. The FIRST, LAST, NEXT, and PREVIOUS commands all move to the corresponding slide. In the right-hand corner is the number of the current slide and the total number of slides available.

Both programs use a file named **objects.vlr** in the current directory. The slide-creation program creates this file. The slide-show program opens it for read-only access.

These sample programs have one bug in them. The VLR package uses the File I/O package, which in turn uses the Error-reporting package. The Error-reporting package, in turn, calls the Pop-up Window package. The pop-up windows are for text mode only, so if a file error occurs when in graphics mode, instead of an error window you will just get garbage. Because of the modularity of the packages, all you need to do is create a different **sayerr()** function for graphics mode, update the header files appropriately, and link in the graphics version of **sayerr()** instead of the text version. This is left to you as an exercise.

Listing 10.1 Source code for file "vlr.h"

```
/*  Variable length record toolkit header file   (vlr.h)     */
extern int openvlr(char *fname, char *access_type, long rs);
extern int readhdr(int fh, long *fs, long *fe, long *ita, long *nl);
extern int writehdr(int fh, long fs, long fe, long ita, long nl);
```

```
extern int getvlr(int fh, vstr *s, long locn);
extern int reuse_vlr(int fh, long locn, vstr *w, int offset, int use_fs);
extern int delvlr(int fh, long locn);
extern int addvlr(int fh, vstr *w, long *locn);
extern int padsize;
```

Listing 10.2 Source code for file "vlr.c"

```
/*************************************************************
 *  Variable length record toolkit  (vlr.c)
 *************************************************************/
#include <stddef.h>
#include <io.h>
#include <stdio.h>
#include <fcntl.h>
#include <string.h>
#include "popup.h"
#include "vstr.h"
#include "fileio.h"
#include "vlr.h"
/* our synchronization code for integrity checking */
#define SYNC_BYTE 253
/* "NULL" link code, and data padding constant */
#define NOLINK 0
/* Each block has 6 bytes of header information, can hold 250 data bytes */
#define BLK_SIZE  256
#define DATA_SIZE 250
int padsize = 10;  /* default padding to 10 bytes */
static int getvlrelem(int fh, long pos, long *nxtlocn,
                      unsigned char *datablk);
static int extend_file(int fh, vstr *s, long *locn, int offset);
int openvlr(char *fname, char *access_type, long rs)
/*
   Opens a variable length record file, using access_type to control
   the file access mode (see openfile function in fileio.c).
   NOTE: DO NOT use any append mode, and be sure to use binary mode !!!.
   If the file is created, then it sets the records to start at rs.
   If just opening, then this parm is ignored.
   Returns new file entry, or -1 if an error occurred.
*/
{
     int fh;
     long zero = 0L;
     /* Open for byte level access */
     if ((fh = openfile(fname,access_type,1)) != -1) {
         if (*access_type == 'w') { /* ie. we're creating */
           outbytes(fh, 0L, (unsigned char *)&rs, 4);    /* freespace */
           outbytes(fh, 4L, (unsigned char *)&rs, 4);    /* file_end  */
```

```
            outbytes(fh, 8L, (unsigned char *)&zero, 4);  /* index_rec */
            outbytes(fh, 12L,(unsigned char *)&zero, 4);  /* nrecs     */
        }
    }
    return fh;
}
int readhdr(int fh, long *fs, long *fe, long *ita, long *nl)
/*
   Reads the header info: FreeSpace, FileEnd, IndxTabAddr,
   and number of Lists.

   Returns = 0 if successful, else, returns a -1
*/
{
    unsigned char datablk[16];
    int rval;
    rval = inbytes(fh, 0L, datablk, 16);
    memcpy((char *)fs, datablk, 4);
    memcpy((char *)fe, datablk+4, 4);
    memcpy((char *)ita, datablk+8, 4);
    memcpy((char *)nl, datablk+12, 4);
    if (rval < 0) return -1; return 0;
}
int writehdr(int fh, long fs, long fe, long ita, long nl)
/*
   Writes the header info: FileStart, FileEnd, IndxTabAddr,
   and number of Lists.

   Returns = 0 if successful, else, returns  a -1
*/
{
    unsigned char datablk[16];
    int rval;
    memcpy(datablk,    (char *)&fs,  4);
    memcpy(datablk+4,  (char *)&fe,  4);
    memcpy(datablk+8,  (char *)&ita, 4);
    memcpy(datablk+12, (char *)&nl,  4);
    rval = outbytes(fh, 0L, datablk, 16);
    if (rval < 0) return -1;
    /* Flush the buffer to insure critical data is written.
       Note we must access stream pointer as stored in file table.
    */
    if (fflush(ft[fh].fp)) {
       sayerr(FERR,"Writing vlr header data in %s\r\n", ft[fh].name);
       return -1;
    }
    return 0;
}
```

```
static int getvlrelem(int fh, long pos, long *nxtlocn,
                      unsigned char *datablk)
/*
 * Reads up to 256 bytes of a block of a VLR.   Thus, datablk should have
 * at least 256 bytes of room in it.  Returns number of bytes read,
 * or returns -1 if an error has occurred.
 *
 * It determines the number of bytes to read from the first byte of block,
 * which gives the length of the block, excluding the byte itself.
 */
{
    int bytesread;
    inbytes(fh, pos, datablk, 1);  /* read length byte */
    bytesread = inbytes(fh, -1L, datablk+1, *datablk);
    if (datablk[1] != SYNC_BYTE) {
       sayerr(SERR,"Sync byte error at %ld\r\n",pos);
       return -1;
    }
    else {
      memcpy((char *)nxtlocn, datablk+2, 4);
    }
    return bytesread;
}
int getvlr(int fh, vstr *s, long pos)
/*
 *  Reads in a variable-length record into virtual string s from file fh,
 *  at pos'n pos.  Returns number of bytes in the record, else returns
 *  -1 if an error occurred.
 */
{
   unsigned char datablk[256];
   unsigned int offset, actual_len, data_size, data_indx;
   int nblks;
   s->currlen = 0;  /* reset string length */
   offset = 0;
   nblks = 0;
   while(pos != 0L) {
     if ((getvlrelem(fh, pos, &pos, datablk)) == -1) {
        /* give up and return what you have */
        s->currlen = offset / s->esize;
        return -1;
     }
     else { /* add data to end of virtual string */
       if (++nblks == 1) { /* if first block, then get actual data length */
          memcpy(&actual_len, datablk+6, 2);
          if (actual_len % s->esize) { /* data types wrong !! */
             sayerr(SERRF,"Data length doesn't jive with vstr type.\r\n"
                          "Data len = %u, element size = %u\r\n",
                          actual_len, s->esize);
```

```
            return -1;
         }
         /* Might have to extend the string. */
         if ((actual_len / s->esize) > s->dimlen) {
            if (!(redimvstr(s, actual_len / s->esize))) return -1;
         }
         data_indx = 8;
         data_size = *datablk-7;  /* compute amt of data in blk */
      }
      else {
         data_indx = 4;
         data_size = *datablk-5;
      }
      memcpy((char *)(s->data)+offset, datablk+data_indx, data_size);
      offset += data_size;
    }
  }
  /* Set current length (in units of elem_size) to the length given
     in the data itself.  Hopefully it divides equally.
  */
  s->currlen = actual_len / s->esize;
  return actual_len;
}
static int extend_file(int fh, vstr *s, long *locn, int offset)
/* Extends the file by adding the data in variable string s to the file,
 * starting with the bytes at the specified offset.  The locn of the
 * start of the data is returned in *locn.
 * Function returns 0 if successful, or -1 otherwise.
 */
{
   long fs,fe,ita,nrecs,link;
   unsigned int i,nb,nl, len;
   unsigned char datablk[256];
   /* Convert length to no. of chars, and subtract offset    */
   /* but if on first block, leave room for two length bytes */
   len = s->currlen * s->esize - offset;
   if (offset == 0) len += 2;
   if (readhdr(fh, &fs, &fe, &ita, &nrecs) == -1) return -1;
   nb = len / DATA_SIZE;
   nl = len - nb*DATA_SIZE;
   link = fe; *locn = fe;
   /* Fill up full blocks first.  If we exhaust the data then link the
    * last block to nowhere.
    */
   if (nb)  {
     for (i = 1; i<=nb; i++) {
       if (i==nb && nl==0) link = 0; else link += BLK_SIZE;
       memcpy(datablk+2, (char *)&link, 4);
       datablk[0] = BLK_SIZE-1;
```

```
      datablk[1] = SYNC_BYTE;
      if (offset == 0) {
         /* stuff in data length bytes on first blk */
         len -= 2;
         memcpy(datablk+6, &len, 2);
         memcpy(datablk+8, ((char *)(s->data)), DATA_SIZE-2);
         offset += DATA_SIZE - 2;
      }
      else {
        memcpy(datablk+6, ((char *)(s->data))+offset, DATA_SIZE);
        offset += DATA_SIZE;
      }
      if (outbytes(fh, fe, datablk, BLK_SIZE) == -1) return -1;
      fe += BLK_SIZE;
    }
  }
  /* For the last non-full block, link it to nowhere, and add up to
   * padsize extra bytes to it, (to help minimize fragmentation when
   * reusing the block).
   */
  if (nl)  {
     link = NOLINK;
     nl += padsize;
     if (nl > DATA_SIZE) nl = DATA_SIZE;
     datablk[0] = nl+5;
     datablk[1] = SYNC_BYTE;
     memcpy(datablk+2, (char *)&link, 4);
     if (offset == 0) {
        /* stuff in data length bytes on first blk */
        len -= 2;
        memcpy(datablk+6, &len, 2);
        memcpy(datablk+8, ((char *)(s->data)), nl-2);
     }
     else {
        memcpy(datablk+6, ((char *)(s->data))+offset, nl);
     }
     if (outbytes(fh, fe, datablk, nl+6) == -1) return -1;
     fe += nl + 6;
  }
  /* Set freespace = file_end, which means no freespace */
  if (writehdr(fh, fe, fe, ita, nrecs) == -1) return -1;
  return 0;  /* <<< success >>> */
}
int reuse_vlr(int fh, long locn, vstr *w, int offset, int use_fs)
/*
 * Reuses the vlr starting at byte pos'n "locn" in file fh, by storing the
 * data in variable string w at the specified offset.  If we run out of
 * room the vlr list, then the list is extended by first using up
 * freespace, and if we run out of that, bytes are appended to the file.
```

```
 * If we do have to use freespace, then this routine is called recursively
 * with "locn" set to the freespace itself, the new vstr offset, and the
 * "use_fs" flag set to 1. This flag tells us whether to try using
 * freespace or to append to the file when we need more room.
 *
 * NOTE: Never call reuse_vlr directly with offset != 0.  This condition
 *       is meant for recursive calls only.  Always use offset = 0.
 *
 * If we have any blocks left over from the old vlr, they are put on the
 * freespace list.  Note however, that the blocks themselves are never split
 * up once they are made.
 *
 * Returns 0 if successful,  -1 otherwise.
 */
{
  unsigned int nb, nu, ls, len;
  unsigned char datablk[256];
  long oldfs,nxtlocn,fs,fe,ita,nrecs,dmy;
  /* Convert to number of chars.  If on first block, */
  /* then add room for two bytes of length code      */
  len = w->currlen * w->esize;
  if (offset == 0) len += 2;
  if (readhdr(fh, &fs, &fe, &ita, &nrecs) == -1) return -1;
  /*****************************************************
   * Walk thru each block of vlr, reusing it's space until
   * we either run out of room, or have added all the data.
   *****************************************************/
  do {
    if (getvlrelem(fh, locn, &nxtlocn, datablk) == -1) return -1;
    nb = *datablk;
    if (nb <= 5) {
       locn = nxtlocn; /* we have block with no room in it, so move on */
    }
    else {              /* we have block with data in it, so reuse it */
       nu = nb-5;
       ls = len - offset;
       if (nu >= ls)  {  /* what's left of our string fits in block */

          /* what's left of our string fits in block, so null at nxtlocn
             since at end, and then copy the data into the block.  If
             we're just starting the vlr, then add the length bytes first.
          */
          memset(datablk+2, 0, 4);  /* null out nxtlocn cause at end */
          if (offset == 0) {  /* if at start of block, add length bytes */
             len -= 2;
             memcpy(datablk+6, &len, 2);  /* add data length code */
             memcpy(datablk+8, ((char *)(w->data)), ls-2); /* and data */
          }
          else {
```

```
            memcpy(datablk+6, ((char *)(w->data))+offset, ls);
        }
        if (outbytes(fh, locn, datablk, *datablk+1) == -1) return -1;
        /* Now, save the old free space pointer, and point freespace
           to the start of any remaining blocks in the chain. If
           we were reusing freespace and we're at it's end, well,
           it's out of space now, so set it equal to the file end.
        */
        oldfs = fs;
        if (nxtlocn)  {
           fs = nxtlocn;
        }
        else {                    /* if we were using freespace, it's */
          if (use_fs) fs = fe;    /* out of room now                  */
        }
        /* Now, if not already using freespace, and there's links
           left in the chain, scan down the chain to the end and
           link the end to the old freespace.  If fs == fe, then there
           really was no freespace, so just leave the end link's
           nxtlocn null.  Then, break out of loop
        */
        if (!use_fs && (nxtlocn != 0)) {
          do {
            locn = nxtlocn;
            if (getvlrelem(fh, locn, &nxtlocn, datablk) == -1) return -1;
          } while (nxtlocn);
          if (oldfs != fe)  {   /* hook up end of chain with fs   */
             memcpy(datablk+2, (char *)&oldfs, 4);
             if (outbytes(fh, locn, datablk, *datablk+1) == -1) return -1;
          }
        }
        writehdr(fh, fs, fe, ita, nrecs);
        break; /* <<< exit loop >>> */
    }
    else {

        /* String doesn't fit into block. So add what you can.
           If at the start of the vlr, then add the length
           bytes to the front
        */
       if (offset == 0) {  /* add len bytes to first block */
          len -= 2;
          memcpy(datablk+6, &len, 2);
          memcpy(datablk+8, ((char *)(w->data)), nu-2);
          offset += nu-2;
       }
       else {
         memcpy(datablk+6, ((char *)(w->data))+offset, nu);
         offset += nu;
```

```
        }
      }
      if (nxtlocn)   {  /* write out new block */
        if (outbytes(fh, locn, datablk, *datablk+1) == -1) return -1;
        locn = nxtlocn;
      }
    }
  } while (nxtlocn);
  /**************** end of block walk loop ********************/
  if (nu < ls) {
     /* We still have some data left, so we need to extend the
      * vlr.  Test to see whether to use freespace or append to
      * file, and set our link to the file-end, or to freespace.
      * Note that even if it says use freespace, there may not
      * be any freespace, but this is checked later.
      */
     if (use_fs) memcpy(datablk+2, (char *)&fe, 4);
            else memcpy(datablk+2, (char *)&fs, 4);
     if (outbytes(fh, locn, datablk, *datablk+1) == -1) return -1;
     /* We may want to append to file, or may have to cause there
      * really isn't any freespace.  Otherwise, recursively reuse the
      * freespace vlr.
      */
     if (use_fs || (fs==fe)) {
        if (extend_file(fh, w, &dmy, offset) == -1) return -1;
     }
     else {
       if (reuse_vlr(fh, fs, w, offset, 1) == -1) return -1;
     }
  }
  return 0;
}
int delvlr(int fh, long locn)
/*
 *  Deletes the vlr which starts at byte pos'n "locn" in file fh.
 *  The record is deleted by placing it on the freespace list.
 *  Returns 0 if successful, -1 otherwise.
 */
{
  unsigned char datablk[256];
  long newfs,fs,fe,ita,nrecs,nxtlocn;
  /* get freespace and file end pointer and number of records */
  if (readhdr(fh, &fs, &fe, &ita, &nrecs) == -1) return -1;
  newfs = locn;  /* vlr's address will be new freespace address */
  /* scan the vlr's blocks until last one found or there's an error */
  nxtlocn = locn;
  do {
    locn = nxtlocn;
    if ((getvlrelem(fh, locn, &nxtlocn, datablk)) == -1) return -1;
```

```
  } while (nxtlocn);
  /* If we have freespace, hook up last block of our vlr to it */
  if (fs != fe)  {
     memcpy(datablk+2, (char *)&fs, 4);
     if (outbytes(fh, locn, datablk, *datablk+1) == -1) return -1;
  }
  /* write out new freespace pointer and number of records */
  if (writehdr(fh, newfs, fe, ita, nrecs-1) == -1) return -1;
  return 0;
}
int addvlr(int fh, vstr *w, long *locn)
/*
 * Takes the data stored in virtual string w and adds it as a
 * vlr to the file fh, and returns the locn of the vlr
 * in *locn.  If there is freespace, that is used before appending
 * to the file.  Returns 0 if successful, -1 otherwise.
 */
{
  long oldfs, fs, fe, ita, nrecs;
  if (readhdr(fh, &oldfs, &fe, &ita, &nrecs) == -1) return -1;
  /* either append bytes to the file, or use up freespace first */
  if (oldfs == fe) {
     if (extend_file(fh, w, &fs, 0) == -1) return -1;
  }
  else {
     if (reuse_vlr(fh, oldfs, w, 0, 1) == -1) return -1;
  }
  /* update number of records in file */
  if (readhdr(fh, &fs, &fe, &ita, &nrecs) == -1) return -1;
  if (writehdr(fh, fs, fe, ita, nrecs+1) == -1) return -1;
  *locn = oldfs; /* our vlr's addr. was the old freespace addr. */
  return 0;      /* successful completion */
}
```

Listing 10.3 Source code for file "vlrex5.c"

```
/*********************************************************
 *  Polygon slide show creation example  (vlrex5.c)
 *
 *  Must link with: popup.obj, mouse.obj, sayerr.obj,
 *                  fileio.obj, sayerr.obj, vstr.obj,
 *                  vlr.obj, graphics.lib
 *********************************************************/
#include <graphics.h>
#include <stdio.h>
#include <string.h>
#include <process.h>
#include "mouse.h"
#include "vstr.h"
```

```
#include "popup.h"
#include "fileio.h"
#include "vlr.h"
#define rectxul 0
#define rectyul 32
typedef struct {
  int x,y;
} point;
typedef struct {
  int x, y;
  char label[10];
} button;
button draw_menu[] = {
  { rectxul,     rectyul-16, "Store" },
  { rectxul+80,  rectyul-16, "Fill"  },
  { rectxul+160, rectyul-16, "Clear" },
  { rectxul+240, rectyul-16, "Quit " }
};
int num_draw_menu_items = sizeof(draw_menu) / sizeof(button);
int mouse_on_entry(button *menu, int nitems);
void main()
{
  int gd=DETECT, gm=0, rectxlr, rectylr;
  unsigned int k;
  vstr v = NULLVSTR, index = NULLVSTR;
  point p = {0,0};
  int first_time = 1, i, command, done, starting_point;
  int fh;
  long locn, fs, fe, ita, nr;
  init_win();
  init_files();
  if ((fh = openvlr("objects.vlr","w+b",32L)) == -1) {
     printf("Error creating objects.vlr\n");
     exit(1);
  }
  initgraph(&gd,&gm,"");
  init_mouse(MOUSE_NEEDED, gd, gm);
  rectxlr = getmaxx();  rectylr = getmaxy();
  clrvstr(&v,30,sizeof(point),5);
  clrvstr(&index,20,sizeof(long),5);
  /* draw menu */
  mouse_off(1);
  for(i=0; i < num_draw_menu_items; i++) {
    outtextxy( draw_menu[i].x, draw_menu[i].y, draw_menu[i].label );
  }
  mouse_on(1);
  /* draw window, and setup window coordinates */
  mouse_off(1);
  rectangle(rectxul, rectyul, rectxlr, rectylr);
```

```
mouse_on(1);
setviewport(rectxul+1,rectyul+1,rectxlr-1,rectylr-1,1);
setfillstyle(8,4);    /* cross hatch fill, red color      */
done = 0;
starting_point = 0;
do {
   while(!(k = mouse_trigger(0)));
   if (k == LEFT_MOUSE_REL) {
      command = mouse_on_entry(draw_menu, num_draw_menu_items);
      switch(command) {
        case 0:
          /* store object, and remember its address */
          addvlr(fh, &v, &locn);
          vstrcat(&index, &locn);
          /* clear object */
          mouse_off(1);
          clearviewport();
          mouse_on(1);
          v.currlen = 0;
          first_time = 1;
        break;
        case 1:
          /* make a closed polygon boundary  */
          /* by adding starting point to end */
          /* then filling in the polygon     */
          vstrcat(&v,((point *)v.data) + starting_point);
          mouse_off(1);
          /* note: this redraws ALL of the polygons in the string */
          fillpoly(v.currlen, (int far *)(v.data));
          mouse_on(1);
          first_time = 1;
        break;
        case 2: /* clear window, reset point string  */
          mouse_off(1);
          clearviewport();
          mouse_on(1);
          v.currlen = 0;
          first_time = 1;
        break;
        case 3: /* finished drawing, so write out index, close file */
          done = 1;
          addvlr(fh, &index, &locn);
          readhdr(fh, &fs, &fe, &ita, &nr);
          writehdr(fh, fs, fe, locn, nr);
          closefile(fh);
        break;
        default:   /* draw line segments */
          if (first_time) {
             mouse_off(1);
```

```
                putpixel(mouse_grph_x - rectxul,
                         mouse_grph_y - rectyul, 15);
                mouse_on(1);
             }
             else {
                mouse_off(0);
                line(p.x, p.y,
                     mouse_grph_x - rectxul, mouse_grph_y - rectyul);
                mouse_on(0);
             }
             p.x = mouse_grph_x - rectxul;
             p.y = mouse_grph_y - rectyul;
             vstrcat(&v,&p);
             if (first_time) starting_point = v.currlen - 1;
             first_time = 0;
         }
      }
  } while (!done);
  mouse_reset();
  closegraph();
}
int mouse_on_entry(button *menu, int nitems)
/* Returns button number that mouse is currently on, or returns -1 */
{
  int i;
  for(i=0; i < nitems; i++) {
    if( mouse_in_box(1,
        menu[i].x, menu[i].y,
        menu[i].x + strlen(menu[i].label)*8 - 1, menu[i].y + 7) )
      return i;
  }
  return -1;
}
```

Listing 10.4 Source code for file "vlrex6.c"

```
/****************************************************************
 *  Polygon slide show browsing program  (vlrex6.c)
 *
 *  Must link with: popup.obj, mouse.obj, sayerr.obj,
 *                  fileio.obj, sayerr.obj, vstr.obj,
 *                  vlr.obj, graphics.lib
 ****************************************************************/
#include <graphics.h>
#include <stdio.h>
#include <string.h>
#include <process.h>
#include "mouse.h"
```

```
#include "vstr.h"
#include "popup.h"
#include "fileio.h"
#include "vlr.h"
#define rectxul 0
#define rectyul 32
typedef struct {
  int x,y;
} point;
typedef struct {
  int x, y;
  char label[10];
} button;
button show_menu[] = {
  { rectxul,      rectyul-16, "First" },
  { rectxul+50,   rectyul-16, "Last"  },
  { rectxul+100, rectyul-16, "Next"  },
  { rectxul+150, rectyul-16, "Prev"  },
  { rectxul+200, rectyul-16, "Quit"  }
};
int num_show_menu_items = sizeof(show_menu) / sizeof(button);
vstr v = NULLVSTR, index = NULLVSTR;
char buffer[20];
int mouse_on_entry(button *menu, int nitems);
char far *bios_video_area = (char far *)0x00400049L;
void main()
{
  int gd=DETECT, gm=0, i, command, obj, fh, rectxlr, rectylr;
  unsigned int k;
  point p;
  long fs, fe, ita, nr;
  init_win();
  init_files();
  if ((fh = openvlr("objects.vlr","rb",32L)) == -1) {
     printf("Error opening file objects.vlr\n");
     exit(1);
  }
  initgraph(&gd,&gm,"");
  init_mouse(MOUSE_NEEDED, gd, gm);
  rectxlr = getmaxx();  rectylr = getmaxy();
  clrvstr(&v,30,sizeof(point),5);
  clrvstr(&index,20,sizeof(long),5);
  /* read in index */
  readhdr(fh, &fs, &fe, &ita, &nr);
  getvlr(fh, &index, ita);
  /* draw menu */
  mouse_off(1);
  for(i=0; i < num_show_menu_items; i++) {
    outtextxy( show_menu[i].x, show_menu[i].y, show_menu[i].label );
```

```
}
mouse_on(1);
/* draw window, and setup window coordinates */
mouse_off(1);
rectangle(rectxul, rectyul, rectxlr, rectylr);
mouse_on(1);
setviewport(rectxul+1,rectyul+1,rectxlr-1,rectylr-1,1);
setfillstyle(8,4);   /* cross hatch fill, red color      */
command = 0;  obj = 0;
do {
   /* change viewports temporarily, so we can clear status field */
   setviewport(rectxlr-60,rectyul-16,rectxlr,rectyul-8,1);
   mouse_off(1);
   clearviewport();
   sprintf(buffer,”%d of %d”,obj+1, index.currlen);
   outtextxy(0,0,buffer);
   mouse_on(1);
   /* back to normal viewport */
   setviewport(rectxul+1,rectyul+1,rectxlr-1,rectylr-1,1);
   while(!(k = mouse_trigger(0)));
   if (k == LEFT_MOUSE_REL) {
      command = mouse_on_entry(show_menu, num_show_menu_items);
      if (command != 4) {
         switch(command) {
           case 0: /* first object */
             obj = 0;
           break;
           case 1: /* last object  */
             obj = index.currlen-1;
           break;
           case 2: /* next object, wrap around to beginning */
             if (++obj == index.currlen) obj = 0;
           break;
           case 3: /* previous object, wrap around to end   */
             if (—obj < 0) obj = index.currlen - 1;
           break;
           default: /* default to first object */
             obj = 0;
         }
         if (command >= 0 && command <= 3) {
            /* get object */
            getvlr(fh, &v, ((long *)(index.data))[obj]);
            /* clear window, and show object */
            mouse_off(1);
            clearviewport();
            fillpoly(v.currlen, (int far *)(v.data));
            mouse_on(1);
         }
      }
```

```
      }
   } while (command != 4);
  mouse_reset();
  closegraph();
  closefile(fh);
}
int mouse_on_entry(button *menu, int nitems)
/* Returns button number that mouse is currently on, or returns -1 */
{
  int i;
  for(i=0; i < nitems; i++) {
    if( mouse_in_box(1,
        menu[i].x, menu[i].y,
        menu[i].x + strlen(menu[i].label)*8 - 1, menu[i].y + 7) )
      return i;
  }
  return -1;
}
```

CHAPTER

11

Turbo C Graphics

The purpose of this chapter is not to rewrite the graphics section of the *Turbo C Additions & Enhancements Guide*, but rather to point out the tricks and traps in using the graphics routines. After a brief introduction, we will plunge right into using the mouse and then show a sample graphics pop-up window package. This is followed by methods for overcoming some of the limitations of Turbo C graphics. This will give us an opportunity to visit many of the graphics routines in a loosely organized, applications-oriented manner. It is assumed that you already have some familiarity with the graphics routines, although we will now take a quick tour.

A QUICK TOUR OF TURBO C GRAPHICS

The Turbo C Graphics package provides support for many different graphics adapters and allows you to write code that is fairly mode-independent. Along with the library file **graphics.lib**, there are several other files which are used by the graphics package. This includes a set of driver files for the different graphics modes and a set of stroked font files:

File	Use
ATT.BGI	Driver file for AT&T Graphics
CGA.BGI	Driver file for CGA Graphics
EGAVGA.BGI	Driver file for EGA and VGA Graphics
HERC.BGI	Driver file for Hercules Graphics
IBM8514.BGI	Driver file for IBM 8514 Graphics
PC3270.BGI	Driver file for IBM 3270 Graphics
GOTH.CHR	File for gothic style stroked fonts
LITT.CHR	File for small stroked fonts
SANS.CHR	File for sansserif style stroked fonts
TRIP.CHR	File for triplex style stroked fonts

> **IMPORTANT:** Before running any of the examples in this chapter, be sure to load all necessary driver and font files into your working directory.

The following program shows the basic code needed to access the Turbo C graphics routines.

```
/*
   Quick tour of Turbo C graphics  (grphex1.c)
   Must link with:  graphics.lib
*/
#include <graphics.h> /* must always include when using graphics */
#include <conio.h>
void main() {
  int gd = DETECT, gm = 0; /* set for auto-detect, highest mode */
  initgraph(&gd,&gm,"");   /* initialize the graphics system    */
                           /* drivers should be in current dir  */
  circle(100,100,50);      /* sample graphics routine           */
  outtextxy(88,100,"abc"); /* sample text output                */
  getch();
  closegraph();            /* go back to text mode              */
}
```

The routine **initgraph()** is used to initialize the graphics system. It does this by loading in the proper graphics driver dynamically at run-time. The driver is determined by the parameter **gd**. When set to DETECT (0), it tells **initgraph()** to automatically detect the type of hardware being used, and to load in the appropriate driver. The **gm** parameter tells it which graphics mode to use. If this parameter is 0 when auto-detecting the driver, it uses the highest resolution possible. Passing both parameters set to 0 is the most common way to initialize the graphics system.

The third parameter determines the directory where the graphics drivers and font tables are found. Turbo C loads these drivers in at run-time by looking in this directory. It is also possible to load them in at link-time, using the routines **registerbgidriver()** and **registerbgifont()**. (See the Turbo C manuals for details.) In the examples of this chapter, we will assume the appropriate drivers and font files are in the current directory.

The call to **circle()** shows a typical graphics function being used. The coordinates of the circle, as well as for any graphics object, are always specified relative to the current *viewport*. A viewport is a region on the screen to which all graphics output is drawn. It is analogous to the text-based window, and we will use the two terms interchangeably here. The default viewport is the whole screen.

The call to **outtextxy()** shows one way to output text in graphics mode. Turbo C provides a bit-mapped font, as well as four stroked fonts. The fonts are very versatile, as you can change their shape, size, color, and justification settings.

Although many functions are provided, the following are perhaps the ones most commonly used:

Basic initialization and viewport functions.

Function	Use
`initgraph()`	Initializes the graphics system
`closegraph()`	Closes the graphics system, goes back to text mode
`setviewport()`	Sets up a viewport
`clearviewport()`	Clears the current viewport
`cleardevice()`	Clears the whole screen
`setcolor()`	Sets the drawing color
`setbkcolor()`	Sets the background color

Basic text output functions

Function	Use
`outtextxy()`	Outputs text at a certain pixel location
`outtext()`	Outputs text at the current pixel location
`settextstyle()`	Sets text font, size, and direction

Basic drawing functions

Function	Use
`drawpixel()`	Draws a pixel
`circle()`	Draws a circle
`line()`	Draws a line
`rectangle()`	Draws a rectangle
`bar()`	Draws a bar for bar graphs
`bar3d()`	Draws a bar for 3D bar graphs
`setfillstyle()`	Sets the fill pattern and color
`setlinestyle()`	Sets the line thickness and style

Animation Support Routines

Function	Use
`getimage()`	Saves a bit mapped image into memory
`putimage()`	Puts a bit mapped memory image onto the screen

You will have an opportunity to see most of these routines in action, as well a few other routines not listed here. So roll up your sleeves and get right to work.

USING THE MOUSE

Just as you used the mouse in text mode, you can use the mouse in graphics mode. The driver supplied with your mouse takes care of almost everything for you. Just make sure you initialize the mouse *after* setting the screen for graphics mode, so that the mouse will be set up properly. The mouse tool kit given earlier was designed to work in graphics mode as well as in text mode.

There are two problems when using the mouse in graphics mode: one is when a Hercules Graphics card is used, the other is when low-resolution modes are used.

The Hercules Graphics card works by emulating the IBM Monochrome Display Adapter in text mode. In addition, it has a special graphics mode which, unfortunately, is not recognized by BIOS, since it is not IBM standard. Because of this, there is no way for the mouse driver to tell when the Hercules graphics mode is being used. The fix is to trick BIOS into thinking you're in a graphics mode.

The BIOS uses a special area of memory located at 0x0040:0x0049 to store various parameters for its video routines. The one located at the start of this area (0x0040:0x0049) is used to store the current video mode. When in Hercules text mode, a **7** is stored there. Unfortunately, if you switch to Hercules graphics mode, it's still a **7**, since BIOS knows nothing about Hercules graphics. By storing a **6** there, the mouse driver will know that a graphics mode is being used (in particular, Hercules graphics). This value assumes you are using page 0 of the Hercules graphics memory. A **5** should be stored at 0x0040:0x0049 if you are using page one of the graphics memory.

Another problem has to do with retrieving the mouse coordinates. The mouse driver assumes a virtual screen width of 640 pixels in all modes except Hercules, where 720 pixels are used. However, there are several low-resolution modes which are only 320 pixels wide. In these cases, the X coordinate, as returned by the mouse driver, must be halved in order to be correct.

Both of these problems are handled as follows: When calling the **init_mouse()** function, you should pass the current driver and graphics mode being currently being used. The values used are the ones returned by the **initgraph()** function of Turbo C. The **init_mouse()** function takes these parameters and determines whether Hercules graphics or low-resolution graphics are being used. For Hercules graphics, it sets the memory location 0x0040:0x0049 to the value **6**, (page zero graphics). For low-resolution graphics, it sets an internal flag so that if the mouse graphics coordinates are requested, they are properly scaled. The following program shows how to set up the mouse correctly:

```
/*
   Using the mouse in graphics mode  (grphex2.c)
   Must link with: mouse.obj, graphics.lib
*/
#include <graphics.h>
#include "mouse.h"
main() {
   int gd = DETECT, gm = 0; /* default modes */
   initgraph(&gd,&gm,"");
   init_mouse(MOUSE_NEEDED, gd, gm);
   while (!mouse_trigger(1));
```

```
    mouse_reset();
    closegraph();
}
```

CHANGING THE MOUSE CURSOR VIA THE MOUSE DRIVER

Instead of the rectangular-shaped mouse cursor used in text mode, the default shape in graphics mode is an arrow pointing up and to the left. Don't worry, there are ways to "roll your own" cursor. There are basically two ways: by calling a special function of the mouse driver or by making your own cursor from scratch. We will show you both ways.

The mouse cursor is defined as a 16-by-16-pixel block in most of the graphics modes. The size of the cursor cannot exceed this, although you can make it smaller by setting up the shape appropriately. To change the shape of the mouse cursor, you can call the mouse driver with function code 9 and pass three parameters to it.

The first two parameters define the "hot spot" coordinates of the cursor. The hot spot determines the origin of the cursor, that is, the spot from which where mouse coordinates are determined. For example, in the default cursor, the hot spot is at the tip of the arrow. The position is given relative to the upper left-hand corner of the 16-by-16 block, and both parameters must be in the range minus 16 to 16. Using negative coordinates, you can define the hot spot to be above and to the left of the actual cursor.

The last parameter specifies the address of two 16-by-16-bit masks used to create the shape of the cursor: the screen mask and the cursor mask. When the mouse cursor is drawn, the screen mask pixels are ANDed with the pixels on the screen. The result is then XORed with the cursor mask. This funny combination gives you the ability to make the cursor either white, the color of the background, transparent, or the inverse of the foreground color. By setting the masks appropriately, you can get any combination of these colors within the same cursor. Figure 11.1 shows this ANDing and XORing process. Table 11.1 shows you how the bit combinations work:

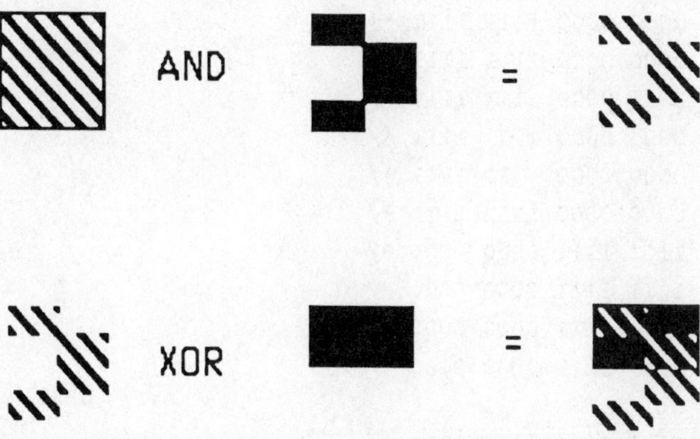

Figure 11.1 The two step cursor masking process (colors inverted)

Table 11.1 Mouse cursor bit combinations

Screen Mask Bit	Cursor Mask Bit	Resulting Color
0	0	Background color
0	1	White
1	0	Transparent
1	1	Foreground color inverted Background becomes white

An example of changing the mouse cursor is given in the following program:

```
/**********************************************************
 *  Example of changing the mouse cursor (grphex3.c)
 *  Must link with: mouse.obj, graphics.lib
 **********************************************************/
#include <dos.h>
#include <conio.h>
#include <graphics.h>
#include <alloc.h>
#include "mouse.h"
unsigned int test_pattern[] = {
  /* Screen Mask */
   0xff00,      /* 1111 1111 0000 0000 */
   0xff00,      /* 1111 1111 0000 0000 */
   0xff00,      /* 1111 1111 0000 0000 */
   0xff00,      /* 1111 1111 0000 0000 */
   0x00ff,      /* 0000 0000 1111 1111 */
   0x00ff,      /* 0000 0000 1111 1111 */
   0x00ff,      /* 0000 0000 1111 1111 */
   0x00ff,      /* 0000 0000 1111 1111 */
   0x00ff,      /* 0000 0000 1111 1111 */
   0x00ff,      /* 0000 0000 1111 1111 */
   0x00ff,      /* 0000 0000 1111 1111 */
   0x00ff,      /* 0000 0000 1111 1111 */
   0xff00,      /* 1111 1111 0000 0000 */
   0xff00,      /* 1111 1111 0000 0000 */
   0xff00,      /* 1111 1111 0000 0000 */
   0xff00,      /* 1111 1111 0000 0000 */
 /* Cursor mask */
   0xffff,      /* 1111 1111 1111 1111 */
   0xffff,      /* 1111 1111 1111 1111 */
   0xffff,      /* 1111 1111 1111 1111 */
```

```
    0xffff,       /* 1111 1111 1111 1111 */
    0xffff,       /* 1111 1111 1111 1111 */
    0xffff,       /* 1111 1111 1111 1111 */
    0xffff,       /* 1111 1111 1111 1111 */
    0xffff,       /* 1111 1111 1111 1111 */
    0x0000,       /* 0000 0000 0000 0000 */
    0x0000,       /* 0000 0000 0000 0000 */
    0x0000,       /* 0000 0000 0000 0000 */
    0x0000,       /* 0000 0000 0000 0000 */
    0x0000,       /* 0000 0000 0000 0000 */
    0x0000,       /* 0000 0000 0000 0000 */
    0x0000,       /* 0000 0000 0000 0000 */
    0x0000        /* 0000 0000 0000 0000 */
};
void setcur(int hotspotx, int hotspoty, void *shape);
void main() {
 int gd = DETECT, gm = 0;
 initgraph(&gd,&gm,"");
 init_mouse(MOUSE_NEEDED, gd, gm);
 /*
    Set background to red, draw a yellow fill patterned box
    to see effects of cursor masks
 */
 mouse_off(1);
 setbkcolor(RED);
 setfillstyle(BKSLASH_FILL,YELLOW);
 bar(100,50,200,75);
 mouse_on(1);
 while(!mouse_trigger(1));
 /* Change to test pattern cursor */
 setcur(0,0,test_pattern);
 while(!mouse_trigger(1));
 mouse_reset();
 closegraph();
}
void setcur(int hotspotx, int hotspoty, void *shape)
/*
   Routine to set the graphics mouse cursor to
   specified shape with specified hot spot coordinates.
*/
{
   union REGS inregs, outregs;
```

```
   struct SREGS segregs;
   inregs.x.ax = 9;  /* Cursor shape function code */
   inregs.x.bx = hotspotx;
   inregs.x.cx = hotspoty;
   inregs.x.dx = FP_OFF(shape);
   segregs.es  = FP_SEG(shape);
   int86x(0x33,&inregs,&outregs,&segregs);
}
```

This program first draws a box with a yellow slashed fill pattern and a cursor with its default shape. Press any mouse button and the cursor changes to a test pattern shape, which has all possible bit combinations in it. Move the cursor over the fill pattern to see the effects of the masks. Press another mouse button to exit the program.

The function **setcur()** calls the mouse driver via **int86x()** to change the cursor shape. You may want to add this routine to your mouse library. Note how the address of the masks is passed. The masks are arranged in a single integer array, the screen mask followed by the cursor mask. The address of this array is passed via registers DX and ES.

While this program will work in any graphics mode, it is most dramatic in the EGA and VGA color modes. The masking effects also show up quite nicely in the CGA high-resolution mode.

ROLLING YOUR OWN CURSOR

By using the Turbo C routines **getimage()** and **putimage()**, you can create your own graphics cursor. This has several advantages. You have more control over the color of the cursor, and you can use any size desired. Probably the main advantage is that you can have a cursor even if you do not have a mouse. The cursor could be moved around with the cursor keys. This does mean you have to explicitly write a driver to move the cursor whereas with the mouse cursor that is done for you by the mouse driver.

Although it is not the simplest way, the following program shows how to create a cursor with the same two masks used with the mouse driver cursor. This is done mainly to show the operations taking place by the mouse driver for its own cursor.

```
/*****************************************************************
 *  Rolling your own mouse cursor  (grphex4.c)
 *  Must link with: graphics.lib
 *****************************************************************/
#include <dos.h>
#include <bios.h>
#include <conio.h>
#include <graphics.h>
#include <alloc.h>
#define UPKEY        0x4800
#define DOWNKEY      0x5000
#define LEFTKEY      0x4b00
#define RIGHTKEY     0x4d00
```

```
#define ESCKEY      0x011b
unsigned int test_pattern[] = {
  /* Screen Mask */
    0xff00,      /* 1111 1111 0000 0000 */
    0xff00,      /* 1111 1111 0000 0000 */
    0xff00,      /* 1111 1111 0000 0000 */
    0xff00,      /* 1111 1111 0000 0000 */
    0x00ff,      /* 0000 0000 1111 1111 */
    0x00ff,      /* 0000 0000 1111 1111 */
    0x00ff,      /* 0000 0000 1111 1111 */
    0x00ff,      /* 0000 0000 1111 1111 */
    0x00ff,      /* 0000 0000 1111 1111 */
    0x00ff,      /* 0000 0000 1111 1111 */
    0x00ff,      /* 0000 0000 1111 1111 */
    0x00ff,      /* 0000 0000 1111 1111 */
    0xff00,      /* 1111 1111 0000 0000 */
    0xff00,      /* 1111 1111 0000 0000 */
    0xff00,      /* 1111 1111 0000 0000 */
    0xff00,      /* 1111 1111 0000 0000 */
/* Cursor mask */
    0xffff,      /* 1111 1111 1111 1111 */
    0xffff,      /* 1111 1111 1111 1111 */
    0xffff,      /* 1111 1111 1111 1111 */
    0xffff,      /* 1111 1111 1111 1111 */
    0xffff,      /* 1111 1111 1111 1111 */
    0xffff,      /* 1111 1111 1111 1111 */
    0xffff,      /* 1111 1111 1111 1111 */
    0xffff,      /* 1111 1111 1111 1111 */
    0x0000,      /* 0000 0000 0000 0000 */
    0x0000,      /* 0000 0000 0000 0000 */
    0x0000,      /* 0000 0000 0000 0000 */
    0x0000,      /* 0000 0000 0000 0000 */
    0x0000,      /* 0000 0000 0000 0000 */
    0x0000,      /* 0000 0000 0000 0000 */
    0x0000,      /* 0000 0000 0000 0000 */
    0x0000       /* 0000 0000 0000 0000 */
};
void make_cursor(unsigned int *curs, void *scrnmsk, void *cursmsk);
void draw_cursor(int x, int y);
void erase_cursor(int oldx, int oldy);
void *scrnmsk, *cursmsk, *save_image;
void main() {
```

```
int gd = DETECT, gm = 0, k, x, y, mx, my;
initgraph(&gd,&gm,"");
save_image = malloc(imagesize(0,0,15,15));
scrnmsk    = malloc(imagesize(0,0,15,15));
cursmsk    = malloc(imagesize(0,0,15,15));
make_cursor(test_pattern,scrnmsk,cursmsk);
outtextxy(0,40,"Bit masks made. Press a key to continue ...");
getch();
cleardevice(); /* erase cursor construction */
/*
   Set background to red, draw a yellow fill patterned box
   to see effects of cursor masks
*/
setbkcolor(RED);
setfillstyle(BKSLASH_FILL,YELLOW);
bar(100,50,200,75);
x = 100; y = 50;
mx = getmaxx()-15; my = getmaxy()-15;
draw_cursor(x,y);
do {
   if (bioskey(1)) {
      k = bioskey(0);
      erase_cursor(x,y);
      switch(k) {
        case UPKEY:
          if (—y < 0) y = 0;
        break;
        case DOWNKEY:
         if (++y > my) y = my;
        break;
        case LEFTKEY:
         if (—x < 0) x = 0;
        break;
        case RIGHTKEY:
         if (++x > mx) x = mx;
        break;
    default: ;
      }
      draw_cursor(x,y);
   }
} while(k != ESCKEY);
closegraph();
```

```
}
void make_cursor(unsigned int *curs, void *scrnmsk, void *cursmsk)
/*
   Makes the cursor masks by forming bit images right on the screen.
   The masks should be allocated before coming in.
*/
{
  int i, j;
  setbkcolor(0);  /* should be black for this to work properly */
  /* create the screen mask right on the screen */
  for (i = 0; i<16; i++) {
      for (j=0; j<16; j++) {
          if ((curs[i] >> (15-j)) & 0x0001)
             putpixel(j,i,WHITE); /* important to use white !! */
      }
  }
  /* now store bit image of it in a buffer */
  getimage(0,0,15,15,scrnmsk);
  /* same for cursor mask */
  for (i = 0; i<16; i++) {
      for (j=0; j<16; j++) {
          if ((curs[i+16] >> (15-j)) & 0x0001)
             putpixel(j,i+20,WHITE); /* important to use white !! */
      }
  }
  getimage(0,20,15,35,cursmsk);
}
void erase_cursor(int oldx, int oldy)
/* Erase cursor by putting back old image */
{
   putimage(oldx,oldy,save_image,COPY_PUT);
}
void draw_cursor(int x, int y)
/* Draw cursor at new position, but save image underneath first */
{
   getimage(x,y,x+15,y+15,save_image);     /* save image      */
   putimage(x,y,scrnmsk,AND_PUT);          /* draw the cursor */
   putimage(x,y,cursmsk,XOR_PUT);
}
```

The program is essentially the same as used in the mouse example, except you must explicitly create, move, and erase our own cursor. The keyboard arrows are used to move the cursor around, and ESC exits the program.

The function **make_cursor()** is responsible for taking the screen and cursor masks and creating the cursor image. It does this by drawing white pixels on a black background using the bit patterns in the masks. Once the image is formed, **getimage()** is called to save the actual memory image of the cursor. Then **putimage()** is used later to draw the cursor at any position.

It is very important to realize the distinction between having a bit mask and having the actual image itself. In the EGA and VGA, each pixel is formed from four bits arranged in planes. These four planes determine the color of the pixel. All four bits need to be set for each pixel so that the AND and XOR operations work properly. This can be done by using a white-on-black color scheme.

This technique of creating images for later use by actually drawing them on the screen first is the typical way of creating your own cursors, icons, and so on. Using this method insures that your images will work for any graphics mode, barring differences in resolution and color. If it bothers you to see them drawn first, you can draw them on a different hidden graphics page first, if your graphics adapter supports it. The Turbo C functions **setactivepage()** and **setvisualpage()** can be used for this purpose.

The functions **draw_cursor()** and **erase_cursor()** are used to draw and erase the cursor. To allow the cursor to be moved, the image underneath is saved before the cursor is drawn, and it is restored when the cursor is erased. It takes four memory transfers to move the cursor: first restore the old position image, then save the new position image, AND the screen mask, then XOR the cursor mask. This is not the best way to move images around.

The most efficient way is by XORing the image with the screen underneath. Two consecutive XOR operations cause the image to be drawn and then erased. Thus, images can be moved simply by using **putimage()** with an XOR operation. There is no need to store the image underneath. How can you get away with this? Due to the way XOR works, the state of the screen *is* stored by altering the color of the pixels. For instance, if a screen pixel is yellow, and it is XORed with a blue pixel, then a yellow pixel results. Another XOR reverts the pixel to yellow. This means that the color of the cursor interacts with what is underneath, which may be undesirable for some applications.

The multiple save, AND, and XOR operation used by the mouse driver allows you greater flexibility with the look of the cursor. You can make portions of it white, inverted, transparent, or the background color. With just XOR, you are at the mercy of the XOR operation. However, the XOR technique is much more efficient, and as always, there are tradeoffs.

A SAMPLE GRAPHICS POP-UP WINDOW PACKAGE

In this section we will present code to do pop-up windows in graphics mode. The code is given in Listings 11.1 and 11.2. It was written by borrowing the text mode pop-up window routines and modifying them slightly to work in graphics mode. Care was taken to keep the calls as close as possible to the text mode routine, but unfortunately, this ideal was not always fulfilled. Although we will not do it here, an interesting exercise would be to write one package that supports both text and graphics modes.

Many of the routines are either the same or very similar to the ones used in the text mode package. Missing are the ones that support writing text to the windows. You will have to supply these yourself. The intent here is not to give you a completed package but rather enough of one to introduce many of the Turbo C graphics features.

Since this package uses the same concepts found in the text mode version, we will focus mainly on the differences in the routines. See Chapter 4 on text mode pop-up windows for more details.

WINDOW STATUS

Turbo C provides more settings for graphics mode than it does for text mode. The wincolors structure defined in the text Pop-up Windows package was modified to handle these additional settings, and is given as:

```
typedef struct wincolors_struct {
  struct linesettingstype lineinfo;  /* line style */
  struct fillsettingstype fillinfo;  /* fill style */
  struct textsettingstype textinfo;  /* font style */
  struct linesettingstype brdinfo;   /* border line style */
  struct viewporttype     viewinfo;  /* window coordinates */
  char border_type;
  unsigned char border_color, text_color, hilite_color, back_color;
} wincolors;
```

The additional structures store the status of the current colors, viewport coordinates, and line and fill styles. The routines used to obtain these settings and their associated structures are:

Routine	Associated Structure

`getfillsettings()`	`struct fillsettingstype {`
	`int pattern;`
	`int color;`
	`}`

`getlinesettings()`	`struct linesettingstype {`
	`int linestyle;`
	`unsigned upattern;`
	`int thickness;`
	`}`

`gettextsettings()`	`struct textsettingstype {`
	`int font;`
	`int direction;`
	`int charsize;`
	`int horiz;`
	`int vert;`
	`}`

`getviewsettings()`	`struct viewporttype {`
	`int left, top, right, bottom;`
	`int clip;`
	`}`

Turbo C has corresponding routines to change these settings:

Function	Use
`setfillpatern()`	Selects a user-defined fill pattern
`setfillstyle()`	Selects a fill pattern and color
`setlinestyle()`	Changes the line width and style
`settextjustify()`	Sets the text justification
`settextstyle()`	Sets the text font, direction, and size
`setviewport()`	Sets the viewport coordinates

Another modification made to the wincolors structure is that there is no title color (titles are not drawn for graphics windows), but a background color was added. The background color mentioned here is *not* the overall background color of the screen (which is set by **setbkcolor()**), but is the color used when the window is cleared.

The **border_type** field works basically as it did before. Setting it to 0 will cause no border to be drawn. Setting it to 1 causes NORM_WIDTH lines (1 pixel wide) to be used for the border. Setting it to 2 causes THICK_WIDTH lines (3 pixels wide) to be used.

With these changes to the window color pack, the window structure itself looks like:

```
typedef struct winstruct {
   char *name;                        /* window title */
   void *image;                       /* ptr to image save area */
   struct winstruct *under,*over;     /* ptrs to window below and
                                         above on pop-up stack */
   wincolors wc;                      /* current drawing settings */
   int wd, ht;                        /* computed width & height  */
   int  xsave,ysave;                  /* saved cursor posn */
   enum windowtype wtype;             /* window type */
} windesc;
```

which is almost the same as the structure for text mode. One change is that although a title is stored, it is never drawn. It is in here mainly for compatibility. The other change is that the coordinates **xul, yul, xlr**, and **ylr** are no longer present. These coordinates are defined in the viewport structure stored in the wincolors structure. To make it easy to port text mode programs to graphics mode, the following macros are defined in the header file:

```
#define xul wc.viewinfo.left
#define yul wc.viewinfo.top
#define xlr wc.viewinfo.right
#define ylr wc.viewinfo.bottom
```

INITIALIZING THE WINDOW PACKAGE

The function **init_win()** is used to initialize the Window package. Like its text mode counterpart, it gets the current screen settings and stores them with the base window.

Unlike the text mode version, the graphics **init_win()** uses three additional global variables. They are defined as:

```
int graphdriver   = 0;
int graphmode     = 0;
char *pathdriver = "";
```

The first two global variables are the graphics driver and graphics mode to be used when initializing the graphics system. The default values given will cause the graphics system to be initialized in the highest mode possible (i.e., autodetection takes place). You can set them to other values before calling **init_win()**, if you wish.

The last variable is the path to the directory where the graphics drivers and fonts are stored. It defaults to "", which means the current directory. As written, the graphics Pop-up Window package loads the graphics drivers and fonts at run-time. If you wish to have them loaded at link-time, you need to change the **init_win()** function accordingly.

DRAWING WINDOWS

The routine **draw_win()** is used to pop up a graphics window, and it is very similar to the one used in the text mode version.

Note how the image save buffer is initialized. Due to the way **draw_win()** is written, a call to **putimage()** is ultimately made (via **swap_image()**) before an image has been saved. Unlike the buffer used with **gettext()** and **puttext()**, the graphics buffers store not only the image itself, but also its size. If **putimage()** is called with an uninitialized buffer, then not only can garbage appear, but it might appear outside the intended region and be of arbitrary size. To counter this, the image buffer is allocated using **calloc()**, which initializes the whole buffer to 0, effectively setting the image size to 0 as well. This image size gets updated as soon as **getimage()** is called.

SWAPPING IMAGES

In the function **swap_image()**, the functions **getimage()** and **putimage()** are used in place of their text mode counterparts, **gettext()** and **puttext()**. One subtle difference, though, is that **getimage()** and **putimage()** use viewport-relative coordinates, whereas the text mode functions use absolute coordinates. In order to access the border of the window (which is outside the viewport), you must switch to the absolute coordinates before calling **getimage()** and **putimage()**. The **chgviewport(base_win)** call does that for us.

CLEARING WINDOWS

The routine **clr_win()** does more than the one used for text mode. It not only clears the current window, but sets the background color and redraws the border. The function **fill_win()** that it calls does all of the work.

Note that you cannot use **setbkcolor()** to set the background color of the window, since that routine sets it for the entire screen. Instead, a call to **bar3d()** is used. This routine is used because it can do two things for you at once. It not only can draw a rectangular border, but it can fill the rectangle with a specified color as well. The fill style is set to SOLID_FILL, and the color, to the window's background color before calling **bar3d()**. As in **swap_image()**, you must use absolute coordinates.

One subtle problem is if lines of THICK_WIDTH are used. Since they are more than one pixel wide, you must use smaller bar coordinates than for lines of NORM_WIDTH, so that the border stays inside the region of the screen that is saved for the window.

CHANGING WINDOWS

The routines **view_win()**, **chg_win()**, and **chgviewport()** are all involved in selecting a new window. The **view_win()** function is identical to the one used in text mode. The **chg_win()** function was modified to save the old color, line, and fill styles, as well as switch to the new ones. The **chgviewport()** function was added, and it handles the different border line widths when calculating new window coordinates.

EXAMPLE OF MOVING WINDOWS

To show the graphics Pop-up Window package in action, the following is the moving windows example used in the text-based pop-up window (Chapter 4), modified to work in graphics mode:

```
/*****************************************************************
 *   Moving Windows Example in Graphics Mode  (grphex5.c)
 *   Must link with: gpopup.obj, mouse.obj, graphics.lib
 *****************************************************************/
#include <stdlib.h>
#include <conio.h>
#include <bios.h>
#include <graphics.h>
#include "gpopup.h"
#include "mouse.h"
#define MAX(a,b)  ((a) > (b) ? (a) : (b))
#define MIN(a,b)  ((a) < (b) ? (a) : (b))
wincolors acolors, bcolors, ccolors;
int mouse_on_border(windesc **w, int *i, int *xofs, int *yofs);
void move_curr_win(int x, int y);
void main() {
 windesc *w[3];
 int x, y, xofs, yofs, i;
 unsigned int k;
 init_win();
 init_mouse(MOUSE_OPTIONAL, graphdriver, graphmode);
 acolors = defcolors;  acolors.back_color = BLACK;
```

```
bcolors = defcolors;  bcolors.back_color = BLACK;
ccolors = defcolors;  ccolors.back_color = BLACK;
w[0] = draw_win(50,60,200,50,"",popup,&acolors);
rectangle(50,15,150,35);
outtextxy(100,25,"1");
w[1] = draw_win(70,90,200,60,"",popup,&bcolors);
circle(100,25,20);
outtextxy(100,25,"2");
w[2] = draw_win(90,110,200,50,"",popup,&ccolors);
ellipse(100,25,0,360,40,15);
outtextxy(100,25,"3");
do {
   while (!(k = mouse_trigger(1)));      /* get event trigger */
   if (k == LEFT_MOUSE_PRESS) {
      if (mouse_on_border(w, &i, &xofs, &yofs)) {
     slct_win(w[i]);  /* mouse on border of window, so select it */
     while(button_state()) {  /* move till button release   */
        mouse_grph_posn(&x,&y);
        move_curr_win(x-xofs,y-yofs);
     }
      }
   }
   else {                         /* possible keyboard press           */
     xofs = 0; yofs = 0;          /* reset mouse/window corner offsets */
     x = curr_win->xul;    /* default to current position */
     y = curr_win->yul;
     switch(k) {
       case UPKEY:
         y -= 5;
         move_curr_win(x,y); /* move_curr_win will do bounds checking */
       break;
       case DOWNKEY:
         y += 5;
         move_curr_win(x,y);
       break;
       case LEFTKEY:
         x -= 5;
         move_curr_win(x,y);
       break;
       case RIGHTKEY:
         x += 5;
```

```
          move_curr_win(x,y);
        break;
        case 0x0231:        /* the "1" key */
          slct_win(w[0]);
        break;
        case 0x0332:        /* the "2" key */
          slct_win(w[1]);
        break;
        case 0x0433:        /* the "3" key */
          slct_win(w[2]);
        break;
        default:                /*send character to current window */
         if (k != RIGHT_MOUSE_PRESS) /*mprintf("%c",lo(k))*/;
      }
    }
 } while (k != ESCKEY && k != RIGHT_MOUSE_PRESS);
 rmv_win(w[2]);
 rmv_win(w[1]);
 rmv_win(w[0]);
 mouse_reset(0);
 closegraph();
}
int mouse_on_border(windesc **w, int *i, int *xofs, int *yofs)
/* Given an array of windows, determines which border the mouse
   is currently on, and returns the window number and the offset
   of the mouse from the top left hand corner
 */
{
  int x, y, j;
  mouse_grph_posn(&x,&y);
  for (j = 0; j<3; j++) {
      if (x >= w[j]->xul && x <= w[j]->xlr &&
          y >= w[j]->yul && y <= w[j]->ylr) { /* in window region */
          if (abs(x - w[j]->xul) < 4 ||
              abs(x - w[j]->xlr) < 4 ||
              abs(y - w[j]->yul) < 4 ||
              abs(y - w[j]->ylr) < 4) {   /* within range of border */
              *i = j;
              *xofs = x - w[j]->xul;
              *yofs = y - w[j]->yul;
              return 1;
```

```
        }
      }
    }
    return 0;
}
void move_curr_win(int x, int y)
/*
   Moves the current window. If coordinates haven't changed,
   then nothing happens. Does bounds checking on the new position.
*/
{
  int xsave, ysave;
  if (x != curr_win->xul || y != curr_win->yul) {
     xsave = getx();
     ysave = gety();
     swap_image(curr_win);  /* hide window */
     curr_win->xul = x;
     curr_win->yul = y;
     curr_win->xul = MAX(curr_win->xul,0);
     curr_win->xul = MIN(curr_win->xul,getmaxx() - curr_win->wd);
     curr_win->yul = MAX(curr_win->yul,0);
     curr_win->yul = MIN(curr_win->yul,getmaxy() - curr_win->ht);
     curr_win->xlr = curr_win->xul + curr_win->wd - 1;
     curr_win->ylr = curr_win->yul + curr_win->ht - 1;
     swap_image(curr_win); /* show window */
     chgviewport(curr_win); /* change window coordinates */
     moveto(xsave, ysave);
  }
}
```

The program works as follows: if you press the number 1, 2, or 3, the corresponding window is selected. If you use the arrow keys, you can then move the selected window around; or if you like, you can press the left mouse button when it is on the border of a window. The window is selected, and you can then move it around while dragging the mouse with the left button pressed. Press ESC or the right mouse button to exit. Figure 11.2 shows a sample screen drawn with this program.

If you are using the EGA or VGA hi-resolution color modes, you will notice that swapping and moving the windows is a pretty slow process, even on a fast 268-based AT. This shows you the reason that text-based windows are probably the only practical way to go until faster graphics cards become widely available on the PC. Also, pop-up graphics windows can chew up a lot more memory than their text-based counterparts. For instance, to save the whole screen in EGA 640x350 16 color mode requires roughly 112K, as compared to only 4K for text mode.

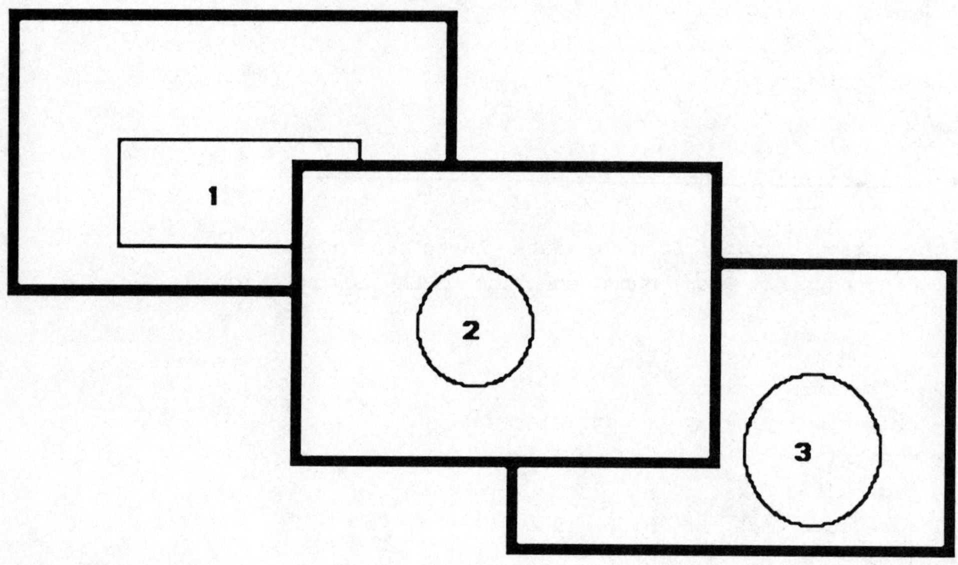

Figure 11.2 Moving windows in graphic mode

TEXT IN GRAPHICS MODE

In this section we will take a look at writing graphics-based text. The easiest way to output text in graphics modes is by calling **putchar()**, **puts()**, or **printf()**. These standard I/O routines eventually call BIOS, which supports printing text in all of the graphics modes (except Hercules). However, the support is minimal. For one thing, it uses the teletype scroll mode for outputting the text, and it does not support color. Also, the use of different fonts and sizes is severely limited. Because of this, Turbo C provides a set of functions for doing more sophisticated text output.

It should be noted that using the standard I/O routines is not all bad. By using them, you can make your programs work either in text or graphics mode without changing anything. A good example is the DOS DIR command, which works no matter what mode you are in. You also retain the ability to do I/O redirection, and using **printf()** gives you built-in formatting capabilities. (You will see a way to do some types of formatting using the Turbo C text routines shortly.)

Turbo C supplies the functions **outtext()** and **outtextxy()** for outputting text in graphics mode. There are also functions for changing colors, fonts, font sizes, and justifying text. These functions are:

Function	Use
setcolor()	Sets the drawing color (which is used for text, among other things)
gettextsettings()	Get current font, size, direction, etc. settings
settextjustify()	Set text justification parameters
settextstyle()	Set font style, direction, and size
setusercharsize()	Set user-defined character sizes
outtext()	Output text at current position
outtextxy()	Output text at pixel position (x,y)
textheight()	Get height of text string using current font size
textwidth()	Get width of text string using current font size

Along with an 8-by-8-bit mapped font, Turbo C supplies four *stroked fonts*. Instead of being written as bit-mapped images, these fonts are composed of a set of line segments. They look much better in larger sizes than the bit-mapped font does, and that is their main advantage.

Although the routines above are quite useful, they have several deficiencies:

- No formatting output function is provided.
- Scrolling is not supported.
- Overwriting text already on the screen does not erase old text.
- Highlighting text is not supported.

We shall now focus on ways to work around these deficiencies.

FORMATTING TEXT

You can get a limited form of text formatting by using **vsprintf()** to format text into a buffer and then calling **outtext()** or **outtextxy()** to write that buffer to the screen. The following program shows how.

```
/*
   Formatting text in graphics mode  (grphex6.c)
   Must link with: graphics.lib
*/
#include <stdio.h>
#include <conio.h>
#include <stdarg.h>
#include <graphics.h>
void outfmttext(int x, int y, char *fmt, ...);
void main() {
  int gd = DETECT, gm = 0, age = 30;
  initgraph(&gd,&gm,"");
  outfmttext(50,50,"Sally is %d years old",age);
  getch();
```

```
  closegraph();
}
void outfmttext(int x, int y, char *fmt, ...)
/*
   Outputs formatted text in graphics mode.
   NOTE: (1) newlines and tabs are not supported.
         (2) Formatting must not exceed 255 characters!!
*/
{
   va_list arg_ptr;
   char t[255];
   va_start(arg_ptr,fmt);       /* point to optional arguments  */
   vsprintf(t,fmt,arg_ptr);     /* format the string */
   va_end(arg_ptr);
   outtextxy(x,y,t);
}
```

Note that this method does *not* support newline or tab characters, since **outtextxy()** treats them as just graphics characters. If you wish to support such control characters, you have to write a loop which outputs one character at a time, checking for, and taking the appropriate action on, any control characters you see.

A more difficult problem is supporting scrolling in a window. This could be done by moving the image up one line via **getimage()** and **putimage()**. The size of image to move can be computed by knowing the size of the window and by using **textheight()** to compute the height of one line of text. You might try such a routine as an exercise.

OVERWRITING TEXT

Another problem is trying to overwrite text already on the screen. To see the problem, try running the following program:

```
/*
   Graphics text overwriting example #1  (grphex7.c)
   Must link with: graphics.lib
*/
#include <conio.h>
#include <graphics.h>
char msg1[] = "Baby, come here";
char msg2[] = "I am the ape man";
void main() {
 int gd = DETECT, gm = 0;
 initgraph(&gd,&gm,"");
 settextstyle(DEFAULT_FONT, HORIZ_DIR, 1);    /* use bit mapped font */
```

```
outtextxy(0,0,msg1);
getch();
outtextxy(0,0,"I am the ape man");
getch();
closegraph();
}
```

You will notice that the text in the second message is just ORed with the first message. The first message is not cleared.

There are several ways around this. One is to define a viewport to be just the size of the first message and then call **clearviewport()** before writing the second message. Another way is to clear the first message by drawing a solid bar just the right size with the color set to the background color. Still another way is to use **getimage()** to get a bit map of the original text and then to use an EXCLUSIVE OR putimage to effectively erase the original text.

Of these ways, drawing a solid bar is probably the best, since you will not affect the current viewport coordinates. Also, you do not have to allocate memory for a bit-map image, and having different colored backgrounds for text is easy to handle. All of the ways require computing the size of the original text. You can do this either by knowing it ahead of time, or by using the **textheight()** and **textwidth()** functions, or perhaps you can just clear the whole screen or a known region of it.

Let us modify our program to draw a solid background color bar over the first message before writing the second:

```
/*
   Graphics text overwriting example #2  (grphex8.c)
   Must link with: graphics.lib
*/
#include <conio.h>
#include <graphics.h>
char msg1[] = "Baby, come here";
char msg2[] = "I am the ape man";
void main() {
 int gd = DETECT, gm = 0, th, tw;
 initgraph(&gd,&gm,"");
 settextstyle(DEFAULT_FONT, HORIZ_DIR, 1);
 outtextxy(0,0,msg1);
 getch();
 th = textheight(msg1);  tw = textwidth(msg1);
 setfillstyle(SOLID_FILL, 0);    /* clear first message        */
 bar(0,th/4,tw,th+th/4);         /* with the background color */
 outtextxy(0,0,"I am the ape man");  /* new message */
 getch();
 closegraph();
}
```

A problem exists if you use a stroked font. Although **textwidth()** and **textheight()** will compute the size of the text properly, the position of the text will be wrong. When writing lowercase letters such as **g** or **y**, the tails of the letters are written below the line. To see this effect, change the font to TRIPLEX_FONT by using the statement:

```
settextstyle(TRIPLEX_FONT, HORIZ_DIR, 1);
```

You will notice that the tails of **y** and the comma are not erased. What is actually happening is that the top of each stroked font character is written several pixels below what they would be if the bit-mapped font were used. This allows the "tails" to appear below the line. The shift turns out to be approximately one-fourth of the height of the text as computed by **textheight()**, although you may have to experiment a little with this number. So, to correct it, try changing the bar statement to:

```
bar(0,th/4,tw,th+th/4);
```

You only want to do this for stroked fonts, so the proper way is to check for the type of font before calling the bar routine. The following code is our example corrected to work for any font:

```
/*
   Graphics text overwriting example #3  (grphex9.c)
   Must link with: graphics.lib
*/
#include <conio.h>
#include <graphics.h>
char msg1[] = "Baby, come here";
char msg2[] = "I am the ape man";
struct textsettingstype txtinfo;
void main() {
 int gd = DETECT, gm = 0, th, tw;
 initgraph(&gd,&gm,"");
 settextstyle(TRIPLEX_FONT, HORIZ_DIR, 0);
 outtextxy(0,0,msg1);
 getch();
 th = textheight(msg1);  tw = textwidth(msg1);
 gettextsettings(&txtinfo);
 /* clear the first message with the background color */
 setfillstyle(SOLID_FILL, 0);
 if (txtinfo.font) bar(0,th/4,tw,th+th/4); else bar(0,0,tw,th);
 outtextxy(0,0,"I am the ape man");
 getch();
 closegraph();
}
```

Verify that it works properly by trying different types and sizes of fonts.

HIGHLIGHTING TEXT

The last section hints at a way to highlight text in graphics mode. Simply compute the size of the text, draw a solid-colored bar of that size, and then output the text. This works as long as you account for the stroked fonts. The following program shows an example:

```
/*
  Text highlighting in graphics mode  (grphex10.c)
  Must link with: graphics.lib
*/
#include <graphics.h>
#include <conio.h>
#include <stdio.h>
void hilite(int x, int y, char *text, int back_color, int fore_color);
void main() {
 int gd = DETECT, gm = 0;
 initgraph(&gd,&gm,"");
 settextstyle(SANS_SERIF_FONT,HORIZ_DIR,0);
 hilite(50,50,"Hello there baby",WHITE,BLACK);
 getch();
 closegraph();
}
void hilite(int x, int y, char *text, int back_color, int fore_color)
/*
   Highlights the text at position (x,y) using the
   specified background and foreground colors.
   The shifted position of stroked fonts is accounted for.
*/
{
  struct textsettingstype txtinfo;
  int th, tw;
  gettextsettings(&txtinfo);
  th = textheight(text);
  tw = textwidth(text);
  if (txtinfo.font) th++;  /* add one just to make sure */
  setfillstyle(SOLID_FILL,back_color);
  bar(x,y,x+tw-1,y+th-1);
  setcolor(fore_color);
  if (txtinfo.font) {
     outtextxy(x,y-th/4,text);
  }
  else {
```

```
      outtextxy(x,y,text);
   }
}
```

Note that contrary to our text overwrite example, instead of shifting the bar down one-quarter of the height, we shift the text down. This is so that the bar will appear in the same place, regardless of whether you use a bit-mapped or stroked font.

With this highlighting routine, you now have the basic ingredient to doing menus in graphics mode. Try doing some!

RUBBER-BANDING LINES FOR THE EGA

Although Turbo C allows you to use OR, AND, NOT, and XOR operations with **putimage()**, unfortunately it does not provide the same ability when drawing pixels, lines, rectangles, and so on. The one operation that is particularly useful is XOR, since it allows you to do animation efficiently. By using XOR when drawing lines, you can get the *rubber-banding* line effect seen in most CAD packages. With rubber-banding lines, you have a pivot point about which a line is stretched and rotated using some pointing device. This allows you to see how a line will look before it is drawn permanently.

To get rubber-banding lines for any general graphics mode, you would have to bypass the Turbo C line routines and write your own. However, in this section we will show you an easy trick for getting rubber-banding lines with the EGA. Although it is beyond the scope of this book to talk about the EGA in detail, we will show you just enough to get rubber-banding lines.

The EGA (as well as the VGA) has many different registers which can be set to give a variety of read and write modes. One such register, the data rotate/function select register, can be used to control the logical operation that is performed with a pixel already on the screen and the pixel about to be used to overwrite it. Table 11.2 shows the possible operations:

Table 11.2 Function select register select update codes

7654 3210	Operation
Bit XXX0 0XXX*	REPLACE
XXX0 1XXX	AND
XXX1 0XXX	OR
XXX1 1XXX	XOR

* X bits are used for other purposes

The bits we are concerned with here are Bits 3 and 4. The X bits are for other purposes and are normally set to 0. To get an XOR operation, we can use a code of 0x18. The normal operation is REPLACE, which is code 0x00.

Setting this register before calling the Turbo C line routine allows us to XOR a line with what is already on the screen. Calling the line routine twice in this fashion will cause the line to be drawn and then erased, restoring the pixels underneath to their original color.

Unfortunately, due to the way Turbo C draws horizontal lines, it does not always restore the pixels properly. (It seems that some pixels in horizontal lines are actually drawn twice, causing the XOR to get out of synchronization.) So you must check for horizontal lines and draw them another way. One way is to use **getimage()** and **putimage()** to save and restore the image underneath the horizontal line. The following rubber-banding line example shows this technique in action.

```
/****************************************************************
 *   Rubber banding lines example  (grphex11.c)
 *   Must link with: mouse.obj, graphics.lib
 *   Works for EGA 640x350 and 640X200 color modes only
 ****************************************************************/
#include <math.h>
#include <dos.h>
#include <conio.h>
#include <graphics.h>
#include <alloc.h>
#include "mouse.h"
void *save_image;
int been_saved = 0;
char msg[] = "This is a test of rubber banding lines";
void rubber_line(int px, int py, int ex, int ey, int drawflag);
void main() {
  int gd = EGA, gm = EGAHI;
  int px, py, ex, ey, mx, my;
  unsigned int k;
  initgraph(&gd,&gm,"");
  init_mouse(MOUSE_NEEDED, gd, gm);
  /* Allocate enough room for a two-pixel high line the width of
     the screen.
  */
  save_image = calloc(imagesize(0,0,getmaxx(),1),1);
  while(!mouse_trigger(1));
  px = mouse_grph_x;  py = mouse_grph_y;
  ex = px;            ey = py;
  mouse_off(1);
  settextstyle(TRIPLEX_FONT,HORIZ_DIR,0);
  outtextxy((getmaxx()-textwidth(msg))/2,getmaxy()/2,msg);
  mouse_on(1);
  setlinestyle(DOTTED_LINE,0,1);
  rubber_line(px,py,ex,ey,1);
  do {
```

```
      mouse_grph_posn(&mx,&my);
      if (k = mouse_trigger(1)) {     /* ie. mouse button release */
         mouse_off(1);
         rubber_line(px,py,ex,ey,0); /* erase, then make line permanent */
         setcolor(GREEN);
         line(px,py,ex,ey);
         setcolor(WHITE);
         mouse_on(1);
         px = ex; py = ey;            /* change pivot point */
      }
      else {
        if (mx != ex || my != ey) {
           mouse_off(1);
           rubber_line(px,py,ex,ey,0);     /* move line via XOR */
           ex = mx; ey = my;
           rubber_line(px,py,ex,ey,1);
           mouse_on(1);
        }
      }
   } while(k != RIGHT_MOUSE_PRESS);
   mouse_reset();
   closegraph();
}
void rubber_line(int px, int py, int ex, int ey, int drawflag)
/*
   XOR's a line in EGA HiRes mode, using Turbo C line routine.
   Must use getimage() and putimage() for horizontal lines
   due to way Turbo C draws horizontal lines.
   Works with any line style, but must use normal width.
*/
{
   int sx, fx;
   if (py == ey) { /* horizontal line */
      if (px > ex) { sx = ex; fx = px; } else {sx=px; fx=ex; }
      if (drawflag) {
         /* must use a two pixel high rectangle */
         getimage(sx,py,fx,py+1,save_image);
         been_saved = 1;
         line(sx,py,fx,py);
      }
      else {
         if (been_saved) putimage(sx,py,save_image,COPY_PUT);
```

```
            been_saved = 0;
        }
    }
    else {
        outp(0x3ce,3);      /* select function register */
        outp(0x3cf,0x18);   /* set it to XOR            */
        line(px,py,ex,ey);  /* then draw the line       */
        outp(0x3ce,3);      /* set it back to replace   */
        outp(0x3cf,0);
    }
}
```

This program first writes a message on the screen and then uses the mouse to draw rubber-banding lines. Clicking the left mouse button causes the current line to be drawn permanently, and the ending point of the line becomes the new pivot point. Clicking the right mouse button exits the program. Although you are using the default solid line style here, the XOR technique works for other line styles as well (such as dotted lines). However, you must use only NORM_WIDTH (single pixel) lines, and not THICK_WIDTH lines.

Although the program is quite short, there are a few subtleties in it. When a horizontal line is drawn, the image underneath it is saved to be restored when the line is erased. However, **getimage()** and **putimage()** do not work for rectangles one pixel-high (the normal size of a line), so a two-pixel-high rectangle is used. Also, although you can pass coordinates to the line routine in any order, with **getimage()** and **putimage()**, a few rules must be observed. The left X coordinate must be smaller than the right, and likewise for the top and bottom coordinates. Thus the coordinates are checked and swapped if necessary.

Another problem is that the saving and restoring of images can get out of step if the mouse button is clicked at the wrong times. Because of this, the flag "been_saved" is used to see whether or not the horizontal line needs to be restored.

The XOR mode is set by outputting to two ports used for the function and data registers. The code sequence

```
outp(0x3ce,3);      /* select function register     */
outp(0x3cf,0x18);   /* set it to XOR                */
line(px,py,ex,ey);  /* then draw the line           */
outp(0x3ce,3);      /* set it back to replace mode  */
outp(0x3cf,0);
```

is used to set the update mode to XOR, draw the line, and then set the mode back to normal. As always, the mouse should be turned off during this time.

SUMMARY

We have seen many of the Turbo C graphics functions in action in this chapter. After reading and understanding the code presented here, you should see some of the power inherent in the graphics functions provided in Turbo C. We have pointed out some of the problems in using the routines and what things to watch out for. We have also given suggestions on how to enhance the routines and how to work around some of their deficiencies.

The routines were presented at a very rapid pace in this chapter, especially if you are a beginner. Even so, we covered just a few of the details. There is not enough room to discuss them all in this book. Be sure to read the graphics section in Turbo C manuals thoroughly for other functions and settings that can be used. You may also want to consider purchasing a good book on graphics, particularly one devoted to Turbo C graphics, although for many applications you can get along fine without one.

Listing 11.1 Source code for header file "gpopup.h"

```
/*  Graphics popup window toolkit header file (gpopup.h)   */
/* Center window code */
#define  CTRWIN  999
/* These help port from text popup windows */
#define xul wc.viewinfo.left
#define yul wc.viewinfo.top
#define xlr wc.viewinfo.right
#define ylr wc.viewinfo.bottom
/* popupwindows save the image underneath, tiled windows don't */
enum windowtype {popup,tile};
/* A structure to hold the box type, and a set of window colors */
typedef struct wincolors_struct {
  struct linesettingstype lineinfo;
  struct fillsettingstype fillinfo;
  struct textsettingstype textinfo;
  struct linesettingstype brdinfo;
  struct viewporttype     viewinfo;
  char border_type;
  unsigned char border_color, text_color, hilite_color, back_color;
} wincolors;
/* A structure to hold information for each window */
typedef struct winstruct {
   char *name;                          /* window title */
   void *image;                         /* ptr to image save area */
   struct winstruct *under,*over;       /* ptrs to window below and above
                                           on popup stack  */
   wincolors wc;                        /* current drawing settings */
   int wd, ht;                          /* computed width & height  */
   int  xsave,ysave;                    /* saved cursor posn */
   enum windowtype wtype;               /* window type */
} windesc;
extern windesc *base_win;    /* can be used to access whole screen */
extern windesc *curr_win;    /* current window in use */
extern wincolors defcolors;  /* some other global variables */
extern int graphdriver;
extern int graphmode;
extern char *pathdriver;
/* macros for easy use in removing and selecting window */
```

```
#define rmv_win(w)  view_win(w,0)
#define slct_win(w) view_win(w,1)
/* Now the prototypes for the popup functions */
extern void init_win(void);
extern windesc *draw_win(int x, int y, int wd, int ht, char *title,
                    enum windowtype wt, wincolors *wc);
extern void view_win(windesc *this, int select);
extern void swap_image(windesc *w);
extern void clr_win(void);
extern void chgviewport(windesc *this);
```

Listing 11.2 Souce code for file "gpopup.c"

```
/*************************************************************
 *   Graphics popup window toolkit for Turbo C  (gpopup.c)
 *************************************************************/
#include <stddef.h>
#include <stdarg.h>
#include <stdio.h>
#include <stdlib.h>
#include <alloc.h>
#include <conio.h>
#include <string.h>
#include <process.h>
#include <graphics.h>
#include "gpopup.h"
#include "mouse.h"
#define MAX(a,b)  ((a) > (b) ? (a) : (b))
#define MIN(a,b)  ((a) < (b) ? (a) : (b))
/*
 * Global data definitions
 */
windesc *base_win  = NULL;    /* The "Base Window" pointer */
windesc *curr_win  = NULL;    /* The current window pointer */
int graphdriver = 0;          /* Default to auto detect, */
int graphmode   = 0;          /* Highest resolution      */
char *pathdriver = "";        /* Current directory       */
/* Window settings */
wincolors defcolors = {
  {SOLID_LINE, 0, NORM_WIDTH}, /* line style - solid line, 1 pixel wide */
  {EMPTY_FILL, 0},             /* empty fill, background color */
  {DEFAULT_FONT, HORIZ_DIR, 1, LEFT_TEXT, TOP_TEXT}, /* text style */
  {SOLID_LINE, 0, THICK_WIDTH},/* border - solid 3 pixel wide line */
  {0,0,0,0,1},     /* viewport loaded by draw_win, but clip set here */
  1,               /* will actually have a border */
  7,7,7,0          /* border and text will be gray, hilite will be white,
                      and background black */
};
static windesc *top_win;   /* window stack pointer */
static void dispose_window_node(windesc *w);
```

```
static windesc *push_window_node(void);
static windesc *make_window_node(void);
static void chg_win(windesc *this);
static void fill_win(windesc *w);
void init_win(void)
/*
  init_win initializes the internal variables for the popup windows
  package. This function creates a base window "base_win" which
  represents the entire screen.
  This function MUST be called before any popup routines are used.
*/
{
  initgraph(&graphdriver, &graphmode, pathdriver);
  base_win = make_window_node();      /* allocate a window node */
  getviewsettings(&base_win->wc.viewinfo);
  base_win->wc.text_color = getcolor();
  getfillsettings(&base_win->wc.fillinfo);
  getlinesettings(&base_win->wc.lineinfo);
  gettextsettings(&base_win->wc.textinfo);
  base_win->wc.brdinfo = base_win->wc.lineinfo;
  base_win->xsave = getx();
  base_win->ysave = gety();
  base_win->wtype = tile;              /* no saved image underneath    */
  base_win->wc.border_type = 0;        /* has no border either         */
  top_win = base_win;                  /* set up window stack          */
  curr_win = base_win;
}
windesc *draw_win(int x, int y, int wd, int ht, char *title,
                  enum windowtype wt, wincolors *wc)
/*
   draw_win creates a new window at a designated screen location.
   The viewport will actually reside inside the border.
   Besides the usual coordinates for (x,y), you can use the following
   codes:
        x = CTRWIN   (Center window in x direction)
        y = CTRWIN   (Center window in y direction)
*/
{
  windesc *w;
  int maxx, maxy;
  w = push_window_node();  /* create and link up a window node */
  maxx = getmaxx();  maxy = getmaxy();
  /* Check for valid window size */
  wd = MAX(wd,3);
  wd = MIN(wd,maxx);
  ht = MAX(ht,3);
  ht = MIN(ht,maxy);
  /* Check for centering coordinates and current coordinates.
     Reminder: these are absolute coordinates !!! */
  if (x == CTRWIN) x = (maxx-wd) / 2;
```

```
  if (y == CTRWIN) y = (maxy-ht) / 2;
  /*
     Check for valid coordinates.
  */
  x = MAX(x,0);
  y = MAX(y,0);
  if ((x+wd) > maxx) x = maxx-wd+1;
  if ((y+ht) > maxy) y = maxy-ht+1;
  /* Store the window parameters */
  w->wc = *wc;  /* set up our window line, fill and color settings */
  w->wd  = wd;                w->ht  = ht;
  w->xul = x;                 w->yul = y;
  w->xlr = x + w->wd - 1;     w->ylr = y + w->ht - 1;
  w->xsave   = 1;               w->ysave    = 1;
  w->wtype   = wt;              w->name     = strdup(title);
  /* allocate and save image underneath if a popup window */
  if (wt == popup) {
     /* use calloc so that the size of the image gets initialized
        to zero!! It will pop up faster first time that way, and
        also keep swap_image from calling put_image with an
        uninitialized buffer */
     w->image =
        calloc(imagesize(w->xul,w->yul,w->xlr,w->ylr),1);
     swap_image(w);
  }
  fill_win(w);     /* draw border and fill window with color */
  chg_win(w);      /* change to new window coords and styles */
  return w;        /* return new window pointer              */
}
static void fill_win(windesc *w)
/* Draws the border,and fills window with background color */
{
  mouse_off(1);
  /* Must go to absolute coordinates so we can get to
     the borders of our window */
  chgviewport(base_win);
  setcolor(w->wc.border_color);
  setlinestyle(w->wc.brdinfo.linestyle,
               w->wc.brdinfo.upattern,
               w->wc.brdinfo.thickness);
  setfillstyle(SOLID_FILL,w->wc.back_color);
  /* Tricky!! If border is more than one pixel thick, we must
     compensate so that rectangle pixels are all inside the
     image region we've saved.
  */
  if (w->wc.border_type && w->wc.brdinfo.thickness == THICK_WIDTH)
     bar3d(w->xul+1,w->yul+1,w->xlr-2,w->ylr-2,0,0);
  else
     bar3d(w->xul,w->yul,w->xlr,w->ylr,0,0);
  chgviewport(curr_win);     /* Back to previous viewport */
```

```
  mouse_on(1);                /* restore mouse state        */
}
void clr_win(void)
/* Clears the current window */
{
   fill_win(curr_win);
}
void view_win(windesc *this, int select)
/* If select = 1, then view_win moves "this" window to the
   top of the stack and makes it the active window.
   If select = 0, then the window is removed from the stack and erased.
   Note that no moves take place if already at the top.
   If this is merely a tiled window, then it is just selected.
*/
{
   windesc *p;
   if (select && this == top_win) return;
   mouse_off(1);    /* make sure mouse hidden */
   /* if this is a popup window, move its image to the top */
   if (this->wtype == popup) {
      p = top_win;
      while(p != this) {    /* hide all window above */
        swap_image(p);
        p = p->under;
      }
      swap_image(this);     /* and then this window */
      p = this;             /* then put rest of windows back */
      while(p != top_win) {
        p = p->over;
        swap_image(p);
      }
   }
   /* link up window underneath this one, with the window above it */
   if (this == top_win) {         /* if this == top_win here, then it is also */
      this->under->over = NULL; /* true that we're removing it for good     */
      top_win = this->under;
   }
   else {
     this->under->over = this->over;
     this->over->under = this->under;
   }
   if (select) {
      top_win->over = this; /* move window to the top */
      this->under = top_win;
      top_win = this;
      swap_image(this);     /* put back it's image. Does nothing if tiled */
      chg_win(this);        /* change window */
   }
   else {
```

```
      chg_win(top_win);          /* might as well select top window */
      dispose_window_node(this); /* but do before free old window   */
    }
    mouse_on(1);        /* restore mouse state */
}
static void chg_win(windesc *this)
/* Internal routine to select a window */
{
   curr_win->xsave = getx();
   curr_win->ysave = gety();
   getfillsettings(&curr_win->wc.fillinfo);
   getlinesettings(&curr_win->wc.lineinfo);
   gettextsettings(&curr_win->wc.textinfo);
   chgviewport(this);
   setcolor(this->wc.text_color);
   setfillstyle(this->wc.fillinfo.pattern,this->wc.fillinfo.color);
   setlinestyle(this->wc.lineinfo.linestyle,this->wc.lineinfo.upattern,
               this->wc.lineinfo.thickness);
   settextjustify(this->wc.textinfo.horiz,this->wc.textinfo.vert);
   settextstyle(this->wc.textinfo.font,this->wc.textinfo.direction,
               this->wc.textinfo.charsize);
   moveto(this->xsave,this->ysave);
   curr_win = this;                /* selected window is active */
}
void chgviewport(windesc *this)
/* Changes to this windows coordinates. Takes care of border thickness
    in it coordinate calculations.
*/
{
   int delta;
   if (this->wc.border_type)
      delta = this->wc.brdinfo.thickness;
      else delta = 0;
   setviewport(this->xul+delta, this->yul+delta,
              this->xlr-delta, this->ylr-delta,
              this->wc.viewinfo.clip);
}
void swap_image(windesc *w)
/*
    This routines swaps the image buffer of a window with what is
    on the screen.  If the window is not a popup window, then
    nothing happens.
*/
{
   char *temp_image;
   int nbytes;
   if (w->wtype == popup) {
      nbytes = imagesize(w->xul,w->yul,w->xlr,w->ylr);
      temp_image = malloc(nbytes);
```

```
      /* Must go to absolute coordinates so we can get to
         the borders of our window */
      chgviewport(base_win);
      mouse_off(1);
      getimage(w->xul,w->yul,w->xlr,w->ylr,temp_image);
      putimage(w->xul,w->yul,w->image,COPY_PUT);
      mouse_on(1);
      /* now back to relative coords */
      chgviewport(w);
      memcpy(w->image,temp_image,nbytes); /* save screen image */
      free(temp_image);
   }
}
static windesc *make_window_node(void)
{
/*
  Make_window_node allocates room for a new window structure,
  and initializes it's links to NULL.
*/
  windesc *q;
  q = (windesc *)malloc(sizeof(windesc));
  q->image = NULL; q->under = NULL; q->over = NULL;
  return q;
}
static windesc *push_window_node(void)
{
/*
  Push_window_node "pushes" the window w onto the window stack.
*/
   windesc *q;
   q = make_window_node();    /* allocate a window node */
   top_win->over = q;          /* link top of stack to new node */
   q->under = top_win;         /* link new node to top of stack */
   top_win = q;                /* set top of stack to new node  */
   return q;
}
static void dispose_window_node(windesc *w)
{
/*
  Dispose_window_node frees up the image save area of the window,
  and the window structure itself.
*/
  if (w != NULL) {    /* safety test for base window   */
     if (w->wtype == popup) free(w->image);
     free(w->name);     /* free up window title */
     free(w);           /* and then the structure itself */
  }
}
```

CHAPTER

12

Advanced Project— A Hypertext System

This chapter is the culmination of many of the things you have learned in this book. Presented is a hypertext system that uses the various tools and techniques developed in earlier chapters. It employs pop-up windows, mouse and keyboard I/O, variable-length dynamic strings, and file I/O with variable-length records.

First, what exactly is hypertext? Essentially, it is text that can be scanned in ways other than the conventional, two-dimensional way that you use when you read a book. As the name may suggest, hypertext allows you to have "hyper-dimensional" text. This is accomplished by having special links in the text from which you can jump to other portions of the text. In general, these links can be bidirectional and can be created on-the-fly while you are browsing through the text. In one approach, the text is organized into **cards** and links refer not to specific locations in the text, but rather to other cards.

The hypertext system developed here has many of the features just discussed. However, to keep it simple, dynamic links are not supported. This means you cannot create hypertext on the run. Instead, you create a special text file which contains commands to organize the text into cards and to provide links between them. This text file is then "compiled" into hypertext and stored in another file. It can then be read by a "browser" program, which allows you to browse through the hypertext.

Our hypertext system is implemented as two programs: a hypertext compiler and a hypertext browser.

THE HYPERTEXT COMPILER

The Hypertext Compiler is a program that reads an ASCII text file and converts it into a VLR file containing special hypertext code. The ASCII file contains lines of text with command lines interspersed throughout. The text is separated into groups of text lines, called *cards*, by command lines starting with **#card**. Figure 12.1 shows an example of such a file. The directive **#card XXXX** tells the compiler that a new card is starting and that the name of the card is **XXXXX**. This name serves as the key by which the card can be referenced.

Listing 12.1 shows the source code for the hypertext compiler. The name of the file to be compiled is given on the command line, with an assumed extension of **.txt**. A hypertext file with the same name is created and is given the same name, but with extension **.htx**.

The compiler works in two passes. The first pass scans the file looking for **#card** lines and collects all the card names. The second pass then takes this list of card names and scans the text looking for matches. Anywhere a match is found, its position in the file is recorded in a key position list, one such list for each card. These lists are used by the browser to detect when a link has been selected. In this manner, the compiler figures out the card links for you automatically. All you do is reference cards by their names in the text.

The **preprocess()** function does the first pass and scans the file looking for **#card** directives. A card name is assumed to follow the directive on the same line. It starts with the first nonspace character on the line and ends with either a space or a newline. It should be no more

```
A sample card text file.

#card Cow
I've seen a lot of cows in my day,
but never like the one i saw riding
a horse out back behind the pig pen.
#card
This is the stuff of an unnamed card.
#card Horse
Talk about a pig of a diff...
oops!!, I meant a horse of a
different color.  Did you know
that a cow doesn't think a horse
is better than a zebra?
#card Zebra
Zebras are a lot of fun, except
when you get to know them. Then
they can be real pen pals, that
is, as in pigs.
#card Pig
Piggy does as piggies do. But
they don't do as horses do.
```

Figure 12.1 Sample hypertext source text file, "cards.txt"

than 20 characters long, although that can be changed via the MAXKEYSIZE macro. If no name is found, then a default name of **_cardNN** is generated, where NN is the current line number in the file.

The **process_cards()** function then rewinds the file and makes another pass through the text, gathering the text into cards. Once the text for a card is collected, the physical size of the card (i.e., character width and number of lines) is recorded, and then the text is passed to a hypertext scanner function.

The function **hypertext_scan()** is used to do the scanning. Each card name is tried in sequence to see if it appears in the text. When a match is found, the position of the match is recorded in a key position list. The matching ignores case. When the card has been completely scanned, the card text and the key position list are each stored in records in the VLR file. The address of both records is stored in an index table.

Once all cards have been processed, the index table itself is added to the VLR file. The index contains the card number, name, size, and addresses of its text and key position data. The file is now ready to be read by the hypertext browser.

Figure 12.2 shows the text file given in Figure 12.1 converted into a VLR file. The file is shown in a hex dump and illustrates what is contained in a VLR file. As an exercise, see if you can decipher the data in the file by using the VLR format given in the VLR file chapter.

THE HYPERTEXT BROWSER

The Hypertext Browser is given in Listing 12.2. It reads a hypertext file and allows you to browse it using the keyboard and/or mouse. Each card is popped up in its own window, with all links highlighted. Clicking the mouse or pressing return on any link allows you to hop to the designated card.

There are two special predefined cards, a Home Card and a Stack Card. The Home Card contains an index of all keys contained in the file. It is itself a hypertext card, so one chooses a new key from the index in the same manner as for any card. The Stack Card contains a history of the last 15 cards you have browsed, in the order in which you visited them. It is also a hypertext card, allowing you to click on any card in the stack and jump there.

A sample screen of cards is shown in Figure 12.3. At the top of each card is its name and a menu of commands. The commands are:

Command	Use
`Home`	`Takes you to the Home Card`
`Stack`	`Takes you to the Stack Card`
`Prev`	`Takes you to the previous card, as defined by the order of cards in the original text file`
`Next`	`Takes you to the next card, as defined by the order of cards in the original text file`
`Delete`	`Removes the current card from the stack (You cannot remove a card if it is the only one)`
`Quit`	`Erases all of the cards and exits`

```
0000  d6 03 00 00 d6 03 00 00-1f 03 00 00 0b 00 00 00  ................
0010  00 00 00 00 00 00 e5 99-cc 10 db 2f 98 0a 00 00  .........../....
0020  81 fd 00 00 00 00 70 00-49 27 76 65 20 73 65 65  ......p.I've see
0030  6e 20 61 20 6c 6f 74 20-6f 66 20 63 6f 77 73 20  n a lot of cows
0040  69 6e 20 6d 79 20 64 61-79 2c 0d 0a 62 75 74 20  in my day,..but
0050  6e 65 76 65 72 20 6c 69-6b 65 20 74 68 65 20 6f  never like the o
0060  6e 65 20 69 20 73 61 77-20 72 69 64 69 6e 67 0d  ne i saw riding.
0070  0a 61 20 68 6f 72 73 65-20 6f 75 74 20 62 61 63  .a horse out bac
0080  6b 20 62 65 68 69 6e 64-20 74 68 65 20 70 69 67  k behind the pig
0090  20 70 65 6e 2e 0d 0a 00-00 00 00 00 00 00 00 00   pen...........
00a0  00 00 29 fd 00 00 00 00-18 00 14 00 01 00 03 00  ..).............
00b0  02 00 03 00 03 00 05 00-04 00 1d 00 03 00 03 00  ................
00c0  06 00 00 00 00 00 00 00-00 00 00 00 39 fd 00 00  ............9...
00d0  00 00 28 00 54 68 69 73-20 69 73 20 74 68 65 20  ..(.This is the
00e0  73 74 75 66 66 20 6f 66-20 61 6e 20 75 6e 6e 61  stuff of an unna
00f0  6d 65 64 20 63 61 72 64-2e 0d 0a 00 6e 65 76 65  med card....neve

0100  72 20 6c 69 6b 65 11 fd-00 00 00 00 00 00 14 00  r like..........
0110  01 00 03 00 02 00 03 00-aa fd 00 00 00 00 99 00  ................
0120  54 61 6c 6b 20 61 62 6f-75 74 20 61 20 70 69 67  Talk about a pig
0130  20 6f 66 20 61 20 64 69-66 66 2e 2e 2e 0d 0a 6f   of a diff.....o
0140  6f 70 73 21 21 2c 20 49-20 6d 65 61 6e 74 20 61  ops!!, I meant a
0150  20 68 6f 72 73 65 20 6f-66 20 61 0d 0a 64 69 66   horse of a..dif
0160  66 65 72 65 6e 74 20 63-6f 6c 6f 72 2e 20 20 44  ferent color.  D
0170  69 64 20 79 6f 75 20 6b-6e 6f 77 0d 0a 74 68 61  id you know..tha
0180  74 20 61 20 63 6f 77 20-64 6f 65 73 6e 27 74 20  t a cow doesn't
0190  74 68 69 6e 6b 20 61 20-68 6f 72 73 65 0d 0a 69  think a horse..i
01a0  73 20 62 65 74 74 65 72-20 74 68 61 6e 20 61 20  s better than a
01b0  7a 65 62 72 61 3f 0d 0a-00 00 00 00 00 00 00 00  zebra?..........
01c0  00 00 00 39 fd 00 00 00-00 28 00 08 00 04 00 03  ...9.....(......
01d0  00 02 00 13 00 02 00 05-00 04 00 1c 00 04 00 05  ................
01e0  00 04 00 12 00 05 00 05-00 05 00 0e 00 01 00 03  ................
01f0  00 06 00 00 00 00 00 00-00 00 00 00 00 86 fd 00  ................
```

Figure 12.2 Hexadecimal dump image of the hypertext file, "cards.htx"

```
0200  00 00 00 75 00 5a 65 62-72 61 73 20 61 72 65 20  ...u.Zebras are
0210  61 20 6c 6f 74 20 6f 66-20 66 75 6e 2c 20 65 78  a lot of fun, ex
0220  63 65 70 74 0d 0a 77 68-65 6e 20 79 6f 75 20 67  cept..when you g
0230  65 74 20 74 6f 20 6b 6e-6f 77 20 74 68 65 6d 2e  et to know them.
0240  20 54 68 65 6e 0d 0a 74-68 65 79 20 63 61 6e 20   Then..they can
0250  62 65 20 72 65 61 6c 20-70 65 6e 20 70 61 6c 73  be real pen pals
0260  2c 20 74 68 61 74 0d 0a-69 73 2c 20 61 73 20 69  , that..is, as i
0270  6e 20 70 69 67 73 2e 0d-0a 00 20 61 20 68 6f 72  n pigs.... a hor
0280  73 65 0d 0a 21 fd 00 00-00 00 10 00 01 00 01 00  se..!..........
0290  05 00 05 00 0b 00 04 00-03 00 06 00 1c 00 04 00  ................
02a0  05 00 04 00 12 00 4e fd-00 00 00 00 3d 00 50 69  ......N.....=.Pi
02b0  67 67 79 20 64 6f 65 73-20 61 73 20 70 69 67 67  ggy does as pigg
02c0  69 65 73 20 64 6f 2e 20-42 75 74 0d 0a 74 68 65  ies do. But..the
02d0  79 20 64 6f 6e 27 74 20-64 6f 20 61 73 20 68 6f  y don't do as ho
02e0  72 73 65 73 20 64 6f 2e-0d 0a 00 68 65 6e 0d 0a  rses do....hen..
02f0  74 68 65 79 20 29 fd 00-00 00 00 18 00 12 00 02  they )..........

0300  00 05 00 04 00 01 00 01-00 03 00 06 00 0f 00 01  ................
0310  00 03 00 06 00 12 00 05-00 05 00 05 00 0e 00 b6  ................
0320  fd 00 00 00 00 a5 00 43-6f 77 00 00 00 be ff 04  .......Cow......
0330  00 01 00 4c 01 00 00 00-00 ce ff b7 20 00 00 00  ...L.......... ...
0340  a2 00 00 00 26 00 03 00-5f 63 61 72 64 37 00 ff  ....&..._card7..
0350  04 00 01 00 4c 01 00 00-00 00 ce ff b7 cc 00 00  ....L...........
0360  00 06 01 00 00 26 00 01-00 48 6f 72 73 65 00 00  .....&...Horse..
0370  ff 04 00 01 00 4c 01 00-00 00 00 ce ff b7 18 01  .....L..........
0380  00 00 c3 01 00 00 22 00-05 00 5a 65 62 72 61 00  ......"...Zebra.
0390  00 ff 04 00 01 00 4c 01-00 00 00 00 ce ff b7 fd  ......L.........
03a0  01 00 00 84 02 00 00 21-00 04 00 50 69 67 00 61  .......!...Pig.a
03b0  00 00 ff 04 00 01 00 4c-01 00 00 00 00 ce ff b7  .......L........
03c0  a6 02 00 00 f5 02 00 00-1e 00 02 00 00 00 00 00  ................
03d0  00 00 00 00 00 00 ff
```

Figure 12.2 Hexadecimal dump image of the hypertext file, "cards.htx" *(continued)*

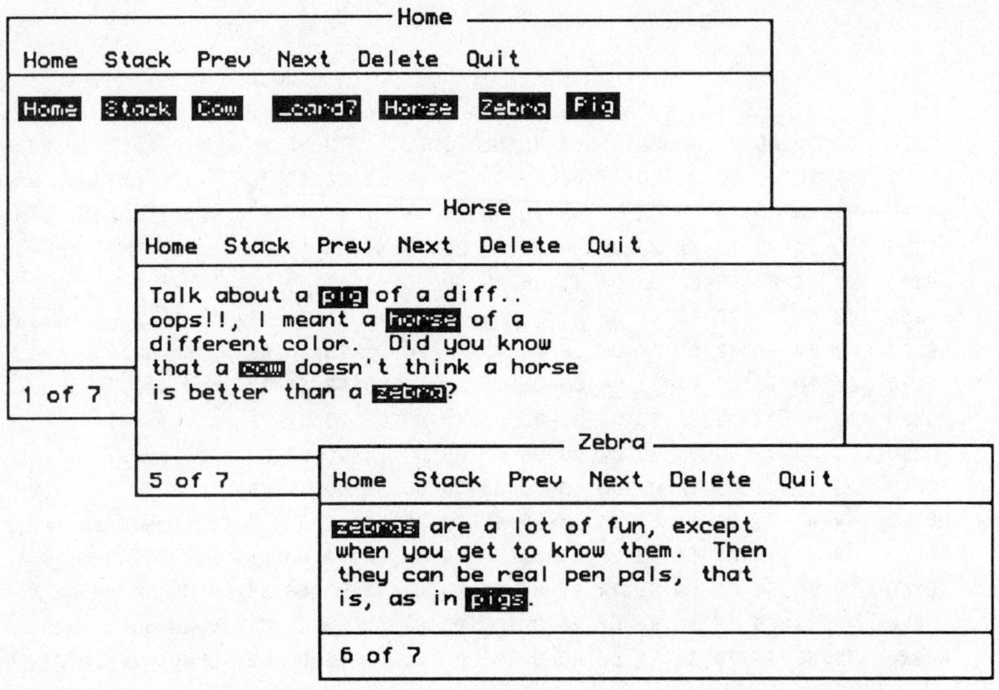

Figure 12.3 Screen image for a sample session with the display of hypertext cards

These commands can be accessed by clicking on them with the mouse, moving the cursor to them and pressing return, or by using the following keys:

Key	Use
Arrows	Moves the cursor around in the card window
Shift Arrows	Allows you to move the card around on the screen. Can also move card by dragging left mouse button on its border. Only works for active cards.
HOME, "h", "H"	Takes you to the Home Card
PGUPKEY, "p", "P"	Takes you to the previous card
PGDNKEY, "n", "N"	Takes you to the next card
BSKEY, DELKEY, "d", "D"	Deletes the top card from the stack
Right Mouse Button, ESCKEY, "q" ,"Q"	Quits the program

The cards are maintained on a window stack in exactly the same manner as we saw in our Move Window example in Chapter 4. In fact, some of the code was borrowed from that example, although slightly changed. Whenever a card is selected that is not already on the screen, it is popped up. If it is already drawn, it is merely moved to the top of the window stack. Whenever a new card is selected, the old card is changed to dim colors in order to reduce screen clutter.

The program maintains two parallel stacks, a card number stack and a window stack. Do not confuse the window stack with the one used in the Pop-up Window package. The window stack in the Hypertext Browser program merely contains a list of window pointers implemented via a dynamic string. It is true, however, that the order of the windows is the same for both window stacks. In fact, if you select the stack card, the list of card names shown there gives you a clear picture of the pop-up order of the windows.

DYNAMIC STRING USE

The Hypertext Browser makes extensive use of dynamic strings and provides a good vehicle for their study. There are six strings maintained by the program. The **index** string is a copy of the index table stored in the VLR file. The **card** string holds the actual text for a card. The **keypos** string holds position information (i.e., starting (x and y) coordinates, width, and key number) for each key shown on the current card. The **keystack** string holds a stack of card numbers recording the history of card visitation. This stack is limited to 15 entries, in order to keep too many windows from being popped up. The **winstack** string is a stack of window pointers that works in parallel with **keystack**. The **indxstk** string is simply of list of card numbers from 1 to N (where N is the number of cards), which is used to generate the Home Card.

Note how we methodically initialize each string at compile time via the NULLVSTR macro. Any time you wish to reuse a string, the **clrvstr()** function is used. As discussed in Chapter 7 (dynamic strings), this method is preferred over using **dimvstr()**. It allows us to reuse the strings inside loops (as is done in this program) without worrying about allocating memory too many times, or even worse, not at all.

FUNCTIONS IN THE HYPERTEXT BROWSER

The most complex functions in the Hypertext Browser Program are briefly discussed in the following paragraphs.

The main() Function

The **main()** function initializes the window and file systems and then opens up the VLR file given in the command line. The file name should be given without an extension, and a **.htx** extension is assumed. The file is opened for read-only access so it cannot inadverdantly be modified. The index table is then read in. Next the card stack is initialized, and the Home Card is popped up.

The WHILE loop is the main loop in the program. It pops up (or moves to the top, if already drawn) the current card and waits for a new selection. The selection maybe a new card reference, or a command from the menu. In either event, the new card number is computed, the card is drawn, and the cycle repeats until the "quit" command is chosen. All of the cards on the screen are then removed and the program exits.

The paint_htx() Function

This function takes the text for a card and prints it in the specified window. In then takes a list of key positions and highlights those positions in the window. Note that the highlighting method is exactly like the one used in our highlighting example in Chapter 4. This is not the most efficient way to do it, however. It would be faster to simply change the attributes by writing directly to the screen. As an exercise, see if you can change the code and get this direct method to work.

The get_next_card() Function

This function serves as the main event trigger. It waits for a key press, mouse button press, or button release. The appropriate action is then selected via a switch statement. The function loops until either a link or a command has been selected by clicking the left mouse button or pressing the return key on an entry. If you press down and hold the left mouse button on the border of the current card, you can drag the card to a new location on the screen. This can also be accomplished using the shift arrow keys. The function returns the key or card number of the selected link. Should the link happen to actually be a command, then the command is coded by using numbers beyond the range of the number of cards in the system. The **main()** function loop then decodes these numbers into either card selections or commands.

The make_index_card() Function

This function is used to generate hypertext for both the Home Card and the Stack Card. A list of card numbers is passed, which is used along with the index table to create lines of text containing the names of the cards in the list. Each name is separated by two spaces, and the lines are made to fit within the given width. The key position list for the card is also generated.

Note that no provision is made for having too many card names to fit on the card, since the browser does not support scrolling.

Other Functions

The **on_key()**, **recolor()**, **mouse_on_border()**, and **move_curr_win()** functions are straightforward and self-explanatory from the listing. Some of these functions were borrowed from earlier examples.

LIMITATIONS TO THE HYPERTEXT SYSTEM

The Hypertext System implemented here, although quite powerful in its own right, does have a few limitations. These limitations are that it does not support text scrolling, allow for link aliases, or allow the dynamic creation and deletion of links.

Because text scrolling is not supported, the cards (although automatically sized) must fit on the screen. The Home and Stack Cards have a fixed size. No checking is done to see if the text will actually fit on the card. If it does not, the text will scroll (since we're using **cprintf()** to print the text), but the link positions will not be updated properly. Because the Home and StackCards are of fixed size, there is an inherent limit to the number of cards you can have in any one hypertext file. The number depends on the lengths of the card names. Note that as far as storing hypertext in a file is concerned, this limitation does not apply.

Although the system allows for upper and lower case to be ignored when searching for links in the text, you must spell the reference the same way as it is in the card name, that is, no aliases are allowed. Also, no blanks can appear in a reference. These limitations could be circumvented by enhancing the compiler to handle aliases. One way to do this is as follows.

Suppose you have a card named **ghost**, and you have a piece of text like:

```
... I just saw Casper, the friendly ghost ...
```

and you wish to turn Casper into a reference for **ghost**. This could be done by using special escape characters, as follows:

```
... I just saw \ghost\Casper\, the friendly ghost ...
```

The **** character would signal to the compiler that an alias follows. The actual reference name is given, followed by another **** delimiter, and finally, the text you would like to appear on the card. When creating the key position list for the card, the compiler could use the appropriate card number, and then delete the delimiters and the actual reference name from the text.

Supporting dynamic linking would be much harder. This would require you to have not only a card browser, but a card editor as well. The editor would allow you to insert and delete text from a card, and set up links (or even delete them) to other cards. Once you have mastered using the VLR files and dynamic strings, you might try doing this.

Listing 12.1 Source code for the hypertext compiler, "hc.c"

```
/*************************************************************
 *  The Hypertext Compiler  (hc.c)
 *
 *  Must link with:  popup.obj, mouse.obj, sayerr.obj,
 *       fileio.obj, vstr.obj,  vlr.obj
 *************************************************************/
#include <stdio.h>
#include <dir.h>
#include <string.h>
#include <process.h>
#include <ctype.h>
#include <errno.h>
#include "popup.h"
#include "fileio.h"
#include "vstr.h"
#include "vlr.h"
#define MAXLINESIZE 128
#define MAXKEYSIZE  21
#define INDEX ((index_elem *)index->data)
typedef struct  {
   char key[MAXKEYSIZE];  /* card name             */
```

```
   long txt_addr;          /* text record addres  */
   long key_addr;          /* keys record addess  */
   int wd,ht;              /* size of card        */
} index_elem;
typedef struct {
  int x, y, wd, keyno;     /* key position info   */
} key_pos_elem;
char infile[MAXPATH];
char outfile[MAXPATH];
char line_buff[MAXLINESIZE];
int fhin;      /* input file is a text file */
int fhout;     /* output file is a vlr file */
vstr index  = NULLVSTR;  /* key table */
vstr card   = NULLVSTR;  /* card data */
vstr posn   = NULLVSTR;  /* key position data */
static void preprocess(int fhin, vstr *index);
static void process_cards(int fhin, int fhout,
            vstr *index, vstr *card, vstr *posn);
static void hypertext_scan(vstr *card, vstr *index, vstr *posn);
void main(int argc, char *argv[]) {
  init_win();        /* initialize window package */
  init_files();      /* initialize our high level file table */
  if (argc < 2) {
     printf("Usage: >hc cardfile\nExtension of 'txt' assumed\n");
     exit(1);
  }
  else {
     strcpy(infile,argv[1]);
     strcat(infile,".txt");
     /* Open input file for character access, text mode, read only */
     if ((fhin = openfile(infile,"rt",1)) == -1) exit(1);
     strcpy(outfile,argv[1]);
     strcat(outfile,".htx");
     /* Rewrite vlr file, or create is doesn't exist. Start recs at 32 */
     if ((fhout = openvlr(outfile,"w+b",32L)) == NULL) exit(1);
     preprocess(fhin,&index);  /* collect keys and posn's */
     process_cards(fhin,fhout,&index,&card,&posn);
     closefile(fhin);
     closefile(fhout);
  }
}
static void preprocess(int fhin, vstr *index)
/* Scan the input file, collect all card names as keys. */
{
   int i, line_no;
   char newkey[MAXKEYSIZE];
   char *p;
   line_no = 0;
```

```
   clrvstr(index,30,sizeof(index_elem),10);  /* start with 30 keys */
   while(!feof(ft[fhin].fp)) {  /* accumulate keys till eof or error */
     if (rdstr(line_buff,MAXLINESIZE,fhin) == -1) break;
     p = line_buff;
     line_no++;
     if (!strncmp(p,"#card",5)) {
        p += 5;
        while (isspace(*p)) p++;  /* look for start of card name */
        if (!*p) {
           sprintf(newkey,"_card%-d",line_no);
           printf("Error: card on line %d has no name, given default\n");
        }
        else {
          i = 0;
          while(!isspace(*p) && i < MAXKEYSIZE-1)  /* extract key */
               newkey[i++] = *p++;
          newkey[i] = 0; /* add null to key name */
        }
        printf("found key '%s'\n", newkey);
        vstrcat(index,&newkey);
     }
   }
   for (i=0; i<index->currlen; i++) {
     printf("key %p\n",(char far *)&(INDEX[i].key));
   }
}
static void process_cards(int fhin, int fhout,
                          vstr *index, vstr *card, vstr *posn)
/*
   For each card, read in the card's text, convert to hypertext, store
   in vlr file.
 */
{
  int i, wd, ht, len;
  long locn, fs, fe, ita, nl;
  rewind(ft[fhin].fp);  /* remember to start file over !!! */
  rdstr(line_buff,MAXLINESIZE,fhin);  /* get things started */
  for (i=0; i<index->currlen; i++) {  /* for each card */
      clrvstr(card,500,sizeof(char),200);      /* init card data */
      while(strncmp(line_buff,"#card",5) && !feof(ft[fhin].fp)) {
         printf("searching ... %s",line_buff);
         rdstr(line_buff,MAXLINESIZE,fhin);
      }
      if (!feof(ft[fhin].fp)) {
         /* collect up the lines of the card */
         do {
            if (rdstr(line_buff,MAXLINESIZE,fhin) == -1) break;
            printf("%s", line_buff);
```

```
            if (strncmp(line_buff,"#card",5)) {
               /* Ready to store line, but must force in
                  a carriage return ahead of the line feed
                  so that cprintf will work properly  */
               len = strlen(line_buff);
               line_buff[len-1] = '\r';  /* put in cr */
               line_buff[len]   = '\n';  /* ahead of lf */
               vstrins(card,card->currlen,line_buff,++len);
            }
            else break;
         } while(1);
         /* add null so numnewlines will work properly */
         vstrcat(card,"");
         numnewlines((char *)(card->data), &ht, &wd); /* get size */
         /* Scan the card for hypertext, add to file */
         hypertext_scan(card, index, posn);
         addvlr(fhout,card,&locn);
         INDEX[i].txt_addr = locn;
         addvlr(fhout,posn,&locn);
         INDEX[i].key_addr = locn;
         INDEX[i].wd = wd;
         INDEX[i].ht = ht;
      }
      else {
         printf("Unexpected end of file\n");
         exit(1);
      }
   }
   /* okay, now store the key table and store its pointer in
      pre-designated location in the file header */
    for (i=0; i<index->currlen; i++) {
      printf("key %s %ld %d %d \n",
             INDEX[i].key,
             INDEX[i].txt_addr,
             INDEX[i].key_addr,
             INDEX[i].wd,
             INDEX[i].ht
            );
    }
   addvlr(fhout,index,&locn);
   printf("index starts at %ld\n",locn);
   readhdr(fhout,&fs,&fe,&ita,&nl);
   ita = locn;
   writehdr(fhout,fs,fe,ita,nl);
}
static void hypertext_scan(vstr *card, vstr *index, vstr *posn)
/*
   Searches for keys in the text, and records their position.
```

```
*/
{
   char *key, *txt;
   unsigned int i, txtpos;
   int keylen, col, row;
   key_pos_elem kp;
   clrvstr(posn,10,sizeof(key_pos_elem),5); /* clear key posn data */
   /* for each key in the table, see if you can find it in the text */
   for (i=0; i<index->currlen; i++) {
        key = INDEX[i].key;
        keylen = strlen(key);
        txt = (char *)card->data;  /* point to text */
        txtpos = 0;  col = 1; row = 1;
        while(txtpos < card->currlen) {
           if (*txt == '\n') {
              col = 1; row++;
              txt++, txtpos++;
           }
           else {
             if (!strnicmp(txt,key,keylen)) {
                /* Match,ignoring case, so record posn */
                kp.x  = col;     kp.y     = row;    kp.wd = keylen;
                kp.keyno = i+2;  /* First two key numbers reserved */
                vstrcat(posn, &kp);
                txt += keylen;
                txtpos += keylen;
                col += keylen;
             }
             else {
                txt++; txtpos++; col++;
             }
           }
        }
   }
}
```

Listing 12.2 Source code for the hypertext browser, "hb.c"

```
/***************************************************************
 *  The Hypertext Browser   (hb.c)
 *
 *  Must link with: popup.obj, sayerr.obj, mouse.obj,
 *                  fileio.obj, vstr.obj, vlr.obj
 ***************************************************************/
#include <stdio.h>
#include <dir.h>
#include <string.h>
#include <process.h>
```

```
#include <ctype.h>
#include <conio.h>
#include <alloc.h>
#include "popup.h"
#include "mouse.h"
#include "fileio.h"
#include "vstr.h"
#include "vlr.h"
#define MAX(a,b)     ((a) > (b) ? (a) : (b))
#define MIN(a,b)     ((a) < (b) ? (a) : (b))
#define MAXLINESIZE 128
#define MAXKEYSIZE  21
#define INDEX        ((index_elem *)(index.data))
typedef struct  {
   char key[MAXKEYSIZE];  /* card name            */
   long txt_addr;         /* text record addres   */
   long key_addr;         /* keys record addess   */
   int wd,ht;             /* size of card         */
} index_elem;
typedef struct {
  int x, y, wd, keyno;    /* key position info    */
} key_pos_elem;
index_elem index_key = { "Home",  0L, 0L, 52, 10 };
index_elem stack_key = { "Stack", 0L, 0L, 52, 10 };
static void paint_htx(windesc *mw, vstr *keypos, vstr *text);
static int  get_next_card(windesc *w, vstr *keypos);
static int  on_key(vstr *keypos, int x, int y);
static void make_index_card(vstr *index, vstr *index_card,
                            vstr *stack, vstr *keypos, int wd);
static void move_curr_win(int x, int y);
static int  mouse_on_border(windesc *, int *xofs, int *yofs);
static void recolor(windesc *w, int attr);
char *cmds[] = {
  "Home", "Stack", "Prev", "Next", "Delete", "Quit"
};
key_pos_elem cmd_menu[6];
vstr index      = NULLVSTR;    /* key table */
vstr card       = NULLVSTR;    /* card data */
vstr keypos     = NULLVSTR;    /* position of keys on screen */
vstr keystack   = NULLVSTR;    /* our keystack through the cards */
vstr winstack   = NULLVSTR;    /* our stack of card windows */
vstr indxstk    = NULLVSTR;    /* an index stack            */
wincolors deadcolors = {1, 7, 7, 7, 7};
char infile[MAXPATH];  /* hypertext file name */
int  fhtx;             /* and handle          */
void main(int argc, char *argv[]) {
  int i, cardno, newcardno, command, dx, wd, ht;
  long fs,fe,ita,nl;
```

```
init_win();      /* initialize window package */
init_files();    /* initialize our high level file table */
init_mouse(MOUSE_OPTIONAL, MOUSE_TEXT_MODE, MOUSE_TEXT_MODE);
if (argc < 2) {
   printf("Usage: >hd hypertxtfile\nExtension of 'htx' assumed\n");
   exit(1);
}
strcpy(infile,argv[1]);
strcat(infile,".htx");
/* open the vlr file */
if ((fhtx = openvlr(infile,"rb",32L)) == -1) exit(1);
clrvstr(&index,30,sizeof(index_elem),10);  /* start with 30 keys */
readhdr(fhtx,&fs,&fe,&ita,&nl);
nl = (nl-1) / 2; /* two recs for every card, minus index rec */
printf("Should be %ld keys\n",nl);
if (getvlr(fhtx,&index,ita) == -1) exit(1);  /* get the keys */
printf("index says there are %d\n", index.currlen);
for(i=0; i<index.currlen; i++) {
   printf("%d %s %ld\n",i, INDEX[i].key,INDEX[i].txt_addr);
}
printf("Press a key to get started ...\n");
getch();
clrscr();
vstrins(&index, 0, &index_key, 1);
vstrins(&index, 1, &stack_key,  1);
/* Initialize the card key and window stacks */
clrvstr(&keystack, 15, sizeof(int), 0);
clrvstr(&winstack, 15, sizeof(windesc *), 0);
/* set up our index list */
clrvstr(&indxstk, 15, sizeof(int), 10);
for (i=0; i<index.currlen; i++) {
    vstrcat(&indxstk, &i);
}
cardno = 0; command = -1;
while(cardno != -1) {
    /* Popup the card, and add to the card key and window stacks    */
    /* If window already up, don't popup a new one, just clear it   */
    for(i=0; i<keystack.currlen; i++) {
       if (((int *)(keystack.data))[i] == cardno) break;
    }
    /* Deaden old window */
    if (keystack.currlen) recolor(curr_win,7);
    if (i < keystack.currlen) {
       slct_win( ((windesc **)(winstack.data))[i] );
       vstrdel(&keystack, i, 1);
       vstrdel(&winstack, i, 1);
    }
    else { /* Add card, but keep stack from growing too big */
```

```
      if (keystack.currlen == 15) {
         rmv_win( ((windesc **)(winstack.data))[winstack.currlen-1] );
         winstack.currlen–;
         keystack.currlen–;
      }
      wd   = MAX(INDEX[cardno].wd+2,52) + 1;
      ht   = MAX(INDEX[cardno].ht+6,7) + 1;
      draw_win(curr_win->xul+2,curr_win->yul+1,
            wd,ht,INDEX[cardno].key,popup,&monocolors);
   }
   vstrcat(&keystack, &cardno);
   vstrcat(&winstack, &curr_win);
   /* Load hypertext into our scratch card */
   clrvstr(&card,500,sizeof(char),100);
   clrvstr(&keypos, 10, sizeof(key_pos_elem), 5);
   if (cardno == 0) {
      make_index_card(&index, &indxstk, &card, &keypos, index_key.wd);
   }
   else {
     if (cardno == 1) {
       make_index_card(&index, &keystack, &card, &keypos, stack_key.wd);
     }
     else {
       getvlr(fhtx, &card,    INDEX[cardno].txt_addr);
       getvlr(fhtx, &keypos, INDEX[cardno].key_addr);
       /* relocate the y coordinate */
       for (i=0; i<keypos.currlen; i++) {
           ((key_pos_elem *)(keypos.data))[i].y += 2;
       }
     }
   }
   vstrcat(&card,"");  /* null terminate so paint pgm works right */
   /* Print out menu and status information */
   prtfstr(1, 1, " ", curr_win->wc.hilite_color, -80);
   for(i=0, dx=1; i<6; i++) {
      cmd_menu[i].keyno = index.currlen + i;
      cmd_menu[i].x      = dx;
      cmd_menu[i].y      = 1;
      prtfstr(dx, 1, cmds[i], curr_win->wc.hilite_color, 80);
      dx               += strlen(cmds[i]);
      cmd_menu[i].wd     = strlen(cmds[i]);
      dx = dx + 2;
   }
   prtfstr(1, 2,          "\xc4", curr_win->wc.border_color, -80);
   prtfstr(1, curr_win->ht-3, "\xc4", curr_win->wc.border_color, -80);
   prtfstr(1, curr_win->ht-2, " ", curr_win->wc.hilite_color, -80);
   prtfstr(1,curr_win->ht-2, "%3d of %3d",
         curr_win->wc.hilite_color, 80, cardno+1, index.currlen);
```

```
      /* paint the hypertext, highlighting all keys */
      paint_htx(curr_win, &keypos, &card);
      /* add the menu commands as keys */
      vstrins(&keypos, keypos.currlen, cmd_menu, 6);
      newcardno = get_next_card(curr_win, &keypos);
      if (newcardno < index.currlen) {
         cardno = newcardno;
         command = -1; /* must set this to something */
      }
      else {  /* must have been a command */
        command = newcardno - index.currlen;
        switch(command) {
          case 0: /* Home card */
            cardno = 0;
          break;
          case 1: /* Stack card */
            cardno = 1;
          break;
          case 2: /* Pgup, up one card, wrap around */
            if (—cardno < 2) cardno = index.currlen-1;
          break;
          case 3: /* Pgdn, down a card, so wrap around */
            if (++cardno == index.currlen) cardno = 2;
          break;
          case 4: /* Delete top card from stack */
            if (keystack.currlen > 1) {
               rmv_win( curr_win );
               keystack.currlen—;
               winstack.currlen—;
            }
            cardno = ((int *)(keystack.data))[keystack.currlen-1];
          break;
          case 5: /* Esc, so force it to quit */
            cardno = -1;
          break;
      default: ;
         }
      }
      if (command == 5) break;
   }
   closefile(fhtx);
   mouse_off(0);
   for (i = winstack.currlen; i>0; i—) rmv_win(curr_win);
}
#define htx ((unsigned char *)(text->data))
static void paint_htx(windesc *w, vstr *keypos, vstr *text)
/*
   Paints the hypertext contained in *text, highlighting all
   the keys.
```

```
 */
{
   int i, j;
   static texel line[80];
   key_pos_elem kp;
   mouse_off(1);
   gotoxy(1,3);
   cprintf("%s",text->data);
   /* hilight the keys */
   for (i=0; i<keypos->currlen; i++) {
       kp = ((key_pos_elem *)(keypos->data))[i];
       kp.x += w->xul;  kp.y += w->yul;
       gettext(kp.x, kp.y, kp.x + kp.wd + 1, kp.y, line);
       for (j=0; j<kp.wd; j++) line[j].attr = w->wc.hilite_color;
       puttext(kp.x, kp.y, kp.x + kp.wd + 1, kp.y, line);
   }
   mouse_on(1);
}
static int get_next_card(windesc *w, vstr *keypos)
/*
   Waits for keypress and mouse button release events. When an event occurs
   on a hypertext key, then the new card number is returned, else we
   keep trying.
*/
{
  int x, y, xofs, yofs, done;
  unsigned int key;
  int keyno;
  x = 1; y = 3; keyno = -1;
  do {
    gotoxy(x,y);
    if ((key = mouse_trigger(0)) || (key = mouse_trigger(1))) {
       done = 1;
       switch(key) {
         case LEFT_MOUSE_PRESS:
           if (mouse_on_border(w, &xofs, &yofs)) {
              while(button_state()) {  /* if yes move till release   */
                mouse_txt_posn(&x,&y);
                move_curr_win(x-xofs,y-yofs);
              }
           }
           done = 0;
        break;
        case LEFT_MOUSE_REL:
           x = mouse_text_x - curr_win->xul;
           y = mouse_text_y - curr_win->yul;
           gotoxy(x,y);
           if ((keyno = on_key(keypos, x, y)) == -1) done = 0;
```

```
break;
case CRKEY:
  if ((keyno = on_key(keypos, x, y)) == -1) done = 0;
break;
case UPKEY :
  if (!(—y)) y = 1;
  done = 0;
break;
case DOWNKEY :
  if (++y > w->ht-2) y = w->ht-2;
  done = 0;
break;
case LEFTKEY :
  if (!(—x)) x = 1;
  done = 0;
break;
case RIGHTKEY :
  if (++x > w->wd-2) x = w->wd-2;
  done = 0;
break;
case HOMEKEY :
case 0x2368  :  /* "h" */
case 0x2348  :  /* "H" */
  keyno = index.currlen;     /* Home card     */
break;
case 0x1f73 :   /* "s" */
case 0x1f53 :   /* "S" */
  keyno = index.currlen + 1; /* Stack Card    */
break;
case PGUPKEY :
case 0x1970 :  /* "p" */
case 0x1950 :  /* "P" */
  keyno = index.currlen + 2; /* Previous Card */
break;
case PGDNKEY :
case 0x316e :  /* "n" */
case 0x314e :  /* "N" */
  keyno = index.currlen + 3; /* Next Card     */
break;
case BSKEY  :
case DELKEY :
case 0x2064 : /* "d" */
case 0x2044 : /* "D" */
  keyno = index.currlen + 4; /* Back One Card */
break;
case RIGHT_MOUSE_REL:
case ESCKEY :
case 0x1071 : /* "q" */
```

```
          case 0x1051 : /* "Q" */
            keyno = index.currlen + 5; /* quit */
          break;
          case SHFTUPKEY:
            move_curr_win(curr_win->xul,curr_win->yul-1);
            done = 0;
          break;
          case SHFTDNKEY:
            move_curr_win(curr_win->xul,curr_win->yul+1);
            done = 0;
          break;
          case SHFTLEFT:
            move_curr_win(curr_win->xul-1,curr_win->yul);
            done = 0;
          break;
          case SHFTRIGHT:
            move_curr_win(curr_win->xul+1,curr_win->yul);
            done = 0;
          break;
      default : ;
        }
    } /* end of looking for trigger */
    else {
      done = 0;
    }
  } while(!done);
  return keyno;
}
static int on_key(vstr *keypos, int x, int y)
/*
   Given a set of key positions, this function checks to see whether
   the point (x,y) is on any of the keys. If it is, it returns the
   key number, else, it return -1.
*/
{
  int i;
  key_pos_elem kp;
  for (i = 0; i<keypos->currlen; i++) {
      kp = ((key_pos_elem *)(keypos->data))[i];
      if ((y == kp.y) && (x >= kp.x) && (x <= kp.x + kp.wd -1))
          return kp.keyno;
  }
  return -1;
}
static void make_index_card(vstr *index, vstr *keystack,
                            vstr *index_card, vstr *keypos, int wd)
/* Given the index table index, a list of keys stack, and a vstr
   to hold the hypertext index_card, this routine creates some
```

```
   hypertext for the list of keys, and makes it fit in a window
   that is wd characters wide.
 */
{
  int i, k, keylen, col, row;
  key_pos_elem kp;
  char *keystr;
  for (i=0, col = 1, row = 3; i<keystack->currlen; i++) {
      k = ((int *)(keystack->data))[i];
      keystr = ((index_elem *)(index->data))[k].key;
      keylen = strlen(keystr);
      if ((col + keylen + 2) > wd) {
         col = 1; row++;
         vstrcat(index_card,"\n");
      }
      kp.x = col;   kp.y = row;
      kp.keyno = k; kp.wd = keylen;
      vstrcat(keypos, &kp);
      col += keylen + 2;
      vstrins(index_card, index_card->currlen, keystr, keylen);
      vstrins(index_card, index_card->currlen, "  ", 2);
  }
}
static void recolor(windesc *w, int attr)
/* Paints the entire window (except borders) with the attr color */
{
   texel *ip;
   int numtexels, i;
   numtexels = (w->xlr - w->xul + 1) * (w->ylr - w->yul + 1);
   ip  = (texel *)malloc(numtexels*2);
   mouse_off(1);
   gettext(w->xul, w->yul, w->xlr, w->ylr, ip);
   for (i=0; i<numtexels; i++) {
       ip[i].attr = attr;
   }
   puttext(w->xul, w->yul, w->xlr, w->ylr, ip);
   mouse_on(1);
   free(ip);
}
static int mouse_on_border(windesc *w, int *xofs, int *yofs)
{
  int x, y;
  mouse_txt_posn(&x,&y);
  if ((x >= w->xul && x <= w->xlr &&
       y >= w->yul && y <= w->ylr) &&
      (x == w->xul || x == w->xlr ||
       y == w->yul || y == w->ylr)) {
      *xofs = x - w->xul;  *yofs = y - w->yul;
```

```
      return 1;
   }
   return 0;
}
static void move_curr_win(int x, int y)
/*
   Moves the current window. If coordinates haven't changed,
   then nothing happens.  Does bounds checking on the new position.
*/
{
   int xsave, ysave;
   x = MAX(x,1);
   x = MIN(x,81-curr_win->wd);
   y = MAX(y,1);
   y = MIN(y,26-curr_win->ht);
   if (x != curr_win->xul || y != curr_win->yul) {
      xsave = wherex();
      ysave = wherey();
      swap_image(curr_win);  /* hide window */
      curr_win->xul = x;
      curr_win->yul = y;
      curr_win->xlr = curr_win->xul + curr_win->wd - 1;
      curr_win->ylr = curr_win->yul + curr_win->ht - 1;
      swap_image(curr_win); /* show window */
      /* change window coordinates */
      window(curr_win->xul+1,curr_win->yul+1,
             curr_win->xlr-1,curr_win->ylr-1);
      gotoxy(xsave, ysave);
   }
}
```

CHAPTER

13

Debugging

Debugging is an integral part of programming that seeks to detect and remove software malfunction. There are as many types of bugs as there are programs. Detecting software bugs employs a variety of techniques ranging from the primitive printf-aided to the sophisticated hardware-assisted debuggers. Debugging methods depends on the type and availability of debuggers, as well as the application in question. Turbo C 2.0 brings a versatile debugger that is integrated in the environment. This shortens the cycle of modifying and debugging the code.

Software bugs result in three general types of errors:

1. **Run-time system crashes** Depending on the application, certain bugs result in either an imminent or a conditional system crash, depending on the location of the error-generating code.
2. **Run-time error** Unlike the first type, this class of errors normally halts the program and returns control to the underlying operating system. Like the previous type, such errors are either imminent or conditional.
3. **Program logic errors** Such errors permit the program to terminate normally, however the desired results and/or actions are not correctly executed. This can be attributed to either or both of the following factors:
    a. Algorithms used are not properly implemented
    b. Mistakes in coding

Error handling in C is employs defensive programming techniques instead of exception-handlers like those found in Ada.

THE TURBO C DEBUGGER

The Turbo C debugger offers valuable debugging tools. In the Turbo C environment, there are three pull-down options in the main menu that are related to debugging.

1. **Run options** The options provided under this menu selection empower you to perform the following:
   a. Run a program either in a normal fashion or until the next preset break point in the program is encountered.
   b. Reset a program to end a debugging session. This empowers you to edit and then resume debugging, redo the last debugging session, or simply run the program.
   c. Tracing options are offered in two flavors: trace through and step over. Tracing through a program means that you are able to follow the execution of statement in every function. This puts the entire debugging session in thorough-debugging mode, so to speak. The step-over option permits you to quickly execute a function call. You are able to alternate between either options at you discretion using the F7 and F8 keyboard function keys.
2. **Debugger options** The corresponding pull-down menu provides a number of options which include:
   a. The Evaluate option which enables you to type in an expression and view its result. You can also assign a new value to the expression. This is valuable when you wish to correct the value of a variable or array location before resuming execution. The entered expression, its result, and the optional new value appear as a separate one-line window. You are only allowed to type in the expression and new value windows.
   b. The Call Stack option displays the list of functions called before the current code location is reached. For a recursive function, this option gives you an exact picture of how many times that function is called.
   c. The Find Function option enables you to quickly locate a function in a long listing.
   d. The Screen Swap option sets one of three conditions for swapping between the environment and the output screen. The options are Always, Smart, and None. The Smart option shows the output screen when it has been written to by a console output function.
3. **Break/Watch options** These options empower you to manage watch variables and break points. Watch variables are placed in a special stack which is displayed in a Watch window. A watch variable may be a simple variable or an expression.

   The following is a sample declaration:

```
int i;
double x;
double dptr = &x;
long numbers[10];
long *lptr = numbers;
char str[] = "Hello world!';
char ptr = str;
struct complex a; /* has double real, imag; fields */
```

   The following list illustrates how the above variables and pointers may be watched:

Watch	Contents viewed
`i`	`value stored in i`
`x`	`value stored in x`
`dptr`	`address of pointer`
`*dptr`	`value stored in x`
`numbers`	`address of array numbers`
`numbers[0]`	`value stored in numbers[0]`
`numbers[2]`	`value stored in numbers[2]`
`numbers[i]`	`value stored in numbers[i]`
`lptr`	`address of pointer`
`*lptr`	`value stored in numbers[0]`
`*(lptr+2)`	`value stored in numbers[2]`
`*(lptr+i)`	`value stored in numbers[i]`
`str`	`the string "Hello wordl!"`
`ptr`	`the string "Hello wordl!"`
`*ptr`	`the character "H" stored in str[0]`
`a`	`address of structre a`
`a.real`	`the value store in a.real`

You can add and edit a watch variable, delete the last added watch variable, and remove all watch variables. Similarly, you can toggle a break point, remove all break points, and move to the next break point. The screen cursor of the Editor is used to point to the toggled break point. Break points are treated as a circular list: when you are at the last one and request to visit the next one, the debugger takes you to the first one in the program.

SELECTED ERRORS

To discuss all types of errors requires a multivolume text book. Program bugs are limited only by the imagination. They can pop up in every aspect of a program! We will discuss the following selection of bugs using simple examples:

1. **Numeric overflow** In this type of error, a numeric expression increases beyond the limit supported by Turbo C. The following example is a double-typed factorial function. Arguments that are between 1 and 170 are valid (using an 80x87 coprocessor). The short program is shown below:

```
/*
  C program that demonstrates the overflow error for
  factorial that exceed 170, using an 80x87 coprocessor
*/
#include <stdio.h>
#include "conio.h"
double factorial(int);
main()
{
   int n;
   clrscr();
```

```
    printf("Enter an integer : ");
    scanf("%d", &n);
    printf("\n\n%d! = %lg\n\n", n, factorial(n));
}
double factorial(int n)
{
    double result = 1.0L;
    while (n > 1)
        result *= (double) n—;
    return result;
}
```

When tracing the execution of the above program, invoke the Watch/Break option and add a watch for the variables n and result. You will notice the values of **n** decrease, while that of **result** increase. If the supplied argument is within the valid range, the function exits gracefully, otherwise a numeric overflow error occurs. In the case of overflow error, the Watch window assigns a NAN to the variable **result**.

2. **Out-of-range errors** This is another class of common bugs. In the case of one-dimensional arrays, the problem manifests itself in attempting to access an element beyond the declared dimension size. In multi-dimensional arrays, you can add another genre of bug: erroneously interchanging indices for the array's dimensions. This is demonstrated by the next program. The example contains an erroneously coded FOR loop. The program does not crash, but it does not return the correct answer either:

```
/*
   C program that demonstrates the out-of-boundary errors
   that are associated with arrays.
*/
#include <stdio.h>
#include "conio.h"
#define MAX_ROW 10
#define MAX_COL 2
main()
{
    int num[2][10] = { 1,2,3,4,5,6,7,8,9,10,
                       4,7,8,6,3,2,1,6,5,4  };
    int i, j = 0, big = num[1][0];
    clrscr();
    /* — should be MAX_ROW —
               vvvvvvv          */
    for (i = 1; i < MAX_COL; i++)
      if (big < num[1][i]) {
    big = num[1][i];
    j = i;
      }
```

```
    printf("Largest element is number %d and is equal to %d\n\n",
      j, big);
}
```

Using the Turbo C debugger, trace the above program while watching the loop index i and the variable big. The FOR loop executes only twice and then exits. This should clearly indicate the nature of the problem. Replacing MAX_COL with MAX_ROW fixes the bug.

3. **Uninitialized variables or pointers** This represents another popular category of bugs. The Turbo C compiler is able to warn you about using uninitialized variables or pointers, but the problem of lacking re-initialization goes undetected. In the next example, a program scans an array to determine the biggest and smallest elements. A pointer is used to scan through the array sequentially. The pointer is properly initialized for the first loop, but it is not reinitialized for the second loop. In effect you have two types of bugs in this program: uninitialized pointer and out-of-bound array access. The latter is due to the fact that as the pointer is incremented in the second FOR loop, it is accessing elements outside the array num:

```
/*
  C program that demonstrates the out-of-boundary errors
  that are associated with arrays.  This version shows
  the error due omitting re-initialization of a pointer.
  The program finds the smallest and largest elements in
  an array using a pointer for scanning the array elements
  in sequence.
*/
#include <stdio.h>
#include "conio.h"
#define MAX_ROW 20
main()
{
    int num[20] = { 12,23,73,84,15,56,67,98,39,10,
                    54,67,98,16,23,32,41,56,65,74  };
    int i, j = 0, *ptr = num, big = *ptr, small = *ptr;
    clrscr();
    ptr++; /* point to second element */
    for (i = 1; i < MAX_ROW; i++, ptr++)
      if (big < *ptr) {
     big = *ptr;
     j = i;
      }
    /* missing statement is show below  */
    /* ptr = num; */
    printf("Largest element is num[%d] = %d\n\n", j, big);
    ptr++; /* point to second element */
    for (i = 1; i < MAX_ROW; i++, ptr++)
```

```
      if (small > *ptr) {
  small = *ptr;
  j = i;
      }
    printf("Smallest element is num[%d] = %d\n\n", j, small);
}
```

Using the Turbo C debugger, watch the variables big, small, and most importantly *ptr. The latter shows the array element accessed by the pointer. You can install a break point after the first printf since the largest element is correctly reported. As you trace through the second FOR loop, the values associated with *ptr are not those of the array num, but of a memory location beyond it. Inserting the missing statement ptr = num; should fix the bug.

Another example of this type of bugs deals with uninitialized variables. The previous program has been modified to fix the pointer-related bug and remove the initial value assigned to the variable big. In addition, the first element of the array has been made the largest. When the program runs as is, the number 98 is reported as the largest number, instead of 120. If you make 120 less than 98, the bug does not manifest itself. Thus, this program also shows a case of conditional bugs associated with an erroneous implementation of an algorithm. The listing is as follows:

```
/*
   C program that demonstrates the out-of-boundary errors
   that are associated with arrays.  This version shows
   the error due omitting  variable initialization.
   The program finds the smallest and largest elements in
   an array using a pointer for scanning the array elements
   in sequence.
   The big variable is not initialized. Consequently, the
   the first element which is the largest is not detected.
*/
#include <stdio.h>
#include "conio.h"
#define MAX_ROW 20
main()
{
    int num[20] = { 120,23,73,84,15,56,67,98,39,10,
                    54,67,98,16,23,32,41,56,65,74 };
    int i, j = 0, *ptr = num, big, small = *ptr;
    clrscr();
    ptr++; /* point to second element */
    for (i = 1; i < MAX_ROW; i++, ptr++)
      if (big < *ptr) {
     big = *ptr;
     j = i;
      }
```

```
    ptr = num; /* re-initialize pointer */
    printf("Largest element is num[%d] = %d\n\n", j, big);
    ptr++; /* point to second element */
    for (i = 1; i < MAX_ROW; i++, ptr++)
      if (small > *ptr) {
     small = *ptr;
     j = i;
      }
    printf("Smallest element is num[%d] = %d\n\n", j, small);
    scanf("%d", &j);
}
```

Trace this program with a watch on variables big and i, and the pointer access *ptr. It quickly becomes evident that the variable big is entering the first FOR loop with no initial value.

4. **Wrong sequence of operators** This type of bug is rather unique to C, since it is associated with errors related to the ++ and — operators. Placing either of these operators on the "logically" wrong side of a variable makes the variable contribute the wrong value to an expression. The next example is a modified version of the factorial function. The — operator is erroneously placed before the function parameter n in the expression:

   `result *= (double) —n;`

   This bug makes the factorial function return the factorial of (n-1) instead of the sought argument n.

```
/*

  C program that demonstrates using the wrong operator sequence.
  The error is located in the factorial function in the line:
         result *= (double) —n;
  which should be:
         result *= (double) n—;
*/
#include <stdio.h>
#include "conio.h"
double factorial(int);
main()
{
   int n;
   clrscr();
   printf("Enter an integer : ");
   scanf("%d", &n);
   printf("\n\n%d! = %lg\n\n", n, factorial(n));
}
double factorial(int n)
{
   double result = 1.0L;
```

```
    while (n > 1 && n < 170)
        result *= (double) —n;
    return result;
}
```

Trace the above program with a watch on variables n and result. The value associated with result shows that the function is actually calculating the factorial of n-1, since the first —n decremented n before contributing its value.

5. **Infinite looping** This type of bug sends program execution in a vicious circle. The problem usually manifests itself with WHILE or DO loops where a loop counter is altered with every iteration. Omitting the loop counter increment/decrement causes the loop to stagnate. The next program illustrates this problem. The program scans a substring in a string using the **pos_str()** function to handle the string-matching code. The first WHILE loop is followed by a i++; statement to increment the loop control variable i. This statement has been enclosed in a comment to illustrated the bug in question:

```
/*
  C program that demonstrates the error of creating an infinite
  loop (a while in this case) by forgetting to increment the
  index that makes the loop body progress.  The program scans
  the location of a substring in a string.  The error is located
  in the string-scanning function str_pos().
*/
#include <stdio.h>
#include "conio.h"
#include <string.h>
main()
{
  char str[] = "The rain in Spain";
  char *substr;
  int pos;
  clrscr();
  printf("String is '%s'\n\n",str);
  printf("Enter substring -> ");
  gets(substr);
  pos = pos_str(str, substr, 1);
  if (pos > 0)
     printf("Substring matches at character %d\n", pos);
   else
     printf("No match found\n");
}
int pos_str(char* str, char* substr, unsigned int start_index)
{
    int i, j, k, last;
    unsigned int sstrlen = strlen(str);
```

```
    unsigned int substrlen = strlen(substr);
    unsigned char nomatch;
    if ((substrlen == 0) || (start_index >= sstrlen))
        return -1;
    k = -1;
    if (sstrlen > substrlen) {
        i = start_index - 1;
        last = sstrlen - substrlen;
        nomatch = 1;
        while ((i <= last) && (nomatch == 1)) {
        /* i++; makes while loop infinite */
            if (substr[0] == str[i]) {
                k = i;
                j = 1;
                i++;
                nomatch = 0;
                while ((j < substrlen) && (nomatch == 0) )
                    if (substr[j] == str[i]) {
                        i++;
                        j++;
                    }
                    else
                     nomatch = 1;
               /* restore index before complete matching was attempted */
                if (nomatch == 1) {
                    i = k + 1;
                    k = -1;
                }
            } /* if (substr[0] == str[i]) */
        } /* while ((i <= last) && (nomatch)) */
    } /* if (sstrlen > substrlen) */
    return k;
}
```

Trace the program with a watch on i, str, substr, str[i], and substr[0]. Enter a string such that its first letter is not T. When the execution reaches the WHILE loop of the function, you will see that without the statement i++; the values of i and str[i] remain the same, since the loop is iterating infinitely!

6. **Infinite recursion** This class of bugs is associated with recursive functions that simply keep calling themselves. Depending on the function and the type of bug, this error may be influenced by certain values of the function's arguments. The next example shows an infinitely looping recursive factorial. The error is due to the erroneously stated condition:

```
if (n > 1 || n < 170)
```

where the || should have been &&:

```
/*
  C program that demonstrates the error of infinite recursion
  in a wrongly coded factorial function.
*/
#include <stdio.h>
#include "conio.h"
double factorial(int);
main()
{
   int n;
   clrscr();
   printf("Enter an integer : ");
   scanf("%d", &n);
   printf("\n\n%d! = %lg\n\n", n, factorial(n));
}
double factorial(int n)
{
  /* correct if test should be
     (n > 1 && n < 170) */
  if (n > 1 || n < 170)
     return (double) (factorial(n-1) * n);
  else
     return 1.0L;
}
```

Trace this program with a watch on n. Observe how the value of n keeps decreasing below zero and into the realm of negative numbers. The watched values make it easy to conclude that the IF statement is not functioning properly and not protecting against infinite recursion as it is supposed to.

APPENDIX A

C Escape Sequences

Sequence	As Hex Value	Decimal Value	Task of Sequence
\a	0x07	7	Bell
\b	0x08	8	Backspace
\f	0x0C	12	Formfeed
\n	0x0A	10	New line
\r	0x0D	13	Carriage return
\t	0x09	9	Horizontal tab
\v	0x0B	11	Vertical tab
\\	0x5C	92	Backslash
\'	0x2C	44	Single quote
\"	0x22	34	Double quote
\?	0x3F	63	Question Mark
\OOO			1 to 3 digits for an octal value
\XHHH and \xHHH	0xHHH		1 to 3 digits for a hexadecimal value

APPENDIX B

Formatted I/O String Control

% [flags] [width] [.precision] [F|N|h|l] <type character>

Flag Character	Effect
-	Justify to the left within the designated field The right side is padded with blanks
+	Display the plus or minus sign of value
blank	Display a leading blank if value is positive. If output is negative a minus sign is used.
#	Display a leading zero for octals Display a leading 0X or 0x for hexadecimals Display the decimal point for reals No effect on integers

Category	Type Character	Output Format
character	c	single character
integer	d	signed decimal int
	i	signed decimal int
	o	unsigned octal int
	u	unsigned decimal int
	x	unsigned hexadecimal int. The numeric character set used is [01234567890abcdef]
	X	unsigned hexadecimal int. The numeric character set used is [01234567890ABCDEF]
pointer	p	prints only offset of near pointers as AAAA and far pointers as SSSS:OOOO
pointer to int	n	stores the number of characters to far to the indicated pointer
real	f	signed value in the form [-]dddd.dddd
	e	signed scientific format using [-]d.dddd e[+|-]ddd
	E	signed scientific format using [-]d.dddd E[+|-]ddd
	g	signed value using either 'e' or 'f' formats, depending on value and specified precision.
	G	signed value using either 'E' or 'f' formats, depending on value and specified precision.
string pointer	s	emits characters until a null- terminator or precision is attained.

APPENDIX C

Predefined Data Types in Turbo C

Simple Data Type	Byte Size	Value Range	Sample Constant(s)
char	1	-128 to 127	-5, 'a'
signed char	1	-128 to 127	5, 'b'
unsigned char	1	0 to 255	5, 'x'
int	2	-32768 to 32767	-234
signed int	2	-32768 to 32767	-344
unsigned int	2	0 to 65535	65000
short int	2	-32768 to 32767	1230
signed short int	2	-32768 to 32767	345
unsigned short int	2	0 to 65535	40000
long int	4	-2147483648 to 2147483647	1000000
signed long int	4	-2147483648 to 2147483647	-2000000
unsigned long int	4	0 to 4294967295	300000000
float	4	3.4E-38 to 3.4E+38 and -3.4E-38 to -3.4E+38	-1.23e-02
long float	8	1.7E-308 to 1.7E+308 and -1.7E-308 to -1.7E+308	2.3e+100
double	8	1.7E-308 to 1.7E+308 and -1.7E-308 to -1.7E+308	-4.32e-
100			
long double	8	1.7E-308 to 1.7E+308 and -1.7E-308 to -1.7E+308	
12.34e+100			

APPENDIX D

Operators in C

Arithmetic Operators

C Operator	Function
+	Unary Plus
-	Unary Minus
+	Add
-	Subtract
*	Multiply
/	Divide
%	Modulus

<table>
<tr><th>C Operator</th><th>Pascal Operator</th></tr>
<tr><td>&&</td><td>AND</td></tr>
<tr><td>||</td><td>OR</td></tr>
<tr><td>!</td><td>NOT</td></tr>
<tr><td>N/A</td><td>XOR</td></tr>
<tr><td><</td><td><</td></tr>
<tr><td><=</td><td><=</td></tr>
<tr><td>></td><td>></td></tr>
<tr><td>>=</td><td>>=</td></tr>
<tr><td>==</td><td>=</td></tr>
<tr><td>!=</td><td><></td></tr>
<tr><td>? :</td><td>N/A</td></tr>
</table>

Bit-manipulating Operators

Arithmetic Assignment Operators

Assignment Operator	Equivalent Long Form
x += y	x = x + y
x -= y	x = x - y
x *= y	x = x * y
x /= y	x = x / y
x %= y	x = x % y

Relational Operators

<table>
<tr><th>C Operator</th><th>Pascal Operator</th></tr>
<tr><td>&</td><td>AND</td></tr>
<tr><td>|</td><td>OR</td></tr>
<tr><td>^</td><td>XOR</td></tr>
<tr><td>~</td><td>NOT</td></tr>
<tr><td><<</td><td>SHL</td></tr>
<tr><td>>></td><td>SHR</td></tr>
</table>

Bit-manipulating Assignment Operators

<table>
<tr><th>C Operator</th><th>Long Form</th></tr>
<tr><td>x &= y</td><td>x = x & y</td></tr>
<tr><td>x |= y</td><td>x = x | y</td></tr>
<tr><td>x ^= y</td><td>x = x ^ y</td></tr>
<tr><td>x <<= y</td><td>x = x << y</td></tr>
<tr><td>x >>= y</td><td>x = x >> y</td></tr>
</table>

Operators in C with their Precedence and Evaluation Direction

Category	Name	Symbol	Eval. Direction	Precedence
Selection	Parentheses	()	left to right	1
	Array indexing	[]	left to right	1
	Field reference	.	left to right	1
		->	left to right	1
Monadic	Post-increment	++	left to right	2
	Post-decrement	—	left to right	2
	Address	&	right to left	2
	Bitwise NOT	~	right to left	2
	Type cast	(type)	right to left	2
	Logical NOT	!	right to left	2
	Negation	-	right to left	2
	Plus sign	+	right to left	2
	Pre-increment	++	right to left	2
	Pre-decrement	—	right to left	2
	Type cast	(type)	right to left	2
	Size of data	sizeof	right to left	2
Multiplicative	Modulus	%	left to right	3
	Multiply	*	left to right	3
	Divide	/	left to right	3
Additive	Add	+	left to right	4
	Subtract	-	left to right	4
Bitwise Shift	Shift left	<<	left to right	5
	Shift right	>>	left to right	5
Relational	Less than	<	left to right	6
	Less or equal	<=	left to right	6
	Greater than	>	left to right	6
	Greater or equal	>=	left to right	6
	Equal to	==	left to right	7
	Not equal to	!=	left to right	7
Bitwise	AND	&	left to right	8
	XOR	^	left to right	9
	OR	|	left to right	10
Logical	AND	&&	left to right	11
	OR	||	left to right	12
Ternary	Cond. Express.	? :	right to left	13
Assignment	Arithmetic	=	right to left	14
		+=		
		-=		
		*=		
		/=		
		%=		
Shift		>>=	right to left	14
		<<=	right to left	14
Bitwise		&=	right to left	14
		|=		
		^=		
Comma		,	left to right	15

APPENDIX E

Memory Models for Turbo C

	Pointer Reference		Number of 64K Segments for			
Model	**to code**	**to data**	**data**	**code**	**total**	**one data object**
tiny	near	near	[share 1]		1	1
small	near	near	1	1	2	1
medium	far	near	1	> 1	> 1	1
compact	near	far	> 1	1	> 1	1
llarge	far	far	> 1	> 1	> 1	1
huge	far	far	> 1	> 1	> 1	> 1

INDEX

If you hate typing, read this!

Many programmers dislike typing source code that is already available in electronic form. They find it a complete waste of time to key in listings and spend even more time hunting for typos.

This offer provides you instant access to the code in this book. It enables you to begin utilizing the book's programs and libraries. You may select one of two disk formats made available for your convenience: Two 5.25" DSDD, or one 5.25" HD.

Send your order to:

Namir C. Shammas
P.O. Box 1297
Glen Allen, VA 23060
Attention: Advanced Turbo C Programmer's Guide

— —

Please send me copies of the Advanced Turbo to C disk. Enclosed is a check or money order for $24.95 (shipping & handling included).

Disk format available:

5.25" DSDD ______ (Default Choice)

5.25" HD ______ (Need AT drive)

Please type or print the information below:

Name ____

Company (for Business Address) ______________________________

Address ____

City ____________________ State ________ Zip Code ____________________

Daytime Phone (_______) _______ - ____________________________